THE COMPLETE
ASIAN
COOKBOOK

THE COMPLETE
ASIAN
COOKBOOK

MURDOCH
B O O K S

Malaysian Chicken Kapitan, page 219

Sesame Chicken and Shanghai Noodles, page 118

Vegetable Pakoras with Spiced Yoghurt, page 66

Contents

MEDITERA
GOURME
PASTA SAUC.

❧

GREEK
OLIVE PIZZA

1   pre-baked pizza crust
    or focaccia bread

1   cup shredded
    mozzarella cheese

1   cup MEDITERANIA
    Sun Dried Tomato
    and Sautéed Onion
    Gourmet Pasta Sauce

1/2   cup crumbled feta
    cheese

10   Greek olives, pitted
    and cut in half

2   teaspoons fresh thyme
    leaves (optional)

Preheat oven to 450°.
Evenly cover pizza crust
with mozzarella cheese
to the edge of the crust.
Bake for five minutes or
until cheese has slightly
melted. Remove pizza
crust from oven. Top
with MEDITERANIA
Sun Dried Tomato and
Sautéed Onion Gourmet
Pasta Sauce, leaving
some of the melted
mozzarella cheese
uncovered. Top with olive
es and feta cheese. Bake
o 10 minutes or until
ese has softened and
is bubbly. Sprinkle
thyme leaves or
fresh chopped
s if desired.

large pizza
ht slices.

SEBUMPS.

r

rness

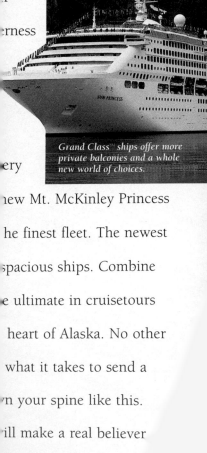

Grand Class™ ships offer more private balconies and a whole new world of choices.

ery

new Mt. McKinley Princess

he finest fleet. The newest

spacious ships. Combine

e ultimate in cruisetours

heart of Alaska. No other

what it takes to send a

n your spine like this.

ill make a real believer

nd for yours today.

-PRINCESS.

Britis

Coriander Noodles with Tuna, page 111

You will find the following cookery ratings on the recipes in this book:

A single pot symbol indicates a recipe that is simple and generally straightforward to make—perfect for beginners.

Two symbols indicate the need for just a little more care and a little more time.

Three symbols indicate special recipes that need more investment in time, care and patience—but the results are worth it.

Beef and Hokkien Noodle Stir-fry, page162

Tofu Kebabs with Miso Pesto, page 81

Saffron Rice, page 116

Coconut Prawn Salad, page 88

The Asian Pantry

BAMBOO SHOOTS
The edible young shoots of bamboo, picked soon after they appear above ground. Fresh shoots are not easy to find and must be peeled and boiled for 5 minutes before use. Canned and bottled shoots are available in supermarkets and Asian food stores.

BEAN SAUCES AND PASTES
Made from fermented and salted yellow or black soy beans, bean pastes have been used as flavourings by the Chinese for thousands of years. It is often difficult to distinguish labels between the varieties but, in fact, black bean, brown bean and yellow bean sauce are pretty much interchangeable in recipes.

Chilli bean paste is also called red bean chilli paste, hot bean paste or chilli bean sauce and is similar to brown bean sauce but hotter because of the chilli.

BESAN
Besan (chickpea flour) is a pale-yellow flour made from ground chickpeas and used most commonly in Indian cuisine, giving a unique texture and flavour. Often used as a thickener in sauces and batters.

BLACK BEANS
Black beans are fermented and heavily salted black soy beans. Rinse them before use. Available in packets or canned (with the canned version being saltier, so drain and rinse well before use). Vacuum-packed black beans need to be rehydrated in a little hot water and rinsed before using. Once opened, store in an airtight container in the refrigerator.

BOK CHOY
(Chinese chard or Chinese white cabbage) This member of the cabbage family has a slightly mustardy taste. Separate the leaves and wash well before use. Use both the leaf and stem in soups and stir-fries, steam and serve with oyster sauce, or fry in oil. A smaller variety is called Shanghai or baby bok choy—use it in the same way.

CHILLI JAM OR PASTE
Chilli jam is a sweet and sourish tangy jam that is sold in jars at Asian food stores and used in sauces, stir-fries and some soups. Both the paste and jam are generally made with tomato, onion, chilli, oil, tamarind, garlic, sugar, salt, spices and vinegar. After opening, store in the fridge. In most recipes they are interchangeable. If you're strictly vegetarian, check the label: some chilli pastes include shrimp paste.

CHINESE RICE WINE
A fermented rice wine with a rich sweetish taste, similar to dry sherry. It is amber-coloured and is made from glutinous rice in Shaosing in southern China.

CRISP-FRIED ONION, GARLIC AND SHALLOTS
Commonly used as a garnish in Southeast Asia, thin slices of onion, garlic or small red Asian shallots are finely sliced and deep-fried until light brown and crisp. They are available from Asian food stores in packets or tubs. Store in the freezer to prevent the oil going rancid. To make your own, finely slice then cook over low heat in oil, stirring until crisp and golden. Drain well and season with salt. Use immediately.

DASHI GRANULES

Made from dried kelp and dried fish (bonito) and available as granules or powder. Dissolve in hot water for Japanese stock.

DRIED SHRIMP

Small sun-dried prawns, available whole or shredded, but usually ground before use. Some can be very salty so soak and rinse before use.

FISH SAUCE

Small fish are packed into barrels, seasoned with salt and fermented for several months. The brown liquid run off is fish sauce.

GALANGAL

A rhizome with brown skin and cream flesh. Related to ginger but with a distinct flavour and aroma. Available fresh, as fresh slices in brine, dried slices in packets, and powdered.

GARLIC CHIVES

Also known as Chinese chives. Thick flat garlic-scented chives, stronger in flavour than their Western counterpart. The flowerbud is edible.

GINGER

Buy firm unwrinkled roots and store in a plastic bag in the fridge. Peel before use.

HOISIN SAUCE

A thick sweet-spicy Chinese sauce made from soy beans, garlic, sugar and spices and used both for cooking and as a dipping sauce. Once opened, store in the fridge.

KAFFIR LIME LEAVES

Available fresh or dried, with double leaves in a figure of eight shape. When a recipe calls for '1 leaf', this means half of the figure of eight shape.

KECAP MANIS

A thick dark sweet soy sauce used in Indonesian and Malaysian cooking. If it is not available, stir a little soft brown sugar into soy sauce until dissolved.

LEMON GRASS

An aromatic herb, best used fresh. Trim the base, remove the tough outer layers and finely chop the inner white layers. The whole stem can also be used to infuse flavour into curries but is lifted out before serving.

MIRIN

A sweet spirit-based rice liquid used in Japanese basting sauces and marinades, but also good in salad dressings and stir-fries.

MISO PASTE

Made from fermented soy beans. Varies in colour but generally the lighter the paste, the milder it will be.

MUSHROOMS

Enoki mushrooms: tiny white Japanese mushrooms on long, thin stalks growing in clumps. Need very little cooking.

Oyster mushrooms: fan or oyster-shell shaped mushroom, pale creamy grey or brown in colour with a slightly peppery flavour that becomes milder when cooked.

Shiitake mushrooms: available fresh or dried—the dried variety must be soaked for 15–20 minutes in boiling water to soften them before use and the tough stems discarded.

MUSTARD SEEDS

Black, brown, yellow and white mustard seeds are a common ingredient in many curries. Mustard seeds are fried before grinding to release essential oils and increase their flavour. Black and brown mustard seeds are the smallest and hottest, whereas yellow and white mustard seeds are larger and have a milder flavour.

NORI SHEETS

A marine algae found on the surface of the sea off Japan, China and Korea is formed into paper-like sheets, compressed and then dried. Colour ranges from green to purple. Wrapped around rice and fillings to make sushi.

PALM SUGAR

A dark, unrefined sugar from the sap of sugar palm trees. Widely used in Southeast Asia, not only in sweet dishes but to balance the flavours in savoury dishes. Shave the sugar off the cake with a sharp knife. Buy in blocks or jars from Asian shops. Thai palm sugar is lighter in colour, softer and more refined than the Indonesian or Malay versions.

SAKE

An alcoholic liquid made by fermenting cooked, ground rice mash. It has a dry, sherry-like taste and is used as a cooking liquid and, in its more refined form, as a drink. Available both clear and amber in colour.

SAMBAL OELEK

A hot paste made from fresh red chillies, sugar, salt and vinegar or tamarind. Used like a relish or as a substitute for fresh chillies in recipes. If covered, it will keep in the fridge for months.

SHRIMP PASTE/SAUCE

A pungent mixture made from fermented prawns. It can be pink, soft and with a liquidy consistency or dried and sold in dark hard bricks. Cover in plastic and store in an airtight container in the fridge. Usually fried or roasted before use.

SICHUAN PEPPERCORNS

Chinese spice made from the red berries of the prickly ash tree and sold whole or ground. Woody flavour with a hot numbing aftertaste. Often the powder is dry-fried to bring out the flavours before use.

SLENDER EGGPLANT

(Japanese eggplant) A cigar-shaped long, thin, purple eggplant.

SNAKE BEANS

(longbean, cowpea or yard-long bean) A long, green, stringless bean usually cut into short lengths for curries and stir-fries. Buy firm deep green beans and use as soon as possible.

SOY SAUCE

Soy sauce is extracted from fermented and salted soy beans. Chinese cooking distinguishes between light and dark soy sauce as they have different flavours and uses. Where a recipe does not specify which soy sauce to use, it generally requires the light type, as this is the type most commonly sold as generic soy sauce.

Light soy sauce, while lighter in colour with a thinner consistency, is actually saltier than dark soy sauce, and is made from the first pressing. It is mainly used in cooking, especially in dishes featuring pale food, such as fish or poultry, where a pale colour is desired.

Dark soy sauce is aged longer than its light counterpart and has a heavier consistency. It is mainly used in braises and stews and is integral to the Chinese 'red' cooking technique as it imparts its deep colour to the food. It is also used as a dipping sauce as it is less salty than light soy sauce.

Mushroom soy sauce is dark soy sauce that has been infused with dried straw mushrooms.

Japanese soy sauce (shoyu) is a much lighter and sweeter form than the Chinese version and must be used in Japanese dishes.

STAR ANISE

A star-shaped fruit comprised of eight segments that is sun-dried until hard and brown. Has a pronounced aniseed aroma and sweet aniseed flavour. Essential flavouring for Chinese five-spice powder. Sold whole or ground.

TAMARIND

A large, brown, bean-like pod with a fruity tart flavour. It is available as a dried shelled fruit, a block of compressed pulp (usually containing seeds), a purée or a concentrate. It is dissolved in hot water and the liquid then strained through a sieve. Lemon juice is a good substitute.

TOFU

Tofu products are made from yellow soy beans that have been soaked, ground, combined with water and then cooked for a short time, until they solidify into a mass.

Firm tofu is rather soft, but will hold its shape during cooking. It is suitable for stir-frying, pan-frying, marinating and baking.

Silken tofu has a smooth, silky texture and, when blended, is similar to cream. It doesn't stir-fry well due to its delicate texture, but it is often added to soups in cubes.

Silken firm tofu is slightly firmer than silken tofu, and holds its shape a little better. Used in soups.

Fried tofu puffs are cubes of tofu with an aerated texture that have been deep-fried. Use for stir-fries, curries and soups.

Tempeh is similar to tofu, but fermented (like miso and soy sauce). It is made by adding a culture to the cooked soy beans and then compressing the mixture into firm blocks. As tempeh is quite bland, it is often available marinated in a mixture of spices.

WASABI PASTE

Very hot pungent paste made from the knobbly green root of the Japanese wasabi plant. Often referred to as 'Japanese horseradish' because of its strong heat. Served as a condiment with sushi, sashimi and noodles.

WATER CHESTNUTS

Small, rounded, crisp vegetables, usually sold canned (if fresh, they need peeling). They give a crunchy texture to many Asian dishes. Any unused water chestnuts will keep fresh for 4 days if immersed in water in the fridge; change the water daily.

WRAPPERS

Gow gee wrappers are round pieces of dough made from wheat flour and water. These wrappers are most commonly used in Chinese steamed dishes.

Rice paper wrappers are paper-thin, brittle rounds made from rice flour, salt and water. They are available dry in sealed packets and will keep indefinitely in this state. Soak each wrapper briefly in warm water before using to soften it.

Won ton wrappers are thin pliable squares or circles of wheat flour and egg dough, used to wrap savoury and sweet fillings that are then steamed or deep-fried in Chinese dishes. They are sold fresh in packs of about 30 and can be kept in the fridge for about three days.

Soups

THAI-STYLE CHICKEN AND CORN SOUP

Preparation time: 10 minutes
Total cooking time: 5 minutes
Serves 4

2 litres chicken stock
420 g (14 oz) can corn kernels, undrained
8 spring onions, sliced
1 tablespoon finely chopped fresh ginger
4 small chicken breast fillets, finely sliced
1 tablespoon sweet chilli sauce
1 tablespoon fish sauce
120 g (4 oz) rice vermicelli noodles
bunch of fresh coriander leaves, chopped
2 teaspoons grated lime rind
2 tablespoons lime juice

1 Bring the chicken stock to the boil in a large saucepan over high heat. Add the corn kernels and liquid, spring onion and ginger, then reduce the heat and simmer for 1 minute.
2 Add the chicken, sweet chilli sauce and fish sauce and simmer for 3 minutes, or until the chicken is cooked through.
3 Meanwhile, place the noodles in a heatproof bowl and pour in enough boiling water to cover. Leave for 4 minutes, or until softened. Drain the noodles and cut them into shorter lengths.
4 Add the noodles, coriander, lime rind and lime juice to the soup and serve immediately.

NUTRITION PER SERVE
Protein 33 g; Fat 5 g; Carbohydrate 35 g;
Dietary Fibre 5.8 g; Cholesterol 63 mg;
1327 kJ (317 cal)

Add the corn kernels, spring onion and ginger to the chicken stock.

Place the noodles in a heatproof bowl and cover with boiling water.

BEEF PHO

Preparation time: 45 minutes
Total cooking time: 4 hours 15 minutes
Serves 4

1 kg (2 lb) beef shin bones
350 g (11 oz) gravy beef
5 cm (2 inch) piece of fresh ginger,
    thinly sliced
1 teaspoon salt
6 black peppercorns
1 cinnamon stick
4 cloves
6 coriander seeds
2 tablespoons fish sauce
400 g (13 oz) thick fresh rice noodles
150 g (5 oz) rump steak, thinly sliced
3 spring onions, finely chopped
1 onion, very thinly sliced
1/4 cup (7 g/1/4 oz) fresh coriander
    leaves
sliced red chillies, bean sprouts, fresh
    purple basil leaves, chopped
    spring onions and lime wedges,
    to garnish
chilli sauce and hoisin sauce, to serve

1 Place the bones, beef, ginger, salt and 2.5 litres water in a large pan. Bring to the boil, reduce the heat to low and simmer for 3½ hours. Skim off any scum that forms on the surface. Add the peppercorns, cinnamon, cloves, coriander and fish sauce and cook for another 40 minutes. Remove the gravy beef and set aside to cool. Drain the stock, discarding the bones and spices, and return to the pan. When the beef is cool enough to touch, slice finely across the grain.

2 Close to serving time, plunge the noodles into boiling water and cook for 10 seconds only. Drain well and divide among large soup bowls.

3 Bring the beef stock to a rapid boil. Place some slices of the cooked meat on top of each bowl of noodles, as well as a few slices of the raw steak. Ladle the boiling stock over the top and sprinkle with the spring onion, onion slices and coriander. Arrange the garnishes on a platter in the centre to be added to the soup by the diner. Serve with chilli and hoisin sauces.

NUTRITION PER SERVE
Protein 36 g; Fat 8 g; Carbohydrate 22 g;
Dietary Fibre 1 g; Cholesterol 80 mg;
1260 kJ (300 cal)

Remove the purple basil leaves from the stems. Prepare the other garnishes.

Strain the stock through a colander, reserving all the liquid.

VEGETABLE SOUP

Preparation time: 45 minutes
Total cooking time: 10 minutes
Serves 6–8

90 g (3 oz) stale white bread, crusts
    removed
500 g (1 lb) pork mince
2 teaspoons chopped fresh coriander
    roots and stems
3 teaspoons chopped fresh coriander
    leaves
1/2 teaspoon five-spice powder
1 teaspoon grated fresh ginger
1 egg white
3 cups (270 g/9 oz) bean sprouts

2 teaspoons sesame oil
2.25 litres chicken stock
1 small red chilli, chopped
2 carrots, cut into strips
2 sticks celery, cut into strips
6 spring onions, cut into strips
1 1/2 tablespoons lime juice
coriander leaves, to serve

1 Line a baking tin with baking paper.
Cover the bread with cold water, then
squeeze out the liquid. Mix with the
mince, coriander, five-spice powder,
ginger, egg white and 1/4 teaspoon
each of salt and pepper.
2 Roll 1/2 tablespoons of the mixture
into balls and lay in the lined tin.
Divide the bean sprouts among bowls.
Mix the sesame oil and stock in a large

saucepan, bring to the boil and add
the pork balls in batches. Return to the
boil and, when they float, divide
among the bowls.
3 Add the chilli, carrot, celery and
spring onion to the stock, bring to the
boil and simmer for 1 minute. Remove
from the heat, season to taste and add
the lime juice. Ladle into bowls and
top with a few coriander leaves.

NUTRITION PER SERVE (8)
Protein 4 g; Fat 8 g; Carbohydrate 10 g;
Dietary Fibre 2 g; Cholesterol 2 mg;
575 kJ (160 cal)

NOTE: Five-spice is a mixture of
Sichuan pepper, star anise, fennel,
cloves and cinnamon.

Coarsely chop the roots and stems from the
coriander and then chop finely.

Cut the vegetables into short lengths, then cut
into fine strips for quick cooking.

Soak the bread in water, then squeeze out the
liquid with your hands.

13

JAPANESE GINGER BROTH WITH SALMON

Preparation time: 10 minutes
Total cooking time: 15 minutes
Serves 6

2 teaspoons dashi powder
3 x 3 cm (1 inch) pieces of fresh
    ginger, cut into fine strips
8 spring onions, thinly sliced on the
    diagonal
750 g (1 1/2 lb) baby bok choy,
    trimmed, leaves separated
3 teaspoons Japanese soy sauce

200 g (6 1/2 oz) soba noodles
2 tablespoons peanut oil
6 small salmon fillets, skin and bones
    removed
lime wedges, to serve

1 Place 1.5 litres water and the dashi powder in a large saucepan. Bring to the boil and add the ginger, spring onion and bok choy. Reduce the heat and simmer, covered, for 5 minutes, or until the bok choy has wilted. Stir in the soy sauce, remove from the heat and keep warm.
2 Meanwhile, cook the noodles in a saucepan of boiling water for

1 minute, or until just tender. Drain and keep warm.
3 Heat the oil in a large frying pan, add the salmon fillets and cook for 3 minutes each side, or until cooked to your liking. (The salmon is best still rare in the middle.) Divide the noodles among six serving bowls. Add the bok choy and spoon on the broth. Top with the salmon fillets and serve with lime wedges.

NUTRITION PER SERVE
Protein 21 g; Fat 20 g; Carbohydrate 8 g;
Dietary Fibre 2.5 g; Cholesterol 0 mg;
1207 kJ (287 cal)

Add the ginger, spring onion and bok choy to the dashi stock and cook until wilted.

Cook the soba noodles in boiling water for just 1 minute, or until tender.

Heat the oil in a large frying pan and cook the salmon to your liking.

WON TON SOUP

Preparation time: 50 minutes
  + 30 minutes soaking
Total cooking time: 40 minutes
Serves 4

2 dried Chinese mushrooms
15 raw prawns
100 g (3½ oz) pork mince
2 spring onions, chopped
1 teaspoon grated fresh ginger
2 tablespoons canned water
    chestnuts, chopped
2 teaspoons chopped lemon grass,
    white part only
1 clove garlic, finely chopped
3 tablespoons soy sauce

225 g (7 oz) won ton wrappers
fresh coriander leaves
1.5 litres beef stock
3 baby carrots, sliced
3 spring onions, sliced

1 Soak the mushrooms in hot water for 30 minutes. Peel and devein the prawns, then cut in half lengthways. Drain the mushrooms, remove the stems and chop the caps.
2 Mix the chopped mushrooms with the pork, spring onion, ginger, water chestnut, lemon grass, garlic and 1 tablespoon of the soy sauce. Work with one won ton wrapper at a time, keeping the rest covered with a damp tea towel to prevent drying out. Put 2–3 coriander leaves, half a prawn and

a heaped teaspoon of the pork mixture in the centre of a wrapper. Brush the edges with water and lay another wrapper on top. Press to seal. Repeat with the remaining wrappers.
3 Bring the stock, remaining soy sauce, carrot and spring onion to the boil. Bring another large pan of water to the boil and cook the won tons in batches for 4–5 minutes; drain. Pour the hot soup over the won tons and serve immediately.

NUTRITION PER SERVE
Protein 20 g; Fat 4 g; Carbohydrate 50 g;
Dietary Fibre 5 g; Cholesterol 90 mg;
1290 kJ (310 cal)

Thinly slice the white part of the lemon grass, then chop finely.

Remove the stems from the soaked mushrooms and finely chop the caps.

Lightly brush the edges of the wrapper with a little water, then lay another wrapper on top.

MULLIGATAWNY SOUP

Preparation time: 20 minutes
Total cooking time: 1 hour 15 minutes
Serves 4

30 g (1 oz) butter
375 g (12 oz) chicken thigh cutlets,
    skin and fat removed
1 large onion, finely chopped
1 apple, peeled, cored and diced
1 tablespoon curry paste
2 tablespoons plain flour
3 cups (750 ml/24 fl oz) chicken stock
3 tablespoons basmati rice

1 tablespoon chutney
1 tablespoon lemon juice
3 tablespoons cream

1 Heat the butter in a large heavy-based pan and brown the chicken for 5 minutes, then remove from the pan. Add the onion, apple and curry paste to the pan. Cook for 5 minutes, or until the onion is soft. Stir in the flour, cook for 2 minutes then add half the stock. Stir until the mixture boils and thickens.
2 Return the chicken to the pan with the remaining stock. Stir until boiling, reduce the heat, cover and simmer for

45 minutes. Add the rice and cook for a further 15 minutes.
3 Remove the chicken, dice the meat finely and return to the pan. Add the chutney, lemon juice, cream and salt and pepper to taste.

NUTRITION PER SERVE
Protein 25 g; Fat 16 g; Carbohydrate 25 g;
Dietary Fibre 2 g; Cholesterol 28 mg;
1396 kJ (333 cal)

STORAGE: Can be kept covered and refrigerated for up to 3 days.

Once the mixture has thickened, return the browned chicken thighs to the pan.

Add the basmati rice to the soup for the last 15 minutes of cooking.

Add the chutney, lemon juice and cream at the end of cooking.

SPICY LAMB SOUP

Preparation time: 40 minutes
Total cooking time: 1 hour 30 minutes
Serves 4–6

2 large onions, roughly chopped
3 red chillies, seeded and chopped (or
    2 teaspoons dried chilli)
3–4 cloves garlic
2.5 cm (1 inch) piece of fresh ginger,
    chopped
1 teaspoon ground black pepper
5 cm (2 inch) lemon grass, white part
    only, finely chopped
1/2 teaspoon ground cardamom
2 teaspoons ground cumin
1/2 teaspoon ground cinnamon
1 teaspoon ground turmeric
2 tablespoons peanut oil

1.5 kg (3 lb) lamb neck chops
2–3 tablespoons vindaloo paste
2 1/2 cups (600 ml/20 fl oz) coconut
    cream
3 tablespoons soft brown sugar
2–3 tablespoons lime juice
4 kaffir lime leaves

1 Put the onion, chilli, garlic, ginger, pepper, lemon grass, cardamom, cumin, cinnamon and turmeric in a food processor and process to a paste. Heat half the oil in a large pan and brown the chops in batches. Drain on paper towels.
2 Add the remaining oil to the pan and cook the spice and vindaloo pastes for 2–3 minutes. Add the chops and 1.75 litres water, cover and bring to the boil. Reduce the heat and simmer, covered, for 1 hour. Remove

the chops from the pan and stir in the coconut cream. Remove the meat from the bones, shred and return to the pan.
3 Add the sugar, lime juice and leaves. Simmer, uncovered, over low heat for 20–25 minutes, until slightly thickened.

NUTRITION PER SERVE (6)
Protein 55 g; Fat 38 g; Carbohydrate 17 g;
Dietary Fibre 3 g; Cholesterol 166 mg;
2602 kJ (622 cal)

STORAGE: Can be stored in an airtight container in the fridge for 2 days. Bring to the boil when reheating, simmer for 2–3 minutes, then serve.

HINT: This soup is quite spicy even without the addition of the vindaloo paste. Vary the amount of paste added if you prefer a milder taste.

Wear disposable gloves when working with chillies to avoid smarting.

Process the onion with the chilli, garlic and spices to make a paste.

Trim away any excess fat from the lamb chops before cooking.

TOM YAM GOONG

Preparation time: 25 minutes
Total cooking time: 45 minutes
Serves 4–6

500 g (1 lb) raw prawns
1 tablespoon oil
2 tablespoons Thai red curry paste
2 tablespoons tamarind purée
2 teaspoons turmeric
1 teaspoon chopped red chillies
4 kaffir lime leaves, shredded
2 tablespoons fish sauce
2 tablespoons lime juice
2 teaspoons soft brown sugar
fresh coriander leaves, to garnish

1 Peel and devein the prawns, leaving the tails intact. Heat the oil in a large pan and cook the prawn shells and heads for 10 minutes over medium-high heat, tossing frequently, until the heads are deep orange.
2 Add 1 cup (250 ml/8 fl oz) water and the curry paste. Boil for 5 minutes, or until reduced slightly. Add 2 litres water and simmer for 20 minutes. Strain, discarding the shells and heads, and return the stock to the pan.
3 Add the tamarind, turmeric, chilli and lime leaves, bring to the boil and cook for 2 minutes. Add the prawns and cook for 5 minutes, or until pink. Add the fish sauce, lime juice and sugar. Garnish with coriander leaves.

NUTRITION PER SERVE (6)
Protein 17 g; Fat 6 g; Carbohydrate 2 g;
Dietary Fibre 0 g; Cholesterol 125 mg;
560 kJ (135 cal)

HINT: If you can't find tamarind purée, soak one quarter of a block of tamarind in warm water for 10 minutes, work the mixture with your fingertips and remove the stones.

Add the red curry paste and a cup of water to the pan.

Add the tamarind, turmeric, chilli and kaffir lime leaves and bring to the boil.

Add the prawns to the boiling soup mixture and cook until they turn pink.

BABY CORN AND CHICKEN SOUP

Preparation time: 30 minutes
Total cooking time: 15 minutes
Serves 4

150 g (5 oz) whole baby corn (see NOTE)
1 tablespoon oil
2 stalks lemon grass, white part only, very finely sliced
2 tablespoons grated fresh ginger
6 spring onions, chopped
1 red chilli, finely chopped
1 litre chicken stock

1¹/₂ cups (375 ml/12 fl oz) coconut milk
250 g (8 oz) chicken breast fillets, thinly sliced
130 g (4 oz) creamed corn
1 tablespoon soy sauce
2 tablespoons finely chopped chives, to serve
1 red chilli, thinly sliced, to serve

1 Cut the baby corn in half or quarters lengthways, depending on their size.
2 Heat the oil in a pan over medium heat and cook the lemon grass, ginger, spring onion and chilli for 1 minute, stirring continuously. Add the stock and coconut milk and bring to the

boil—do not cover or the coconut milk will curdle.
3 Add the corn, chicken and creamed corn and simmer for 8 minutes, or until the corn and chicken are just tender. Add the soy sauce, season well and serve garnished with the chives and chilli.

NUTRITION PER SERVE
Protein 20 g; Fat 25 g; Carbohydrate 15 g;
Dietary Fibre 3 g; Cholesterol 30 mg;
1520 kJ (360 cal)

NOTE: Canned baby corn can be substituted for fresh corn. Add during the last 2 minutes of cooking.

Grate the peeled fresh ginger on the fine side of the grater.

Cut the baby corn lengthways into halves or quarters, depending on its size.

Add the baby corn, chicken and canned creamed corn to the pan.

CHINESE HOT AND SOUR SOUP

Preparation time: 15 minutes +
  30 minutes soaking
Total cooking time: 15 minutes
Serves 4

8 dried shiitake mushrooms
2 teaspoons cornflour
2 teaspoons sesame oil
1 litre vegetable stock
125 g (4 oz) bamboo shoots, cut into
  thin strips
125 g (4 oz) silken firm tofu, cut into
  long thin strips

2 teaspoons light soy sauce
3 tablespoons white wine vinegar
1/2 teaspoon white pepper
spring onions, thinly sliced, to garnish

1 Soak the mushrooms in a bowl
with 1/2 cup (125 ml/4 fl oz) hot water
for 30 minutes. Drain and reserve the
liquid in a small bowl. Discard the
stems and cut the caps into quarters.
2 Whisk the cornflour, sesame oil and
2 tablespoons of the stock together.
3 Place the remaining stock and
reserved mushroom liquid in a large
saucepan and bring to the boil. Add
the mushrooms and bamboo shoots.
Season with salt, reduce the heat and

simmer for 5 minutes.
4 Add the tofu, soy sauce, vinegar and
white pepper. Return the soup to a
simmer. Stir in the cornflour mixture
and cook until the soup thickens
slightly. Pour into individual serving
bowls and garnish with spring onion.

NUTRITION PER SERVE
Protein 3.5 g; Fat 4 g; Carbohydrate 6 g;
Dietary Fibre 1 g; Cholesterol 0 mg;
320 kJ (75 cal)

HINT: For a hotter soup, add extra
white pepper before serving.

Cut the silken firm tofu into long thin strips of an
even size.

Discard the stems, then cut the soaked shiitake
mushrooms into quarters.

Stir in the cornflour mixture and cook until the
soup thickens slightly.

BEEF BALLS IN CHINESE LONG SOUP

Preparation time: 1 hour
Total cooking time: 20 minutes
Serves 6

500 g (1 lb) lean beef mince
2 egg whites, lightly beaten
1 tablespoon iced water
2 tablespoons soy sauce
1 teaspoon sesame oil
2 teaspoons cornflour
2 tablespoons finely chopped fresh coriander
2 spring onions, finely chopped
1/4 teaspoon ground white pepper
1/4 teaspoon five-spice powder

LONG SOUP
1 litre beef stock
500 g (1 lb) assorted Chinese vegetables, thinly sliced
375 g (12 oz) fresh thin egg noodles, cooked

1 Process the mince in a food processor in small batches for 30 seconds, or until it forms a fine paste. Transfer to a bowl and add the remaining beef ball ingredients.
2 Roll level tablespoons of the mixture into balls with wet hands. Half-fill a wok with water, cover and bring to the boil. Arrange the balls in a steamer lined with lightly oiled greaseproof paper, cover and steam over the wok for 20 minutes.

3 Bring the stock to the boil, add the vegetables and cook for 2 minutes. Pour into a tureen and add the noodles and beef balls.

NUTRITION PER SERVE
Protein 26 g; Fat 10 g; Carbohydrate 46 g;
Dietary Fibre 2 g; Cholesterol 65 mg;
1600 kJ (380 cal)

STORAGE: The beef balls can be made a day in advance and reheated in the boiling stock just before serving.

VARIATION: For combination long soup, add 125 g (4 oz) each of peeled, cooked prawns, sliced barbecued pork and cooked chicken.

Process the mince to a paste and then mix with the other meatball ingredients.

Arrange the beef balls in a lined steamer over a wok of boiling water.

Bring the stock to the boil, add the sliced Chinese vegetables and cook for 2 minutes.

SEAFOOD LAKSA

Preparation time: 45 minutes
Total cooking time: 45 minutes
Serves 4–6

1 kg (2 lb) raw prawns
1/2 cup (125 ml/4 fl oz) oil
2–6 red chillies, seeded
1 onion, roughly chopped
3 cloves garlic, halved
2 cm (3/4 inch) piece of fresh ginger
   or galangal, quartered
1 teaspoon ground turmeric
1 tablespoon ground coriander
3 stalks lemon grass, white part only,
   chopped
1–2 teaspoons shrimp paste
2 1/2 cups (600 ml/20 fl oz) coconut
   cream
2 teaspoons grated palm sugar
4 kaffir lime leaves
200 g (6 1/2 oz) packet fish balls
190 g (6 1/2 oz) packet fried bean curd
   pieces
250 g (8 oz) fresh thin egg noodles
250 g (8 oz) bean sprouts
1/3 cup (20 g/1 oz) chopped fresh
   mint, to serve
1/4 cup (7 g/1/4 oz) fresh coriander
   leaves, to serve

1 Peel and devein the prawns, keeping the shells, heads and tails.
2 To make the prawn stock, heat 2 tablespoons of the oil in a large, heavy-based pan and add the prawn shells, heads and tails. Stir until the heads are bright orange, then add 1 litre water. Bring to the boil, reduce the heat and simmer for 15 minutes. Strain through a fine sieve, discarding the shells. Wipe the pan clean.
3 Put the chillies, onion, garlic, ginger (or galangal), turmeric, coriander, lemon grass and 1/4 cup (60 ml/2 fl oz) of the prawn stock in a food processor and process until finely chopped.
4 Heat the remaining oil in the clean pan and add the chilli mixture and shrimp paste. Stir over low heat for 3 minutes, or until fragrant. Pour in the remaining stock and simmer for 10 minutes. Then add the coconut cream, palm sugar, kaffir lime leaves and 2 teaspoons of salt. Simmer for a further 5 minutes.
5 Add the prawns and simmer for 2 minutes, until they are just pink. Remove and set aside. Add the fish balls and bean curd and simmer gently until just heated through.
6 Bring a pan of water to the boil and cook the noodles for 2 minutes, then drain and place in a bowl. Lay the bean sprouts and prawns on the noodles and pour the soup over the top. Sprinkle with the chopped mint and coriander leaves to serve.

NUTRITION PER SERVE (6)
Protein 50 g; Fat 50 g; Carbohydrate 40 g; Dietary Fibre 8 g; Cholesterol 270 mg; 3340 kJ (800 cal)

HINT: For a really fiery soup, garnish with extra sliced red chilli.

NOTE: Laksa originated in Singapore and can also be made with fresh or dried rice noodles. Shredded cucumber can be added with the bean sprouts.

VARIATION: Laksa can be made without the fish balls or bean curd. Instead, use a combination of seafood or replace the seafood with bite-sized pieces of chicken or pork.

Wearing rubber gloves, halve the chillies lengthways and remove the seeds.

Stir-fry the prawn shells, heads and tails until they turn bright orange.

Put the chillies, onion, garlic, lemon grass, spices and stock in a food processor.

Add the shrimp paste to the pan and stir in with a wooden spoon.

Add the coconut cream, palm sugar, salt and kaffir lime leaves and simmer.

Stir the fish balls into the simmering soup, then add the bean curd.

CRAB DUMPLING SOUP

Preparation time: 25 minutes
Total cooking time: 20 minutes
Serves 4

170 g (5¹/₂ oz) can crab meat, well
    drained
2 tablespoons finely chopped spring
    onions
2 cloves garlic, finely chopped
2 teaspoons sesame oil
3 teaspoons chopped fresh ginger
12 small gow gee or won ton
    wrappers
2 spring onions, extra
1.25 litres chicken stock
1 tablespoon soy sauce
1 tablespoon mirin (see NOTE)
1 teaspoon sugar

1 To make the crab filling, mix the
crab with the chopped spring onion,
1 clove of garlic, 1 teaspoon of sesame
oil and 1 teaspoon of the ginger.
2 Place 2 teaspoons of filling on one
half of each wrapper. Moisten the edge
with some water and fold over to form
a crescent. Press the edges together
firmly. Lay the dumplings on a lightly
floured surface.
3 Cut the extra spring onions into thin
strips and set aside. Heat the remaining
sesame oil in a pan, add the remaining
garlic and ginger and cook over
medium heat for 3–4 minutes, or until
the garlic is lightly golden. Add the
stock, soy sauce, mirin and sugar.
Bring to the boil, add the spring onion
strips and simmer for 2–3 minutes.
4 Bring a large pan of water to the
boil, add 3–4 dumplings at a time and
cook for 5 minutes, or until just
cooked. Place in bowls, ladle the stock
over the dumplings and serve.

NUTRITION PER SERVE
Protein 30 g; Fat 20 g; Carbohydrate 35 g;
Dietary Fibre 5 g; Cholesterol 50 mg;
1800 kJ (430 cal)

NOTE: Mirin is a Japanese sweetened
rice wine which is used frequently
in cooking.

Be sure to drain the crab meat thoroughly so that
the filling is not too liquid.

Using a sharp knife, peel the ginger, cut into
strips, then chop finely.

Fold over the wrapper to enclose the filling and
press firmly.

Cut the spring onions into lengths, then into thin
strips for quick cooking.

SOBA NOODLE SOUP

Preparation time: 15 minutes +
  5 minutes soaking
Total cooking time: 10 minutes
Serves 4

250 g (8 oz) soba noodles
2 dried shiitake mushrooms
2 litres vegetable stock
120 g (4 oz) snow peas, cut into thin
  strips
2 small carrots, cut into thin strips
6 spring onions, cut into short lengths
  and thinly sliced lengthways

2 cloves garlic, finely chopped
2.5 cm (1 inch) piece of fresh ginger,
  cut into thin strips
1/3 cup (80 ml/2 3/4 fl oz) soy sauce
1/4 cup (60 ml/2 fl oz) mirin or sake
1 cup (90 g/3 oz) bean sprouts

1 Cook the noodles according to the
packet instructions and drain.
2 Soak the mushrooms in 1/2 cup
(125 ml/4 fl oz) boiling water until
soft. Drain, reserving the liquid.
Remove the stalks and slice the
mushroom caps.
3 Combine the vegetable stock,
mushrooms, mushroom liquid, snow

peas, carrot, spring onion, garlic and
ginger in a large saucepan. Bring
slowly to the boil, then reduce the
heat to low and simmer for 5 minutes,
or until the vegetables are tender. Add
the soy sauce, mirin and bean sprouts.
Cook for a further 3 minutes.
4 Divide the noodles among four
large serving bowls. Ladle the hot
liquid and vegetables over the top and
serve immediately.

NUTRITION PER SERVE
Protein 13 g; Fat 1.5 g; Carbohydrate 30 g;
Dietary Fibre 6 g; Cholesterol 11 mg;
1124 kJ (270 cal)

Cut the ginger into thin strips the size and shape
of matchsticks.

After soaking the mushrooms, drain and finely
slice them.

Simmer the vegetables for 5 minutes, or until they
are tender.

MISO SOUP

Preparation time: 5–10 minutes
Total cooking time: 5 minutes
Serves 4

2 teaspoons dashi granules or powder
   (see NOTES)
3 tablespoons miso paste (see
   NOTES)
250 g (8 oz) silken tofu
2 spring onions

1 Mix the dashi granules or powder with 1 litre cold water in a pan and bring to the boil. Reduce the heat and whisk in the miso paste.
2 Cut the tofu into small cubes and add to the soup. Slice the spring onions diagonally, separate the layers and add to the soup. Simmer gently for 2–3 minutes before serving.

NUTRITION PER SERVE
Protein 5 g; Fat 3 g; Carbohydrate 5 g;
Dietary Fibre 0 g; Cholesterol 0 mg;
255 kJ (60 cal)

NOTES: Dashi is a basic stock used in Japanese cooking which is made by boiling dried kelp (seaweed) and dried bonito (fish). Instant dashi granules are sold in conveniently sized jars or packets and vary in strength. Add more dashi to your soup if you want a stronger stock.

You can use yellow, white or red miso paste for this soup. Yellow miso is sweet and creamy; red miso is strong and salty.

Put the cold water in a pan and add the dashi granules or powder.

Add the miso paste to the pan and whisk until it has dissolved.

Slice the spring onions diagonally and separate the layers.

TOM KHA GAI

Preparation time: 20 minutes
Total cooking time: 20 minutes
Serves 4

5 cm (2 inch) piece of fresh galangal or
   5 slices of dried galangal (see
   NOTE)
6 kaffir lime leaves
1 stalk lemon grass, white part only,
   quartered
2 cups (500 ml/16 fl oz) coconut milk
2 cups (500 ml/16 fl oz) chicken stock
3 chicken breast fillets, cut into thin
   strips
1 teaspoon finely chopped red chilli

1/4 cup (60 ml/2 fl oz) lime juice
2 tablespoons fish sauce
1 teaspoon soft brown sugar
1/4 cup (15 g/1/2 oz) fresh coriander
   leaves

1 Peel the galangal and cut into thin slices. Mix the galangal, kaffir lime leaves and lemon grass with the coconut milk and stock in a saucepan. Bring to the boil, reduce the heat to low and simmer for 10 minutes, stirring occasionally.
2 Add the chicken strips and chilli and simmer for 8 minutes. Mix in the lime juice, fish sauce and sugar. Serve with a few coriander leaves floating on top of the soup.

NUTRITION PER SERVE
Protein 40 g; Fat 30 g; Carbohydrate 5 g;
Dietary Fibre 0 g; Cholesterol 80 mg;
1840 kJ (440 cal)

NOTE: If you can't find fresh galangal, you can use 5 large slices of dried galangal instead. Soak in 1 cup (250 ml/8 fl oz) of boiling water for 10 minutes, drain, then cut the galangal into thin slices.

Using a sharp knife, cut the chicken breast fillets into thin strips.

Using a vegetable peeler, peel the fresh galangal and slice thinly.

Add the soft brown sugar to the soup and stir until it has dissolved.

CURRIED LENTIL AND VEGETABLE SOUP WITH SPICED YOGHURT

Preparation time: 30 minutes
Total cooking time: 40 minutes
Serves 6

2 tablespoons olive oil
1 small leek, chopped
2 cloves garlic, crushed
2 teaspoons curry powder
1 teaspoon ground cumin
1 teaspoon garam masala
1 litre vegetable stock
1 fresh bay leaf
1 cup (185 g/6 oz) brown lentils
450 g (14 oz) butternut pumpkin,
    peeled and diced
400 g (13 oz) can chopped tomatoes
2 zucchini, cut in half lengthways
    and sliced
200 g (6¹/₂ oz) broccoli, cut into small
    florets
1 small carrot, diced
¹/₂ cup (90 g/3 oz) peas
1 tablespoon chopped fresh mint

SPICED YOGHURT
1 cup (250 g/8 oz) thick plain yoghurt
1 tablespoon chopped fresh coriander
    leaves
1 clove garlic, crushed
3 dashes Tabasco

1 Heat the oil in a saucepan over medium heat. Add the leek and garlic and cook for 4–5 minutes, or until soft and lightly golden. Add the curry powder, cumin and garam masala and cook for 1 minute, or until fragrant.
2 Add the stock, bay leaf, lentils and pumpkin. Bring to the boil, then reduce the heat to low and simmer for 10–15 minutes, or until the lentils are tender. Season well.
3 Add the tomatoes, zucchini, broccoli, carrot and 500 ml (16 fl oz) water and simmer for 10 minutes, or until the vegetables are tender. Add the peas and simmer for 2–3 minutes.
4 To make the spiced yoghurt, place the yoghurt, coriander, garlic and Tabasco in a small bowl and stir until combined. Dollop a spoonful of the yoghurt on each serving of soup and garnish with the chopped mint.

NUTRITION PER SERVE
Protein 17 g; Fat 10 g; Carbohydrate 26 g;
Dietary Fibre 10 g; Cholesterol 6.5 mg;
1100 kJ (260 Cal)

Stir in the curry powder, cumin and garam masala and cook until fragrant.

Simmer the lentils and vegetables over low heat until the vegetables are tender.

Combine the yoghurt, coriander, garlic and Tabasco sauce.

HOT AND SOUR LIME SOUP WITH BEEF

Preparation time: 20 minutes
Total cooking time: 30 minutes
Serves 4

1 litre beef stock
2 stalks lemon grass, white part only, halved
3 cloves garlic, halved
2.5 cm (1 inch) piece of fresh ginger, sliced
90 g (3 oz) fresh coriander, leaves and stalks separated
4 spring onions, thinly sliced
2 strips lime rind
2 star anise
3 small fresh red chillies, seeded and finely chopped
500 g (1 lb) fillet steak, trimmed
2 tablespoons fish sauce
1 tablespoon grated palm sugar
2 tablespoons lime juice
fresh coriander leaves, to garnish

1 Put the stock, lemon grass, garlic, ginger, coriander stalks, 2 spring onions, lime rind, star anise, 1 teaspoon chopped chilli and 1 litre water in a saucepan. Bring to the boil and simmer, covered, for 25 minutes. Strain and return the liquid to the pan.
2 Heat a chargrill pan until very hot. Brush lightly with olive oil and sear the steak on both sides until browned but very rare in the centre.
3 Reheat the soup, adding the fish sauce and palm sugar. Season with salt and black pepper. Add the lime juice to taste (you may want more than 2 tablespoons) to achieve a hot and sour flavour.
4 Add the remaining spring onion and the chopped coriander leaves to the soup. Slice the beef across the grain into thin strips. Curl the strips into a decorative pattern, then place in the centre of four deep wide serving bowls. Pour the soup over the beef and garnish with the remaining chilli and a few extra coriander leaves.

NUTRITION PER SERVE
Protein 31 g; Fat 7 g; Carbohydrate 7 g; Dietary Fibre 0.5 g; Cholesterol 84 mg; 900 kJ (215 cal)

Bring the soup to the boil, then reduce the heat and simmer for 25 minutes.

Brown the fillet steak on a hot chargrill pan, keeping it very rare in the centre.

Slice the beef along the grain and curl the strips into a decorative pattern.

CHICKEN NOODLE SOUP

Preparation time: 20 minutes +
 10 minutes soaking
Total cooking time: 10 minutes
Serves 4

3 dried Chinese mushrooms
185 g (6 oz) dried thin egg noodles
1 tablespoon oil
4 spring onions, cut into thin strips
1 tablespoon soy sauce
2 tablespoons rice wine, mirin or
 sherry
1.25 litres chicken stock
1/2 small barbecued chicken,
 shredded
60 g (2 oz) sliced ham, cut into strips

1 cup (90 g/3 oz) bean sprouts
fresh coriander leaves and thinly sliced
 red chilli, to garnish

1 Soak the mushrooms in boiling water for 10 minutes to soften them. Squeeze dry, then remove the tough stems from the mushrooms and slice the caps thinly.
2 Cook the noodles in a large pan of boiling water for 3 minutes, or according to the packet directions. Drain and cut the noodles into shorter lengths with scissors.
3 Heat the oil in a large heavy-based pan. Add the mushrooms and spring onion. Cook for 1 minute, then add the soy sauce, rice wine and stock. Bring slowly to the boil and cook for

1 minute. Reduce the heat then add the noodles, shredded chicken, ham and bean sprouts. Heat through for 2 minutes without allowing to boil.
4 Use tongs to divide the noodles among four bowls, ladle in the remaining mixture, and garnish with coriander leaves and sliced chilli.

NUTRITION PER SERVE
Protein 25 g; Fat 10 g; Carbohydrate 35 g;
Dietary Fibre 3 g; Cholesterol 80 mg;
1426 kJ (340 cal)

NOTE: Rice wine and mirin are avaiable at Asian food stores.

VARIATION: Udon noodles can be used instead of egg noodles.

The easiest way to shred the meat from the barbecued chicken is with a fork.

Put the mushrooms in a bowl, cover with boiling water and leave to soak.

Cut the noodles into shorter lengths to make them easier to eat.

CRAB AND CORN SOUP

Preparation time: 15 minutes
Total cooking time: 10 minutes
Serves 4

1¹/₂ tablespoons oil
6 cloves garlic, chopped
6 red Asian shallots, chopped
2 stalks lemon grass, white
   part only, finely chopped
1 tablespoon grated fresh ginger
1 litre chicken stock

1 cup (250 ml/8 fl oz) coconut milk
2¹/₂ cups (375 g/12 oz) frozen corn
   kernels
2 x 170 g (5¹/₂ oz) cans crab meat,
   drained
2 tablespoons fish sauce
2 tablespoons lime juice
1 teaspoon shaved palm sugar
   or soft brown sugar

1 Heat the oil in a large saucepan, then add the garlic, shallots, lemon grass and ginger and cook, stirring, over medium heat for 2 minutes.

2 Pour the chicken stock and coconut milk into the saucepan and bring to the boil, stirring occasionally. Add the corn and cook for 5 minutes.

3 Add the drained crab meat, fish sauce, lime juice and sugar and stir until the crab is heated through. Season to taste. Ladle into bowls and serve immediately.

NUTRITION PER SERVE
Protein 15 g; Fat 11 g; Carbohydrate 21.5 g;
Dietary Fibre 3.5 g; Cholesterol 71.5 mg;
1016 kJ (240 cal)

Peel off the outer layers of the Asian shallots before chopping.

Shave off thin slices of the palm sugar with a sharp knife.

When the soup comes to the boil, add the corn kernels and cook for 5 minutes.

LOW-FAT CHICKEN LAKSA

Preparation time: 30 minutes
Total cooking time: 25 minutes
Serves 4

1 large onion, roughly chopped
5 cm (2 inch) piece of fresh ginger,
   chopped
8 cm (3 inch) piece of fresh galangal,
   peeled and chopped
1 stem lemon grass, white part only,
   roughly chopped
2 cloves garlic
1 fresh red chilli, seeded and chopped
2 teaspoons vegetable oil
2 tablespoons mild curry paste
500 g (1 lb) chicken breast fillets,
   diced
2 cups (500 ml/16 fl oz) chicken stock
60 g (2 oz) rice vermicelli
50 g (1³/4 oz) dried egg noodles
400 ml (13 fl oz) light coconut milk
10 snow peas, halved
3 spring onions, finely chopped
1 cup (90 g/3 oz) bean sprouts
¹/2 cup (15 g/¹/2 oz) fresh coriander
   leaves

1 Process the onion, ginger, galangal, lemon grass, garlic and chilli in a food processor until finely chopped. Add the oil and process until the mixture has a paste-like consistency. Spoon into a large wok, add the curry paste and stir over low heat for 1–2 minutes, until aromatic. Take care not to burn.
2 Increase the heat to medium, add the chicken and stir for 2 minutes, or until the chicken is well coated. Stir in the chicken stock and mix well. Bring slowly to the boil, then simmer for 10 minutes, or until the chicken is cooked through.
3 Meanwhile, cut the vermicelli into shorter lengths with scissors. Cook the vermicelli and egg noodles separately in large pans of boiling water for 5 minutes each. Drain and rinse under cold water.
4 Just before serving add the light coconut milk and snow peas to the chicken and heat through. To serve, divide the vermicelli and noodles among warmed serving bowls. Pour the hot laksa over the top and garnish with the spring onion, bean sprouts and coriander leaves.

NUTRITION PER SERVE
Protein 30 g; Fat 8 g; Carbohydrate 4.5 g;
Dietary Fibre 3 g; Cholesterol 65 mg;
945 kJ (225 cal)

Stir the curry paste into the onion mixture, over low heat, until aromatic.

Just before serving, stir the coconut milk into the chicken until heated.

COCONUT PRAWN SOUP

Preparation time: 20 minutes +
    15 minutes soaking
Total cooking time: 45 minutes
Serves 4

CURRY PASTE
6 long dried red chillies
1 teaspoon cumin seeds
2 teaspoons coriander seeds
1/2 teaspoon paprika
1 teaspoon ground turmeric
1/2 teaspoon black peppercorns
4 red Asian shallots, chopped
4 cloves garlic, roughly chopped
2.5 cm (1 inch) piece of fresh ginger,
    sliced
4 fresh coriander roots
2 tablespoons chopped fresh
    coriander stems
1 teaspoon grated lime rind
2 stems lemon grass, while part only,
    sliced
2 kaffir lime leaves, finely shredded
1 teaspoon shrimp paste
2 tablespoons oil

STOCK
750 g (1 1/2 lb) raw prawns
4 red Asian shallots, chopped
1 clove garlic
green ends of lemon grass stalks
6 black peppercorns

2 tablespoons oil
2 x 400 ml (13 fl oz) cans coconut milk
1/4 cup (60 m/2 fl oz) fish sauce
fresh coriander and strips of lime rind,
    to garnish

1 For the curry paste, soak the chillies in boiling water for 10–15 minutes, then drain. Toss the spices and peppercorns in a dry frying pan over medium heat for 1 minute, or until fragrant. Grind to a powder in a spice grinder or mortar and pestle, then transfer to a food processor and add the remaining paste ingredients and 1 teaspoon salt. Process until smooth. Add a little water, if necessary.

2 For the stock, peel and devein the prawns, leaving the tails intact. Refrigerate. Keep the heads and shells.

3 Dry-fry the prawn heads and shells in a wok or large saucepan over high heat for 5 minutes until orange. Add the remaining stock ingredients and 1.5 litres water and bring to the boil. Reduce the heat and simmer for 15–20 minutes, then strain, reserving the liquid.

4 Heat the oil in a wok and add 3 tablespoons curry paste (freeze the leftover in an airtight container) and stir constantly over medium heat for 1–2 minutes, until fragrant. Stir in the stock and coconut milk. Bring to the boil, then reduce the heat and simmer for 10 minutes. Add the prawns and cook, stirring, for 2 minutes, or until the prawns are cooked. Stir in the fish sauce and garnish with coriander leaves and strips of lime rind.

NUTRITION PER SERVE
Protein 40 g; Fat 60 g; Carbohydrate 12 g;
Dietary Fibre 3 g; Cholesterol 355 mg;
2972 kJ (705 cal)

Grind the cumin and coriander seeds, paprika, turmeric and peppercorns.

Process the ground spices with the remaining paste ingredients until smooth.

Simmer the stock for 15–20 minutes to reduce the liquid.

Appetisers

PORK AND LEMON GRASS WON TONS

Preparation time: 40 minutes +
    1 hour refrigeration
Total cooking time: 20 minutes
Makes 56

400 g (13 oz) lean pork mince
1 teaspoon finely chopped fresh
    ginger
1 stalk lemon grass, white part only,
    finely sliced
220 g (7 oz) can water chestnuts,
    drained and finely chopped
2 tablespoons finely chopped fresh
    garlic chives
1/2 teaspoon chilli paste
2 tablespoons plum sauce
1 teaspoon chilli oil
1 teaspoon sesame oil
1 tablespoon cornflour
56 x 8 cm (3 inch) won ton wrappers
oil, for deep-frying

DIPPING SAUCE
1/2 cup (125 ml/4 fl oz) light soy sauce
1/4 cup (60 ml/2 fl oz) balsamic vinegar
1 teaspoon finely grated fresh ginger
1 teaspoon chilli oil

1 In a bowl, combine the pork mince, ginger, lemon grass, water chestnuts, garlic chives, chilli paste, plum sauce, chilli and sesame oils and the cornflour. Mix well with your hands. Cover and refrigerate for 1 hour.
2 To make the dipping sauce, stir together the soy sauce, balsamic vinegar, ginger and chilli oil.
3 Work with one won ton wrapper at a time, keeping the rest covered with a damp tea towel to prevent drying out. Place about 2 teaspoons of the filling onto the centre of each wrapper and lightly brush the edges of the wrapper with water. Gather up the corners, bring the edges together in the centre and press firmly to seal. Repeat with the remaining wrappers and filling.
4 Deep-fry the won tons, in batches, in moderately hot oil for 3–4 minutes, or until lightly browned. Remove with a slotted spoon and drain well on paper towels. Serve hot with the dipping sauce.

NUTRITION PER WON TON
Protein 3 g; Fat 2 g; Carbohydrate 5 g;
Dietary Fibre 1 g; Cholesterol 5 mg;
200 kJ (50 cal)

Mix all the ingredients for the filling in a large bowl
and then cover and refrigerate.

Place a ball of the mixture on a wrapper and
brush the edge with water.

SPRING ROLLS

Preparation time: 40 minutes
Total cooking time: 25 minutes
Makes 18

2 tablespoons oil
2 cloves garlic, chopped
2.5 cm (1 inch) piece of fresh ginger, grated
100 g (3^1/$_2$ oz) lean pork mince
100 g (3^1/$_2$ oz) chicken mince
60 g (2 oz) raw prawns, minced
2 celery sticks, finely sliced
1 small carrot, finely chopped
^{1}/$_2$ cup (90 g/3 oz) chopped water chestnuts
4 spring onions, chopped
1 cup (75 g/2^1/$_2$ oz) finely shredded cabbage
^{1}/$_2$ cup (125 ml/4 fl oz) chicken stock
4 tablespoons cornflour
2 tablespoons oyster sauce
1 tablespoon soy sauce
2 teaspoons sesame oil
36 spring roll wrappers
oil, for deep-frying
sweet chilli sauce, for serving

1 Heat 1 tablespoon oil in a wok or pan and cook the garlic and ginger for 30 seconds. Add the pork, chicken and prawn minces and cook for 3 minutes, or until the minces are brown. Transfer to a bowl.
2 Wipe the pan, then heat the remaining tablespoon of oil and add the celery, carrot, water chestnuts, spring onion and cabbage. Stir over medium heat for 2 minutes. Combine the chicken stock, 1 tablespoon cornflour, oyster and soy sauces and salt and pepper, add to the vegetables and stir until thickened. Stir the sesame oil and vegetables into the

meat mixture and cool. Mix the remaining cornflour with ^{1}/$_3$ cup (80 ml/2^3/$_4$ fl oz) water until smooth.
3 Place 1 small square spring roll wrapper on the bench with a corner towards you. Brush all the edges with a little cornflour paste and cover with another wrapper. Brush the edges of the second wrapper and spread about 1^1/$_2$ tablespoons of the filling across the bottom corner of the wrapper. Fold the bottom corner up over the

filling, fold in the sides and roll up firmly. Repeat with the remaining wrappers and filling. Heat the oil in a deep pan and fry the rolls, in batches, for 2–3 minutes, or until golden. Drain and serve with sweet chilli sauce.

NUTRITION PER SPRING ROLL
Protein 2 g; Fat 7 g; Carbohydrate 5 g;
Dietary Fibre 1 g; Cholesterol 7 mg;
390 kJ (90 cal)

Add the pork, chicken and prawn minces to the wok or pan and fry until brown.

Mix the stock, 1 tablespoon of cornflour, oyster and soy sauces and seasoning.

Fold the bottom corner over the filling and fold in the sides before rolling up.

COMBINATION DIM SIMS

Preparation time: 1 hour + 1 hour
  refrigeration
Total cooking time: 30 minutes
Makes about 30

6 dried Chinese mushrooms
200 g (6¹/₂ oz) lean pork mince
30 g (1 oz) pork fat, finely chopped
100 g (3¹/₃ oz) raw prawn meat, finely
  chopped
2 spring onions, finely chopped
1 tablespoon sliced bamboo shoots,
  finely chopped
1 celery stick, finely chopped
3 teaspoons cornflour

2 teaspoons soy sauce
1 teaspoon caster sugar
30 won ton or egg noodle wrappers

1 Soak the mushrooms in 1 cup
(250 ml/8 fl oz) hot water for
10 minutes, drain and chop the caps
finely, discarding the hard stalks.
2 Mix together the mushrooms, pork
mince, pork fat, prawn, spring onion,
bamboo shoots and celery. Mix the
cornflour, soy, sugar and salt and
pepper into a smooth paste and then
stir into the pork mixture, cover and
refrigerate for 1 hour.
3 Work with one wrapper at a time,
keeping the rest covered with a damp
tea towel to prevent drying out. Place

1 tablespoon of filling in the centre of
each wrapper. Moisten the edges with
water and fold the corners into the
centre. Press the corners together to
seal. Place on a lightly floured surface.
4 Line the base of a bamboo steamer
with a circle of baking paper. Arrange
the dim sims on the paper in batches,
cover and cook over a pan of
simmering water for 8 minutes, or until
the wrappers are firm and the filling is
cooked. Serve with chilli or soy sauce.

NUTRITION PER DIM SIM
Protein 3 g; Fat 2 g; Carbohydrate 1 g;
Dietary Fibre 0 g; Cholesterol 10 mg;
77 kJ (18 cal)

Soak the dried mushrooms in hot water to
rehydrate them.

Fold the corners into the centre and press
together to seal.

Arrange a circle of baking paper in the base of a
bamboo steamer.

WON TON CHICKEN RAVIOLI WITH THAI DRESSING

Preparation time: 35 minutes
Total cooking time: 15 minutes
Serves 4 as a starter

400 g (13 oz) chicken mince
2 spring onions, finely chopped
3 kaffir lime leaves, very finely shredded
2 tablespoons sweet chilli sauce
3 tablespoons chopped fresh coriander leaves
1¹/2 teaspoons sesame oil
2 teaspoons grated lime rind

270 g (9 oz) packet won ton wrappers
¹/2 cup (125 ml/4 fl oz) fish sauce
2 tablespoons grated palm sugar
1 tablespoon peanut oil
1 tablespoon lime juice
finely chopped red chilli and fresh coriander leaves, to garnish

1 Combine the mince, spring onion, lime leaves, chilli sauce, coriander, sesame oil and lime rind in a bowl.
2 Work with one won ton wrapper at a time, keeping the rest covered with a damp tea towel to prevent drying out. Place a tablespoon of the filling in the centre of a wrapper, brush the edges lightly with water and top with another wrapper, pressing down

around the edges to stop the ravioli from opening during cooking.
3 Cook the ravioli in batches in a large saucepan of boiling water for 5 minutes, or until the wrappers are soft and the mince is cooked. Drain well and place on serving plates.
4 Combine the fish sauce, palm sugar, peanut oil and lime juice in a bowl. Pour over the ravioli and garnish with the chilli and coriander.

NUTRITION PER SERVE
Protein 25 g; Fat 15 g; Carbohydrate 11 g;
Dietary Fibre 1 g; Cholesterol 50 mg;
1145 kJ (275 cal)

Put a tablespoon of filling on a wrapper and brush the edges with water.

Top with another wrapper and press the edges together firmly to seal.

Cook until the mince is cooked and the wrappers are softened.

ASIAN OYSTERS

Preparation time: 15 minutes
Total cooking time: 5 minutes
Serves 4 as a starter

12 fresh oysters
2 cloves garlic, finely chopped
2.5 cm (1 inch) piece of fresh ginger,
    cut into thin strips
2 spring onions, finely sliced
    on the diagonal
1/4 cup (60 ml/2 fl oz) Japanese soy
    sauce
1/4 cup (60 ml/2 fl oz) peanut oil
fresh coriander leaves, to garnish

1 Arrange the oysters in a lined bamboo steamer. Place the garlic, ginger and spring onion in a bowl, mix together well and then sprinkle over the oysters. Spoon 1 teaspoon soy sauce over each oyster, cover the steamer with a lid and place over a wok of simmering water. Make sure the water is not touching the steamer. Steam for 2 minutes.

2 Heat the peanut oil in a small saucepan until smoking and carefully drizzle a little over each oyster. Garnish with the coriander leaves and serve immediately.

NUTRITION PER SERVE
Protein 3 g; Fat 15 g; Carbohydrate 1 g;
Dietary Fibre 0.5 g; Cholesterol 12 mg;
612 kJ (145 cal)

Sprinkle the oysters with garlic, ginger and spring onion, then with soy sauce.

Heat the peanut oil until it is smoking, then drizzle over the oysters.

THAI POTATO CAKES

Preparation time: 20 minutes
Total cooking time: 25 minutes
Serves 4 as a starter

750 g (1½ lb) waxy potatoes, peeled
1–2 small red chillies, finely chopped
8 cm (3 inch) piece of lemon grass,
    white part only, finely chopped
1 cup (60 g/2 oz) chopped fresh
    coriander leaves

8 spring onions, chopped
2 eggs, lightly beaten
3 tablespoons plain flour
oil, for shallow-frying
sweet chilli sauce, for serving

1 Grate the potatoes, then squeeze dry in a tea towel to remove as much moisture as possible. Mix with the chilli, lemon grass, coriander, spring onion, egg and flour.
2 Heat 1.5 cm (⅝ inch) of oil in a frying pan. Use 2 heaped tablespoons of mixture per cake and cook three or four cakes at a time, for 3–4 minutes over medium heat. Turn and cook for another 3 minutes, or until crisp and cooked through. Drain on paper towels and keep warm while cooking the remaining mixture. Serve hot with sweet chilli sauce.

NUTRITION PER SERVE
Protein 9 g; Fat 15 g; Carbohydrate 30 g;
Dietary Fibre 4 g; Cholesterol 90 mg;
1340 kJ (320 cal)

Coarsely grate the potatoes and then squeeze them as dry as you can.

Add the egg, chilli, lemon grass, coriander, spring onion and flour to the potato and mix through.

Turn the potato cakes over and cook until crisp and cooked through.

SESAME TEMPURA PRAWNS

Preparation time: 15 minutes
Total cooking time: 10 minutes
Serves 6 as a starter

SOY DIPPING SAUCE
1 tablespoon grated fresh ginger
1 cup (250 ml/8 fl oz) Japanese soy
   sauce
1 tablespoon sesame seeds, toasted
1 tablespoon caster sugar

oil, for deep-frying
1 cup (125 g/4 oz) tempura flour
2 tablespoons sesame seeds
750 g (1 1/2 lb) raw prawns, peeled and
   deveined, tails left intact

1 Combine the soy dipping sauce ingredients in a small bowl.
2 Fill a deep, heavy-based saucepan one-third full of oil and heat to 180°C (350°F), or until a cube of bread dropped in the oil browns in 15 seconds. Place the tempura flour and the sesame seeds in a bowl and

gradually stir in 3/4 cup (185 ml/6 fl oz) iced water with chopsticks until just combined. (The batter should still be lumpy.)
3 Dip the prawns, 3–4 at a time, into the batter and deep-fry for 1–2 minutes, or until golden brown. Drain on crumpled paper towels and serve at once with the dipping sauce.

NUTRITION PER SERVE
Protein 32 g; Fat 4 g; Carbohydrate 30 g;
Dietary Fibre 2 g; Cholesterol 186 mg;
1203 kJ (287 cal)

Mix together the ginger, soy sauce, sesame seeds and sugar to make a sauce.

Mix the tempura batter with chopsticks until it is just combined but still lumpy.

Deep-fry the prawns in small batches until they are golden brown.

CHICKEN SAN CHOY BAU

Preparation time: 10 minutes
Total cooking time: 5 minutes
Serves 4 as a starter

1 tablespoon oil
750 g (1¹/₂ lb) chicken mince
2 cloves garlic, finely chopped
100 g (3¹/₂ oz) can water chestnuts,
    drained and chopped
1¹/₂ tablespoons oyster sauce

3 teaspoons soy sauce
1 teaspoon sugar
5 spring onions, finely sliced
4 iceberg lettuce leaves

1 Heat a wok or frying pan over high heat, add the oil and swirl to coat. Add the chicken mince and garlic and stir-fry for 3–4 minutes, or until browned and cooked through, breaking up any lumps with the back of a spoon. Pour off any excess liquid.
2 Reduce the heat and add the water chestnuts, oyster sauce, soy sauce, sugar and spring onion.
3 Trim the lettuce leaves around the edges to neaten them and to form a cup shape. Divide the chicken mixture among the lettuce cups and serve hot, with extra oyster sauce.

NUTRITION PER SERVE
Protein 40 g; Fat 9 g; Carbohydrate 6 g;
Dietary Fibre 2 g; Cholesterol 88 mg;
1142 kJ (273 cal)

VARIATION: Drizzle some hoisin sauce over the top before serving.

Stir-fry the chicken mince and garlic until browned, breaking up any lumps.

Add the water chestnuts, oyster sauce, soy sauce, sugar and spring onion.

Trim the lettuce leaves around the edges to neaten them into cup shapes.

ASIAN RISSOLES

Preparation time: 15 minutes
Total cooking time: 30 minutes
Serves 4 as a starter

600 g (1¹/₄ lb) chicken mince
2 tablespoons sweet chilli sauce
2 tablespoons fresh coriander, roughly
   chopped
2 stalks lemon grass, white part only,
   finely chopped
2 egg whites, lightly beaten

1¹/₃ cups (120 g/4 oz) fresh
   breadcrumbs
²/₃ cup (100 g/3¹/₂ oz) sesame seeds
2–3 tablespoons oil

1 Preheat the oven to 200°C (400°F/
Gas 6). Combine the mince, sweet
chilli sauce, coriander, lemon grass,
egg white and breadcrumbs. Season
well. Divide the mixture into eight
equal portions and shape into rissoles.
Coat with sesame seeds.
2 Heat the oil in a frying pan and
cook the rissoles, in batches, for

3–4 minutes each side, or until the
crust is golden.
3 Place the rissoles on a lined oven
tray and bake for 15 minutes, or until
cooked through.

NUTRITION PER SERVE
Protein 45 g; Fat 33 g; Carbohydrate 20 g;
Dietary Fibre 4 g; Cholesterol 75 mg;
2325 kJ (555 cal)

NOTE: The rissoles can be made a day
in advance, shaped and kept covered
in the refrigerator before cooking.

Divide the mixture into eight equal portions and
coat with the sesame seeds.

Cook the rissoles in batches for a few minutes on
each side, until the crust is golden.

Once you've fried the rissoles, put them on a
lined oven tray and bake to cook through.

VEGETABLE TEMPURA PATTIES

Preparation time: 25 minutes
Total cooking time: 15 minutes
Serves 4 as a starter

WASABI MAYONNAISE
2 teaspoons wasabi paste
1 teaspoon Japanese soy sauce
1/2 cup (125 g/4 oz) mayonnaise
1 teaspoon sake

1/2 carrot, cut into thin strips
1/2 onion, finely sliced
100 g (3 1/2 oz) orange sweet potato, grated
1 small zucchini, grated
1 small potato, cut into thin strips
4 spring onions, cut into short lengths
4 nori sheets, shredded
2 cups (250 g/8 oz) tempura flour, sifted
2 cups (500 ml/16 fl oz) chilled soda water
oil, for deep-frying
2 tablespoons shredded pickled ginger, for serving

1 To make the wasabi mayonnaise, stir together all the ingredients.
2 To make the patties, place the carrot, onion, orange sweet potato, zucchini, potato, spring onion and nori in a bowl. Toss together.
3 Place the tempura flour in a large bowl and make a well in the centre. Add the soda water and loosely mix together with chopsticks or a fork until just combined—the batter should still be lumpy. Add the vegetables and quickly fold through until just combined with the batter.
4 Fill a wok or deep heavy-based saucepan one-third full of oil and heat to 180°C (350°F), or until a cube of

bread dropped into the oil browns in 15 seconds.
5 Gently drop 1/4 cup (60 ml/2 fl oz) of the vegetable mixture into the oil, making sure that the patty is not too compact, and cook for 1–2 minutes, or until golden and crisp. Drain on paper towels and season with sea salt. Repeat with the remaining mixture to make 12 patties. Serve immediately, topped with the wasabi mayonnaise and the pickled ginger.

NUTRITION PER SERVE
Protein 5.8 g; Fat 20 g; Carbohydrate 64 g; Dietary Fibre 3.5 g; Cholesterol 10 mg; 1948 kJ (465 cal)

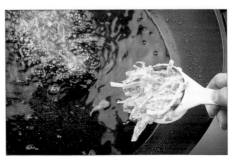
Gently drop the vegetable patty mixture into the hot oil.

Deep-fry the patties until they are lightly brown and crisp.

CALIFORNIA ROLLS

Preparation time: 35 minutes +
    15 minutes standing
Total cooking time: 15 minutes
Makes 30

500 g (1 lb) short-grain white rice
1/2 cup (60 ml/2 fl oz) rice vinegar
1 tablespoon caster sugar
5 nori sheets
1 large Lebanese cucumber, cut
    lengthways into long batons
1 avocado, thinly sliced
1 tablespoon black sesame seeds,
    toasted
30 g (1 oz) pickled ginger slices
1/2 cup (125 g/4 oz) mayonnaise
3 teaspoons wasabi paste
2 teaspoons soy sauce

1 Wash the rice under cold running water, tossing, until the water runs clear. Put the rice and 3 cups (750 ml/ 24 fl oz) water in a saucepan. Bring to the boil over low heat and cook for 5 minutes, or until tunnels form in the rice. Remove from the heat, cover and leave for 15 minutes.
2 Place the vinegar, sugar and 1 teaspoon salt in a small saucepan and stir over low heat until the sugar and salt dissolve.
3 Transfer the rice to a non-metallic bowl and use a wooden spoon to separate the grains. Make a slight well in the centre, slowly stir in the vinegar dressing, then cool a little.
4 Lay a nori sheet, shiny-side-down, on a bamboo mat or flat surface and spread out one-fifth of the rice, leaving a clear border at one end. Arrange one-fifth of the cucumber, avocado, sesame seeds and ginger lengthways over the rice, 2.5 cm (1 inch) from the border. Spread with some of the combined mayonnaise, wasabi and soy sauce and roll to cover the filling. Continue rolling tightly to join the edge, then hold in place for a few seconds. Trim the ends and cut into slices. Serve with wasabi mayonnaise.

NUTRITION PER ROLL
Protein 1.5 g; Fat 3 g; Carbohydrate 15 g;
Dietary Fibre 1 g; Cholesterol 1.5 mg;
380 kJ (90 cal)

Cook the rice until tunnels appear, then cover and leave for 15 minutes.

Slowly pour the vinegar dressing into the rice and stir it through.

Spread the wasabi mayonnaise mixture over the vegetables and start rolling.

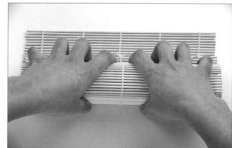

Roll the mat tightly to join the edge, then hold in place for a few seconds.

POTATO AND CORIANDER SAMOSAS

Preparation time: 1 hour
Total cooking time: 30 minutes
Makes 24

50 g (1³/₄ oz) butter
2 teaspoons grated fresh ginger
2 teaspoons cumin seeds
1 teaspoon Madras curry powder
¹/₂ teaspoon garam masala
500 g (1 lb) waxy potatoes, peeled
    and finely diced
¹/₄ cup (30 g/1 oz) sultanas
¹/₂ cup (90 g/3 oz) frozen baby peas
¹/₂ cup (15 g/¹/₂ oz) fresh coriander
    leaves
3 spring onions, sliced
1 egg, lightly beaten
oil, for deep-frying
thick plain yoghurt, to serve

SAMOSA PASTRY
3³/₄ cups (465 g/15 oz) plain flour,
    sifted
1 teaspoon baking powder
1¹/₂ teaspoons salt
110 g (3¹/₂ oz) butter, melted
¹/₂ cup (125 g/4 oz) thick plain yoghurt

1 Heat the butter in a large non-stick frying pan, add the ginger, cumin seeds, curry powder and garam masala and fry lightly for 1 minute. Add the potato and 3 tablespoons water and cook over low heat for 15–20 minutes, or until the potato is tender. Toss the sultanas, peas, coriander leaves and spring onion through the potato, remove from the heat and set aside to cool.
2 To make the samosa pastry, combine the flour, baking powder and salt in a large bowl. Make a well in the centre and add the butter, yoghurt and ³/₄ cup (185 ml/6 fl oz) of water. Using a flat-bladed knife, bring the dough together. Turn out onto a lightly floured surface and bring together to form a smooth ball. Divide the dough into four to make it easier to work with. Roll one piece out until it is very thin. Cover the remaining pastry until you are ready to use it.
3 Using a 12 cm (5 inch) diameter bowl or plate as a guide, cut out six circles. Place a generous tablespoon of potato filling in the centre of each circle, brush the edges of the pastry with egg and fold over to form a semi-circle. Make repeated folds on the rounded edge by folding a little piece of the pastry back as you move around the edge. Continue with the remaining pastry and filling.
4 Heat the oil in a deep heavy-based pan or deep-fryer to 180°C (350°F), or until a cube of bread dropped into the oil browns in 15 seconds. It is important not to have the oil too hot or the samosas will burn before the pastry has cooked. Add the samosas two or three at a time and cook until golden. If they rise to the surface as they puff up, you may need to use a large, long-handled slotted spoon to hold them in the oil to cook the other side. Drain on paper towels. Serve with yoghurt.

NUTRITION PER SAMOSA
Protein 3 g; Fat 6 g; Carbohydrate 20 g;
Dietary Fibre 1 g; Cholesterol 15 mg;
570 kJ (135 cal)

HINT: The samosa pastry becomes very tough if overworked. Use lightly floured hands when working the dough to prevent it sticking and work as quickly as you can.

Toss the sultanas, peas, coriander leaves and spring onion through the potato.

Mix the butter, yoghurt and water into the flour mixture to make a batter.

Cut six circles from each sheet of pastry, using a bowl or plate as a guide.

Use a generous tablespoon of filling mixture for each samosa.

Make folds on the edge of the pastry, folding a piece back as you move around.

Remove the cooked samosas from the oil with a slotted spoon.

VIETNAMESE VEGETARIAN ROLLS

Preparation time: 30 minutes +
　10 minutes standing
Total cooking time: 10 minutes
Serves 4 as a starter

75 g (2¹/₂ oz) dried rice vermicelli
200 g (6¹/₂ oz) firm tofu
1 teaspoon sesame oil
1 tablespoon peanut oil
1 packet 15 cm (6 inch) square rice-
　paper wrappers
¹/₂ small Lebanese cucumber, cut into
　matchsticks
¹/₂ carrot, cut into matchsticks

¹/₂ cup (10 g/¹/₄ oz) fresh mint
¹/₃ cup (50 g/1³/₄ oz) roasted salted
　cashews, roughly chopped
3 tablespoons hoisin sauce
2 tablespoons kecap manis
1 tablespoon lime juice

1 Place the vermicelli in a bowl, cover with boiling water and leave for 10 minutes. Drain well.
2 Pat the tofu dry and cut into four slices. Heat the oils in a large frying pan and cook the tofu over medium heat for 3 minutes each side, or until golden. Drain on paper towels. Cut each slice into four widthways.
3 Fill a bowl with warm water. Dip one wrapper at a time into the water

for about 15 seconds, or until pliable.
4 Place the wrapper on a work surface, top with some vermicelli, tofu, cucumber, carrot, mint and cashews. Roll tightly, folding in the sides, and put on a plate, seam-side-down. Cover with a damp cloth and repeat.
5 To make the dipping sauce, place the hoisin sauce, kecap manis and lime juice in a bowl and mix. Serve immediately with the spring rolls.

NUTRITION PER SERVE
Protein 6 g; Fat 12 g; Carbohydrate 16 g;
Dietary Fibre 2 g; Cholesterol 0 mg;
580 kJ (136 cal)

Cook the tofu over medium heat, turning once, until golden brown on both sides.

Dip one wrapper at a time into the water until soft and pliable.

Fold the sides of the wrappers in and roll up tightly, enclosing the filling.

ONION BHAJIS WITH SPICY TOMATO SAUCE

Preparation time: 30 minutes
Total cooking time: 35 minutes
Makes about 25

SPICY TOMATO SAUCE
2–3 red chillies, chopped
1 red capsicum, diced
425 g (14 oz) can chopped tomatoes
2 cloves garlic, finely chopped
2 tablespoons soft brown sugar
1¹/₂ tablespoons cider vinegar

1 cup (125 g/4 oz) plain flour
2 teaspoons baking powder
¹/₂ teaspoon chilli powder
¹/₂ teaspoon ground turmeric
1 teaspoon ground cumin
2 eggs, beaten
1 cup (60 g/2 oz) chopped fresh
    coriander leaves
4 onions, very thinly sliced
oil, for deep-frying

1 To make the sauce, combine all the ingredients with 3 tablespoons water in a saucepan. Bring to the boil, then reduce the heat and simmer for 20 minutes, or until the mixture thickens. Remove from the heat.
2 To make the bhajis, sift the flour, baking powder, spices and 1 teaspoon salt into a bowl and make a well in the centre. Gradually add the combined egg and 3 tablespoons water, whisking to make a smooth batter. Stir in the coriander and onion.
3 Fill a deep heavy-based saucepan one-third full of oil and heat until a cube of bread dropped into the oil browns in 15 seconds. Drop dessertspoons of the mixture into the oil and cook in batches for 90 seconds each side, or until golden. Drain on paper towels. Serve with the spicy tomato sauce.

NUTRITION PER BHAJI
Protein 1.5 g; Fat 2 g; Carbohydrate 7 g;
Dietary Fibre 1 g; Cholesterol 14 mg;
218 kJ (52 cal)

Peel the four onions and use a sharp knife to slice them very thinly.

Simmer the spicy tomato mixture for 20 minutes, or until it thickens.

Whisk together a smooth batter, then add the sliced onion and coriander and stir to coat.

Drop spoonfuls of the batter into the oil and cook in batches until golden.

VEGETABLE CURRY WITH COCONUT PANCAKES

Preparation time: 25 minutes
Total cooking time: 45 minutes
Serves 4 as a starter

1/2 cup (60 g/2 oz) plain flour
1 egg
275 ml (9 fl oz) coconut milk
1 tablespoon butter, melted
2 cups (500 ml/16 fl oz) coconut
   cream
30 g (1 oz) ghee or butter
1 onion, cut into thin wedges
2 cloves garlic, crushed
1 teaspoon garam masala
1 teaspoon ground cardamom
1 tablespoon Madras curry paste
1/2 cup (125 ml/4 fl oz) vegetable
   stock
4 sticks cassia bark
5 cardamom pods
400 g (13 oz) pumpkin, diced
2 small zucchini, halved lengthways
   and sliced on the diagonal
1 potato, diced
1/2 cup (90 g/3 oz) frozen peas
2 teaspoons soft brown sugar
raita, to serve (see NOTE)

1 Sift the flour into a bowl and gradually whisk in the combined egg, 150 ml (5 fl oz) of the coconut milk and the butter until smooth.
2 Heat an 18 cm (7 inch) non-stick crêpe pan or frying pan and grease. Pour some batter into the pan, swirling to thinly coat the base, then pour off any excess. Cook for 30 seconds, or until the edges curl. Turn and brown the other side. Transfer to a plate and line with paper towels. Keep warm. Repeat, making 7 more pancakes. (If the batter thickens, add water.)
3 To make the filling, add the coconut cream to a wok and bring to the boil over high heat. Boil for 10 minutes, stirring occasionally, or until the coconut cream starts to separate.
4 Meanwhile, heat the ghee in a frying pan and cook the onion over high heat for 2–3 minutes, or until soft. Add the garlic and spices and cook for 1 minute, or until fragrant.
5 Add the curry paste to the coconut cream and stir for 3–4 minutes, or until

fragrant. Add the stock, remaining coconut milk, cassia and cardamom pods, bring to the boil and cook for 5 minutes. Stir in the onion mixture, pumpkin, zucchini, potato and peas and simmer for 15 minutes, or until the vegetables are tender and the curry is thick. Stir in the sugar. Remove the cassia bark and cardamom pods. To serve, place 1/3 cup of the filling in the centre of each pancake and roll up. Serve topped with raita. Spoon any remaining curry over the top.

NUTRITION PER SERVE
Protein 12 g; Fat 55 g; Carbohydrate 35 g; Dietary Fibre 8.5 g; Cholesterol 80 mg; 2823 kJ (674 cal)

NOTE: Raita is a cooling mixture of yoghurt, cucumber and spices. Follow the recipe on page 228.

Cook the pancakes for 30 seconds, or until the edges curl, then turn over.

Cook the coconut cream on the boil for 10 minutes, or until it starts to crack.

THAI OMELETTES

Preparation time: 5 minutes
Total cooking time: 10 minutes
Serves 4 as a starter

2 tablespoons soy sauce
2 tablespoons kecap manis
2 tablepoons dry sherry
4 tablespoons peanut oil
8 spring onions, sliced on the diagonal
1 tablespoon grated fresh ginger
500 g (1 lb) button mushrooms, sliced
12 eggs
4 tablespoons chopped fresh
    coriander leaves

1 Put the soy sauce, kecap manis and sherry in a small bowl and mix well. Heat half the peanut oil in a saucepan, add the spring onion and ginger, and cook over low heat for 3–4 minutes, or until the onion is soft but not brown. Add the soy sauce mixture and the mushrooms and stir over medium heat for 3 minutes, or until the mushrooms are soft. Keep warm.
2 Break 3 of the eggs into a bowl and lightly beat with 1 tablespoon water. Season with salt and pepper. Heat 1 teaspoon of the remaining peanut oil in a small non-stick frying pan, add the beaten eggs and cook over medium heat for 2–3 minutes, or until just set.
3 Spoon a quarter of the mushroom mixture onto one half of the omelette and top with a few chopped coriander leaves. Fold the omelette over and gently slide onto a warm plate. Top with a few more coriander leaves. Serve immediately for someone else to eat while you cook the remaining three omelettes.

NUTRITION PER SERVE
Protein 24 g; Fat 35 g; Carbohydrate 4.5 g; Dietary Fibre 4 g; Cholesterol 540 mg; 1780 kJ (425 cal)

VARIATION: Fresh shiitake or oyster mushrooms can be used instead of button mushrooms. For a main course, add chopped cooked barbecue pork.

Add the soy mixture and the mushrooms to the saucepan and stir for 3 minutes.

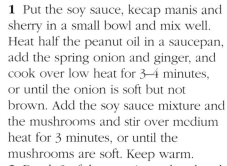

Pour the beaten egg into a small frying pan and cook until lightly set.

Add the warm mushroom mixture to the omelette and top with half the coriander.

SPICY POTATO AND CHICKPEA PANCAKES

Preparation time: 30 minutes + resting
Total cooking time: 20 minutes
Serves 4 as a starter

600 g (1¼ lb) waxy potatoes
1 small onion
3 tablespoons chopped fresh
  coriander
2 spring onions, finely sliced
4 tablespoons besan (chickpea flour)
2 teaspoons harissa (see NOTE)
¾ teaspoon salt
¼ teaspoon ground black pepper
pinch of cayenne pepper
1 egg, beaten
vegetable oil, for shallow-frying
1 teaspoon ground coriander
¼ teaspoon ground turmeric
¾ teaspoon cumin seeds

1 Grate the potatoes and onion, place in a bowl and cover with cold water.
2 Put the fresh coriander, spring onion, besan, harissa, salt, pepper and cayenne into another bowl. Mix together and stir in the egg. Heat 2 tablespoons of oil in a large non-stick frying pan and fry the ground coriander, turmeric and cumin seeds over medium-high heat, stirring, for 25–30 seconds. Add to the bowl.
3 Drain the potato and onion and wring out in a tea towel to dry. Add to the other ingredients and mix with your hands. Cover and set aside for 30 minutes. Wipe out the frying pan with paper towel and preheat the oven to very slow 120°C (250°F/Gas ½).
4 Heat 1–2 tablespoons of the oil in the frying pan. Spoon a heaped tablespoon of potato mixture into the pan and flatten to a rough circle. Cook for 2–3 minutes on each side, or until golden. Keep warm while cooking the remainder of the mixture.

NUTRITION PER SERVE
Protein 10 g; Fat 15 g; Carbohydrate 30 g;
Dietary Fibre 6 g; Cholesterol 45 mg;
1315 kJ (315 cal)

NOTE: Harissa should be available from large supermarkets, otherwise try speciality shops.

Grate the potato and onion and soak in cold water to remove the starch.

Use about a heaped tablespoonful of mixture to make each pancake.

DEEP-FRIED PRAWN TOASTS WITH WASABI MAYONNAISE

Preparation time: 45 minutes
Total cooking time: 25 minutes
Makes 25

WASABI MAYONNAISE
1/2 cup (125 g/4 oz) mayonnaise
1 teaspoon wasabi paste
2 teaspoons Japanese soy sauce

1 loaf day-old unsliced white bread
25 small raw prawns
3 sheets nori (dried seaweed)
3 eggs
1/2 cup (90 g/3 oz) sesame seeds
oil, for deep-frying

1 Mix together the wasabi mayonnaise ingredients in a small bowl, cover and refrigerate.
2 Remove the crusts from the bread and cut the bread into 2.5 cm (1 inch) cubes (you will need 25 cubes in total). Peel and devein the prawns, leaving the tails intact.
3 Using a sharp knife, make an incision in the top of each bread cube to about three-quarters of the way through. Gently ease a prawn, tail-end-out, into each slit in the bread cubes. Cut 25 strips of nori measuring 2 x 15 cm (1 x 6 inches) from the nori sheets. Wrap a strip around the outside of each bread cube and secure each with a toothpick. Lightly beat the eggs in a small bowl and put the sesame seeds in a separate bowl. Dip the bread cubes in egg, draining off any excess, then coat in the sesame seeds (you can leave the tails uncoated).
4 Fill a wok or a deep saucepan one-third full of oil and heat to 180°C (350°F), or until a small cube of bread browns in 15 seconds. Deep-fry in batches for 1–2 minutes, or until the prawns are pink and cooked. Drain well and season with salt. Remove the toothpicks and serve with the wasabi mayonnaise.

NUTRITION PER TOAST
Protein 28 g; Fat 4 g; Carbohydrate 13 g;
Dietary Fibre 1 g; Cholesterol 48 mg;
510 kJ (120 cal)

Hold the bread firmly and ease a prawn into the slit in each cube of bread.

Wrap nori around each bread cube and thread a toothpick through to secure.

Dip the cubes in egg, drain off any excess, then coat in sesame seeds.

Deep-fry the cubes until the prawns are pink and cooked through.

WON TON WRAPPED PRAWNS

Preparation time: 20 minutes +
   20 minutes refrigeration
Total cooking time: 10 minutes
Makes 24

24 raw prawns
1 teaspoon cornflour
24 won ton wrappers
oil, for deep-frying
1/2 cup (125 ml/4 fl oz) sweet chilli
   sauce
1 tablespoon lime juice

1 Peel and devein the prawns, leaving the tails intact.
2 Mix the cornflour with 1 teaspoon water in a small bowl. Work with one won ton wrapper at a time, keeping the rest covered with a damp tea towel to prevent drying out. Fold a wrapper in half to form a triangle. Wrap a prawn in the wrapper, leaving the tail

exposed. Seal at the end by brushing with a little of the cornflour mixture, then pressing gently. Spread the wrapped prawns on a baking tray, cover with plastic wrap and refrigerate for 20 minutes.
3 Fill a deep heavy-based saucepan one-third full of oil and heat to 180°C (350°F), or until a cube of bread dropped into the oil browns in 15 seconds. Cook the prawns in batches for 1¹/₂ minutes each batch, or until crisp, golden and cooked through. The cooking time may vary

depending on the size of the prawns. Check the time by cooking one prawn and testing it before continuing. Remove the prawns from the oil with a slotted spoon and drain on crumpled paper towels.
4 Stir the sweet chilli sauce and lime juice together in a small bowl. Serve with the prawns.

NUTRITION PER PRAWN
Protein 5 g; Fat 2 g; Carbohydrate 6 g;
Dietary Fibre 0.5 g; Cholesterol 27 mg;
245 kJ (60 cal)

Seal the wrapped prawns at the end with a dab of cornflour mixture.

Remove the cooked prawns from the oil with a slotted spoon.

STEAMED PRAWN NORI ROLLS

Preparation time: 15 minutes +
  1 hour refrigeration
Total cooking time: 5 minutes
Makes 25

500 g (1 lb) peeled raw prawns,
  deveined
1¹/₂ tablespoons fish sauce
1 tablespoon sake
2 tablespoons chopped fresh
  coriander
1 large fresh kaffir lime leaf,
  finely shredded
1 tablespoon lime juice

2 teaspoons sweet chilli sauce
1 egg white, lightly beaten
5 sheets nori

DIPPING SAUCE
¹/₄ cup (60 ml/2 fl oz) sake
¹/₄ cup (60 ml/2 fl oz) soy sauce
1 tablespoon mirin
1 tablespoon lime juice

1 Process the prawns in a food
processor or blender with the fish
sauce, sake, coriander, kaffir lime leaf,
lime juice and sweet chilli sauce until
smooth. Add the egg white and mix
for a few seconds to just combine.
2 Lay the nori sheets on a flat surface
and spread some prawn mixture over

each sheet, leaving a clear border at
one end. Roll up tightly, cover and
refrigerate for 1 hour to firm. Using a
very sharp knife, trim the ends, then
cut into slices.
3 Place the rolls in a lined bamboo
steamer, cover and steam over a wok
of simmering water, making sure it
doesn't touch the water. Steam for
5 minutes, or until heated through.
4 For the dipping sauce, thoroughly
mix all the ingredients together in a
small bowl. Serve with the nori rolls.

NUTRITION PER ROLL
Protein 4 g; Fat 0.5 g; Carbohydrate 0.5 g;
Dietary Fibre 0.5 g; Cholesterol 39.5 mg;
95 kJ (23 cal)

Spread prawn mixture over each nori sheet,
leaving a clear border at one end.

Roll each sheet up tightly, then cover and
refrigerate to firm.

Cut the nori rolls into slices with a very sharp knife
before steaming.

SAN CHOY BAU

Preparation time: 20 minutes
Total cooking time: 10 minutes
Serves 4 as a starter

1 tablespoon peanut oil
1 teaspoon sesame oil
1–2 cloves garlic, crushed
1 tablespoon grated fresh ginger
4 spring onions, chopped
500 g (1 lb) lean pork mince
1 red capsicum, seeded and diced
220 g (7 oz) can water chestnuts,
    drained and roughly chopped
1–2 tablespoons soy sauce
1 tablespoon oyster sauce
2 tablespoons dry sherry
4 iceberg lettuce leaves

1 Heat the oils in a large, non-stick frying pan or wok. Add the garlic, ginger and spring onion and stir-fry for about 2 minutes. Add the pork mince and cook over medium heat until well browned, breaking up any lumps with a fork or wooden spoon.
2 Stir in the capsicum, chestnuts, soy and oyster sauces and sherry. Simmer over medium heat until the liquid reduces and thickens. Keep warm.
3 Trim the edges of the lettuce leaves to make cup shapes and arrange on a plate. Spoon the pork filling into the lettuce leaves.

NUTRITION PER SERVE
Protein 32 g; Fat 13 g; Carbohydrate 25 g;
Dietary Fibre 7 g; Cholesterol 60 mg;
1456 kJ (350 cal)

Drain the can of water chestnuts and roughly chop them.

Add the garlic, ginger and spring onion to the wok and stir for about 2 minutes.

Stir in the capsicum, water chestnuts, soy and oyster sauces and sherry.

VIETNAMESE PORK AND PRAWN SPRING ROLLS

Preparation time: 40 minutes
Total cooking time: 10 minutes
Serves 6 as a starter

8–12 large sheets dried rice paper
1 tablespoon peanut oil
1 stem lemon grass, white part only, chopped
2 cloves garlic, finely chopped
500 g (1 lb) pork mince
500 g (1 lb) raw prawns, peeled and deveined
2 tablespoons fish sauce
1 tablespoon soy sauce
1 tablespoon sweet chilli sauce
1 tablespoon toasted sesame seeds
8 butter lettuce leaves, washed, dried and chilled
1 Lebanese cucumber, cut into matchsticks
1 large carrot, finely grated
1/2 cup (10 g/1/3 oz) fresh small mint leaves (or large chopped leaves)
4 tablespoons finely chopped roasted peanuts

DIPPING SAUCE
2 cloves garlic, crushed
1 tablespoon minced fresh red chilli
1 tablespoon sugar
2 tablespoons soy sauce
1 tablespoon fish sauce
1 tablespoon rice wine vinegar
1 tablespoon crunchy peanut butter
1 tablespoon finely chopped fresh coriander

1 Brush each rice paper sheet on both sides with some water and spread out on damp tea towels. Cover with more damp towels and leave until softened.
2 Heat the peanut oil in a pan, add the lemon grass and garlic and fry for 1 minute. Add the pork mince and prawns and stir for 3–4 minutes, or until they change colour. Stir in the sauces and sesame seeds and simmer for 4–5 minutes.
3 Place a lettuce leaf on a rice paper sheet, top with the pork and prawn mixture, cucumber, carrot, mint and nuts, fold in the sides and roll up. Repeat with the remaining rice paper sheets and ingredients.
4 To make the dipping sauce, mix all the ingredients in a small bowl. Serve with the spring rolls.

NUTRITION PER SERVE
Protein 30 g; Fat 9 g; Carbohydrate 10 g; Dietary Fibre 2 g; Cholesterol 40 mg; 800 kJ (200 cal)

Cut the Lebanese cucumber into fine matchsticks with a sharp knife.

Use a pastry brush to moisten each rice paper sheet with water.

Fill the roll, then fold in the sides of the sheet and roll up into a parcel.

SALT-AND-PEPPER SQUID

Preparation time: 30 minutes +
  15 minutes marinating
Total cooking time: 10 minutes
Serves 6 as a starter

1 kg (2 lb) squid hoods, halved
  lengthways
1 cup (250 ml/8 fl oz) lemon juice
1 cup (125 g/4 oz) cornflour
1¹/₂ tablespoons salt
1 tablespoon ground white pepper
2 teaspoons caster sugar
4 egg whites, lightly beaten

oil, for deep-frying
fresh coriander sprigs and lemon
  wedges, for serving

1 Open out the squid hoods, wash
and pat dry. Score a shallow diamond
pattern on the inside, then cut into
5 x 3 cm (2 x 1 inch) pieces. Place in a
flat non-metallic dish and pour on the
lemon juice. Cover and refrigerate for
15 minutes. Drain well and pat dry.
2 Combine the cornflour, salt, white
pepper and sugar in a bowl. Dip the
squid into the egg white and lightly
coat with the cornflour mixture,
shaking off any excess.

3 Fill a deep heavy-based pan one-
third full of oil and heat to 180°C
(350°F), or until a cube of bread
dropped into the oil turns golden
brown in 15 seconds. Deep-fry the
squid, in batches, for 1 minute each
batch, or until the squid turns white
and curls up. Drain on crumpled
paper towels. Garnish with coriander
sprigs and serve with lemon wedges.

NUTRITION PER SERVE
Protein 31 g; Fat 9 g; Carbohydrate 22 g;
Dietary Fibre 0.5 g; Cholesterol 332 mg;
1225 kJ (290 cal)

Lightly score the squid with a diamond pattern
and then cut into small rectangles.

Lightly coat the squid in the cornflour mixture,
shaking off any excess.

When the squid is golden and curled up, remove
from the oil with a slotted spoon.

THAI FISH CAKES

Preparation time: 20 minutes
Total cooking time: 20 minutes
Serves 6 as a starter

500 g (1 lb) redfish fillets, chopped
1 stem lemon grass, white part only,
    chopped
2 tablespoons fish sauce
5 spring onions, chopped
3 tablespoons chopped fresh
    coriander
1 clove garlic, crushed
150 ml (5 fl oz) can coconut milk
1 tablespoon sweet chilli sauce
1 egg
5 snake beans, finely sliced
oil, for shallow-frying
200 g (6¹/₂ oz) mixed lettuce leaves,
    for serving

SAUCE
¹/₃ cup (90 g/3 oz) sugar
2 tablespoons sweet chilli sauce
¹/₂ small Lebanese cucumber, diced

1 Place the fish, lemon grass, fish sauce, spring onion, coriander, garlic, coconut milk, sweet chilli sauce and egg in a food processor and mix until smooth. Transfer to a bowl and fold in the snake beans. With wet hands, shape into twelve 8 cm (3 inch) cakes. Cover on a plate and refrigerate until ready to use.
2 For the sauce, stir the sugar and ¹/₃ cup (80 ml/2³/₄ fl oz) water in a small saucepan over low heat for 2 minutes, or until all the sugar has dissolved. Increase the heat and simmer for 5 minutes, or until slightly thickened. Remove from the heat and stir in the sweet chilli sauce. Cool and stir in the diced cucumber.

3 Heat the oil in a large, deep, heavy-based frying pan and cook the fish cakes in batches over medium heat for 1–2 minutes on each side, or until cooked through.
4 Divide the lettuce among the plates and arrange the fish cakes on top. Serve with the sauce.

NUTRITION PER SERVE
Protein 21 g; Fat 11 g; Carbohydrate 19 g;
Dietary Fibre 1.5 g; Cholesterol 89 mg;
1055 kJ (250 cal)

With wet hands to prevent sticking, shape the mixture into 12 patties.

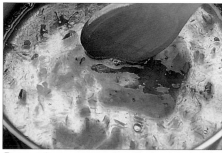

Remove the sugar syrup from the heat and stir in the sweet chilli sauce.

Cook the fish cakes on both sides, turning with a spatula, until cooked through.

SASHIMI TIMBALES

Preparation time: 25 minutes +
    15 minutes standing
Total cooking time: 15 minutes
Serves 6 as a starter

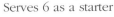

SUSHI RICE
2 cups (440 g/14 oz) short- or
    medium-grain rice
1½ tablespoons sugar
½ cup (125 ml/4 fl oz) Japanese rice
    vinegar
2 tablespoons mirin

WASABI MAYONNAISE
1 cup (250 g/8 oz) mayonnaise
2 tablespoons Japanese rice vinegar
3 teaspoons wasabi paste

3 sheets nori
300 g (10 oz) salmon, very thinly sliced
1 avocado
toasted black sesame seeds, for
    serving
pickled ginger, finely sliced, for serving
Japanese soy sauce, for serving

1 Rinse the rice under cold water until the water runs clear. Place in a saucepan with 2½ cups (625 ml/20 fl oz) water. Cover, bring to the boil, then reduce the heat and simmer for 8–10 minutes, or until all the water is absorbed and holes form on top. Remove from the heat and leave, covered, for 15 minutes, or until cooked through.
2 Meanwhile, put the sugar, vinegar, mirin and ½ teaspoon salt in a small saucepan and stir over medium heat for 2–3 minutes, or until the sugar has dissolved. Lay the rice out on a flat non-metallic tray, pour the vinegar mixture over the top and stir through.

3 For the wasabi mayonnaise, mix all the ingredients together in a bowl.
4 Cut circles from the nori to fit the bases of six 1 cup (250 ml/8 fl oz) ramekins. Cover the base of each ramekin with a sixth of the salmon. Spread 2 teaspoons of the wasabi mayonnaise over each salmon layer. Top with nori, then fill each ramekin three-quarters full, using about ⅔ cup (125 g/4 oz) sushi rice. Refrigerate until just before serving.
5 Cut the avocado into cubes. Dip a

knife in hot water and run around the ramekin edges to loosen the rice. Turn out, top with avocado and sprinkle with sesame seeds. Serve with the mayonnaise, ginger and soy sauce.

NUTRITION PER SERVE
Protein 21 g; Fat 26 g; Carbohydrate 72 g;
Dietary Fibre 3 g; Cholesterol 38 mg;
2495 kJ (595 cal)

Remove the rice from the heat when all the water is absorbed and holes form on top.

Using the ramekins as a guide, cut circles from the nori with a sharp knife.

To release the rice, dip a knife in hot water and run it around the edges.

LARB

Preparation time: 20 minutes
Total cooking time: 8 minutes
Serves 6 as a starter

1 tablespoon oil
2 stems lemon grass, white part only,
  thinly sliced
2 fresh green chillies, finely chopped
500 g (1 lb) lean pork or beef mince
1/4 cup (60 ml/2 fl oz) lime juice
2 teaspoons finely grated lime rind
2–6 teaspoons chilli sauce
6 iceberg lettuce leaves
1/3 cup (10 g/1/3 oz) fresh coriander
  leaves
1/4 cup (5 g/1/4 oz) fresh mint leaves
1 small onion, very finely sliced
60 g (2 oz) roasted peanuts, chopped
3 tablespoons crisp-fried garlic

1 Heat the oil in a wok and stir-fry the
lemon grass, chilli and mince over
high heat for 6 minutes, or until
cooked through, breaking up any
lumps of mince. Allow to cool.
2 Add the lime juice, rind and chilli
sauce to the mince mixture. Arrange
the lettuce leaves on a serving plate.
Stir most of the coriander and mint
leaves, onion, peanuts and fried garlic
through the mince mixture. Spoon
over the lettuce and sprinkle the rest
of the leaves, onion, peanuts and
garlic over the top.

NUTRITION PER SERVE
Protein 22 g; Fat 9 g; Carbohydrate 3 g;
Dietary Fibre 2 g; Cholesterol 40 mg;
750 kJ (180 cal)

NOTE: Crisp-fried garlic is available
from Asian food stores or you can
make your own (see page 6).

Finely slice the white part of the lemon grass with
a sharp knife.

Stir-fry the lemon grass, chilli and mince, breaking
up the mince as it cooks.

Add the lime juice and rind with the chilli sauce to
the cooled mince.

SPICY PORK WON TONS

Preparation time: 25 minutes
Total cooking time: 10 minutes
Serves 6 as a starter

1 teaspoon sesame oil
1 teaspoon peanut oil
2 cloves garlic, crushed
2 spring onions, finely chopped
2 small red chillies, finely chopped
2 teaspoons grated fresh ginger
300 g (10 oz) pork mince
1 tablespoon hoisin sauce
2 tablespoons unsalted peanuts,
   chopped
1 tablespoon chopped fresh coriander
250 g (8 oz) won ton wrappers
oil, for deep-frying

DIPPING SAUCE
1/2 cup (125 ml/4 fl oz) salt-reduced
   soy sauce
1 tablespoon soft brown sugar
1 teaspoon chilli oil

1 Heat both oils in a non-stick frying
pan. Add the garlic, spring onion, chilli
and ginger and cook over medium
heat for 2 minutes. Increase the heat to
high, add the pork mince and cook,
breaking up any lumps with a fork or
wooden spoon, for 5 minutes, or until
the mince is brown.
2 Remove the pan from the heat and
stir in the hoisin, peanuts and
coriander. Place 2 teaspoons of the
mixture into the centre of a wrapper.
Brush the edge of the won ton lightly
with water and place another wrapper

on top. Repeat with the remaining
wrappers and pork mince.
3 Deep-fry the won tons in batches
for 3 minutes, or until crisp and
golden. Drain on paper towels.
4 To make the sauce, place the soy
sauce, brown sugar and chilli oil in a
small pan and simmer over medium
heat for 5 minutes, or until the sauce
thickens slightly. Pour into a bowl and
serve with the won tons.

NUTRITION PER SERVE
Protein 20 g; Fat 12 g; Carbohydrate 30 g;
Dietary Fibre 2 g; Cholesterol 32 mg;
1280 kJ (300 cal)

Take the pan off the heat and stir the hoisin,
peanuts and coriander into the mince.

Brush the edge of a won ton with water and
place another wrapper on top.

Deep-fry the won tons until crisp. Place on paper
towels to drain off the excess oil.

ORANGE CHILLI CHICKEN IN LETTUCE CUPS

Preparation time: 40 minutes
Total cooking time: 15 minutes
Serves 4 as a starter

500 g (1 lb) chicken mince
1 tablespoon soy sauce
1 tablespoon rice wine vinegar
1 tablespoon sesame oil
peanut oil, for deep-frying
60 g (2 oz) dried rice vermicelli
    noodles, broken up
1 red capsicum, finely chopped
120 g (4 oz) can water chestnuts,
    drained and coarsely chopped
2 spring onions, finely sliced
1 teaspoon grated fresh ginger
1 iceberg or romaine lettuce

SAUCE
2 tablespoons soy sauce
1 tablespoon teriyaki sauce
1 tablespoon mild-hot chilli sauce
2 tablespoons hoisin sauce
1 teaspoon sesame oil
2 teaspoons finely grated orange rind
1 teaspoon cornflour

1 Mix together the chicken mince, soy sauce, vinegar and sesame oil, cover and refrigerate.
2 Half-fill a wok, deep-fryer or large, heavy-based pan with oil and heat to moderately hot. Add the rice noodles in small batches (they increase in size rapidly, causing the oil to rise) and fry for 1–2 seconds, or until puffed. Remove and drain on paper towels.
3 To make the sauce, combine all the ingredients and stir until the cornflour

has dissolved. Set aside.
4 Heat a little peanut oil in a wok or large pan. Add the chicken mixture and fry for 3–4 minutes, breaking up any lumps with a fork or wooden spoon. Add the capsicum, water chestnuts, spring onion and ginger to the pan and toss for 1–2 minutes. Add the sauce to the pan and stir for about 1 minute, or until slightly thickened. Remove from the heat and mix in the noodles, reserving a few for garnish. Form the lettuce leaves into 8 cups by trimming the edges and divide the chicken mixture among them. Sprinkle the reserved noodles on top.

NUTRITION PER SERVE
Protein 30 g; Fat 13 g; Carbohydrate 15 g;
Dietary Fibre 3 g; Cholesterol 60 mg;
1220 kJ (290 cal)

Finely slice 2 spring onions, including the green tops.

Use a slotted spoon to remove the cooked noodles from the pan.

Use a wooden spoon or fork to break up any lumps of mince as it cooks.

TERIYAKI CHICKEN PACKAGES

Preparation time: 50 minutes + soaking
Total cooking time: 25 minutes
Makes 24

5 Chinese dried mushrooms
1 tablespoon vegetable oil
2 cloves garlic, crushed
1 teaspoon finely grated fresh ginger
350 g (12 oz) chicken mince
1 small leek, finely sliced
1 tablespoon soy sauce
2 tablespoons dry sherry
1 tablespoon sake
1 tablespoon white sugar
1–2 teaspoons chilli sauce

100 g (3½ oz) fresh rice noodles, finely sliced
15 sheets filo pastry
90 g (3 oz) butter, melted
2 tablespoons sesame seeds

1 Put the mushrooms in a bowl, cover with boiling water and leave to soak for 30 minutes. Drain and chop finely. Heat the oil in a large pan, add the garlic, ginger, chicken mince and leek and stir-fry for 4–5 minutes. Add the soy sauce, sherry, sake, sugar and chilli sauce. Fold in the mushrooms and rice noodles and remove from the heat. Preheat the oven to moderate 180°C (350°F/Gas 4).
2 Unfold the filo, remove a sheet and cover the rest with a damp tea towel to prevent drying out. Brush the sheet of filo lightly with melted butter. Top with another 2 sheets, brushing each with butter. Cut crossways into 8 cm (3 inch) strips and spoon 1 tablespoon of the filling onto one end of each strip. Fold the ends over to form a triangle and continue folding to the end of each strip. Repeat with the remaining pastry and filling.
3 Place the triangles on a lightly oiled baking tray, brush with melted butter and sprinkle with sesame seeds. Bake for 12–15 minutes, or until golden.

NUTRITION PER PACKAGE
Protein 5 g; Fat 5 g; Carbohydrate 7 g; Dietary Fibre 1 g; Cholesterol 20 mg; 390 kJ (90 cal)

Fold in the mushrooms and rice noodles and remove the mixture from the heat.

Place 3 lightly buttered filo sheets on top of each other and cut into strips.

Fold the ends over the filling to form a triangle and keep folding to the end of the strip.

TOFU AND VEGETABLE KOFTAS WITH YOGHURT DIPPING SAUCE

Preparation time: 25 minutes
Total cooking time: 20 minutes
Serves 4 as a starter

YOGHURT DIPPING SAUCE
200 g (6¹/₂ oz) plain soy yoghurt
1 clove garlic, crushed
2 tablespoons finely chopped fresh
   mint

250 g (8 oz) firm tofu
4 tablespoons olive oil
1¹/₂ cups (185 g/6 oz) grated pumpkin
   (see NOTE)
³/₄ cup (100 g/3¹/₂ oz) grated zucchini
1 onion, chopped
4 cloves garlic, crushed

4 small spring onions, finely chopped
3 tablespoons chopped fresh
   coriander leaves
1 tablespoon Madras curry powder
1 cup (150 g/5 oz) wholemeal flour
¹/₂ cup (60 g/2 oz) grated Parmesan
oil, for deep-frying

1 To make the dipping sauce, place the yoghurt, garlic and mint in a small bowl, season and mix together well. Add a little water if needed.
2 Blend the tofu in a food processor or blender until finely processed.
3 Heat the oil in a frying pan. Add the pumpkin, zucchini, onion and garlic and cook over medium heat, stirring occasionally, for 10 minutes, or until the vegetables are tender. Cool.
4 Add the spring onion, coriander, curry powder, ¹/₂ cup of the whole-meal flour, the Parmesan, tofu and

1 tablespoon salt and mix well. Roll a tablespoon of the mixture between your hands to form a ball, then repeat with the remaining mixture. Coat the balls in the remaining flour.
5 Fill a deep heavy-based saucepan one-third full of oil and heat to 180°C (350°F), or until a cube of bread dropped into the oil browns in 15 seconds. Cook the tofu and vegetable koftas in small batches for 2–3 minutes, or until golden brown. Drain on paper towels. Serve with the dipping sauce.

NUTRITION PER SERVE
Protein 20 g; Fat 20 g; Carbohydrate 30 g;
Dietary Fibre 7.5 g; Cholesterol 20 mg;
1553 kJ (370 cal)

NOTE: Buy a piece of pumpkin that weighs about 400 g (13 oz).

Cook the pumpkin, zucchini, onion and garlic until tender.

Roll tablespoons of the tofu and vegetable mixture into balls.

Deep-fry the koftas in small batches until golden brown all over.

VEGETABLE PAKORAS WITH SPICED YOGHURT

Preparation time: 30 minutes +
   15 minutes standing
Total cooking time: 20 minutes
Serves 4 as a starter

SPICED YOGHURT
1 teaspoon cumin seeds
200 g (6¹/2 oz) plain yoghurt
1 clove garlic, crushed
¹/2 cup (15 g/¹/2 oz) fresh coriander
   leaves, chopped

¹/3 cup (30 g/1 oz) besan (chickpea
   flour)
¹/3 cup (40 g/1¹/2 oz) self-raising flour
¹/3 cup (45 g/1¹/2 oz) soy flour
¹/2 teaspoon ground turmeric
1 teaspoon cayenne pepper
¹/2 teaspoon ground coriander
1 small fresh green chilli, seeded and
   finely chopped
oil, for deep-frying
200 g (6¹/2 oz) cauliflower, cut into
   small florets
150 g (5 oz) orange sweet potato,
   thinly sliced
180 g (6 oz) eggplant, thinly sliced
180 g (6 oz) fresh asparagus, cut into
   short lengths

1 To make the spiced yoghurt, heat a small frying pan over medium heat. Add the cumin seeds and deep-fry for 1–2 minutes, or until aromatic—shake the pan frequently to prevent the seeds from burning. Place in a mortar and pestle or spice grinder and roughly grind. Whisk into the yoghurt with the garlic. Stir in the coriander and season with salt and pepper.
2 Place the besan, self-raising and soy flours, ground turmeric, cayenne pepper, ground coriander, chilli and 1 teaspoon salt in a bowl. Gradually whisk in 1 cup (250 ml/8 fl oz) cold water to form a batter. Leave to stand for 15 minutes. Preheat the oven to very slow 120°C (250°F/Gas ¹/2).
3 Fill a small saucepan one-third full with oil and heat to 170°C (325°F), or until a cube of bread dropped into the oil browns in 20 seconds. Dip the vegetables in the batter and deep-fry in small batches, for 1–2 minutes, or until pale gold. Remove with a slotted spoon and drain on paper towels. Keep warm in the oven until all the vegetables are deep-fried.
4 Serve the hot vegetable pakoras with the spiced yoghurt.

NUTRITION PER SERVE
Protein 11 g; Fat 15 g; Carbohydrate 17 g;
Dietary Fibre 6 g; Cholesterol 0 mg;
1025 kJ (245 cal)

Roughly crush the cumin seeds in a mortar and pestle or spice grinder.

Whisk the mixture together to form a smooth batter, then leave to stand.

Deep-fry the pakoras in small batches until they are pale gold.

BLACK BEAN AND CORIANDER PANCAKES WITH BOK CHOY

Preparation time: 30 minutes +
10 minutes soaking
Total cooking time: 20 minutes
Serves 4 as a starter

250 g (8 oz) baby bok choy, cut into
quarters
1/2 cup (60 g/2 oz) fermented black
beans
3/4 cup (90 g/3 oz) plain flour
3/4 cup (90 g/3 oz) soy flour
1 teaspoon baking powder
4 eggs, lightly beaten
3/4 cup (185 ml/6 fl oz) milk
1 cup (90 g/3 oz) bean sprouts
4 spring onions, thinly sliced
1/2 cup (15 g/1/2 oz) fresh coriander
leaves, finely chopped
1 tablespoon finely chopped fresh
ginger
3 cloves garlic, finely chopped
2 small fresh red chillies, finely
chopped
1 tablespoon sherry
3 tablespoons oil
1 clove garlic, crushed
sweet chilli sauce, to serve

1 Bring a large saucepan of salted water to the boil. Add the bok choy and cook for 2 minutes. Drain well and plunge into iced water. Soak the black beans in water for 10 minutes.
2 Sift the flours and baking powder into a bowl and make a well in the centre. Combine the egg and milk, then whisk into the flour mixture until it forms a smooth paste. Add the black beans, sprouts, spring onion, coriander, ginger, garlic, chilli and sherry and mix well.

3 Heat 2 teaspoons oil in a large frying pan, wiping the surface lightly with paper towels to remove any excess oil. When hot, add about 1/3 cup of the batter, spreading out to form a 10 cm (4 inch) wide pancake—depending on the size of your pan, you should be able to cook two at a time. Cook over medium heat for 1–2 minutes, or until small bubbles appear on the surface. Turn and cook for a further minute. Remove and keep warm. Repeat with the remaining batter to make 8 pancakes—add an

extra 2 teaspoons oil, if necessary.
4 Heat the remaining oil in a frying pan or wok. Add the bok choy and stir-fry over medium heat for 2 minutes. Add the garlic and cook for a further minute. Season well. Arrange two pancakes on a serving plate, top with the bok choy and serve with sweet chilli sauce.

NUTRITION PER SERVE
Protein 20 g; Fat 26 g; Carbohydrate 26 g; Dietary Fibre 7 g; Cholesterol 180 mg; 1724 kJ (412 cal)

Using tongs, plunge the blanched bok choy into iced water.

Whisk the milk mixture into the dry ingredients to form a smooth paste.

Fry the pancakes until small bubbles appear on the surface and the underside is golden.

PEKING DUCK PANCAKES

Preparation time: 30 minutes
Total cooking time: 20 minutes
Makes about 15 pancakes

3/4 cup (90 g/3 oz) plain flour
1/3 cup (40 g/1 1/2 oz) cornflour
2 eggs
3 tablespoons milk
2 teaspoons caster sugar
1 tablespoon oil
1/2 large Chinese barbecued duck
3 tablespoons hoisin sauce
1 tablespoon Shaosing (Chinese) wine
6 spring onions, cut into short lengths
    and finely sliced lengthways

1 Combine the flour and cornflour in a large bowl. Whisk together the eggs, milk and sugar with 3/4 cup (185 ml/6 fl oz) water. Make a well in the centre of the flour and gradually add the egg mixture, stirring continuously with a wooden spoon to form a smooth batter.
2 Heat the oil in a frying pan and add 2 tablespoons of batter. Swirl the pan gently to form a round pancake. Cook over medium heat for 2 minutes or until crisp and golden underneath. Turn over and cook the other side for 10 seconds only. Transfer to a plate and place in a low oven to keep warm. Repeat with the remaining batter.
3 Using a Chinese cleaver or large sharp knife, remove the duck drumsticks. Cut the duck skin and meat into small thin slices, discarding the carcass when finished. Remove the skin and bone from the drumsticks and chop the meat into small thin slices.
4 Place heaped tablespoons of meat and skin on each pancake, top with the combined hoi sin sauce and wine, then sprinkle with shredded spring onions. Roll up and serve immediately.

NUTRITION PER PANCAKE
Protein 9 g; Fat 11 g; Carbohydrate 10 g;
Dietary Fibre 1 g; Cholesterol 66 mg;
715 kJ (170 cal)

Gradually add the egg mixture to the dry ingredients, stirring to form a smooth batter.

Use a cleaver or large sharp knife to cut away the drumstick from the duck.

Cut the flesh of the duck into thin slices with a sharp knife.

Assemble the pancakes with the duck slices, spring onions and sauces.

STICKY RICE POCKETS

Preparation time: 1 hour
Total cooking time: 2 hours
Makes 20

20 dried bamboo leaves
1/2 cup (125 ml/4 fl oz) oil
6 spring onions, chopped
400 g (13 oz) eggplant, diced
1/2 cup (90 g/3 oz) water chestnuts,
    chopped
1 tablespoon mushroom soy sauce
3 small red chillies, diced
2 teaspoons sugar
3 tablespoons chopped fresh
    coriander leaves
4 cups (800 g/1 lb 10 oz) white
    glutinous rice, washed and drained
2 tablespoons soy sauce

1 Soak the bamboo leaves in boiling water for 10 minutes, or until soft.
2 Heat half the oil in a wok. Cook the spring onion and eggplant over high heat for 4–5 minutes, or until golden. Stir in the water chestnuts, soy sauce, chilli, sugar and coriander. Cool.
3 Bring 3 cups (750 ml/24 fl oz) water to a simmer. Heat the remaining oil in a saucepan, add the rice and stir for 2 minutes, or until coated. Stir in 1/2 cup (125 ml/4 fl oz) of the hot water over low heat until absorbed. Repeat until all the water has been added (about 20 minutes). Add the soy sauce and season with white pepper.
4 Fold one end of each bamboo leaf on the diagonal to form a cone. Hold securely in one hand and spoon in 2 tablespoons of rice. Make an indent in the rice, add 1 tablespoon eggplant filling, then top with 1 tablespoon of rice. Fold the other end of the bamboo leaf over to enclose the filling. Secure with a toothpick and tie with string.
5 Place in a single layer inside a double bamboo steamer. Cover and steam over a wok half-filled with simmering water for 1 1/2 hours, or until the rice is tender, adding more boiling water as needed. Serve hot.

NUTRITION PER POCKET
Protein 1.5 g; Fat 6 g; Carbohydrate 13 g;
Dietary Fibre 1 g; Cholesterol 0 mg;
465 kJ (111 cal)

Stir-fry the vegetables, soy sauce and coriander over high heat.

Fold one end of the bamboo leaf over on the diagonal to form a cone shape.

Spoon 2 tablespoons of the rice mixture into each bamboo leaf cone.

Fold over the excess bamboo leaf to totally enclose the filling.

SAAG PANIR

Preparation time: 20 minutes +
    overnight refrigeration
Total cooking time: 30 minutes
Serves 4 as a starter

2 litres milk
1/3 cup (80 ml/2¾ fl oz) lemon juice
2 tablespoons plain yoghurt
500 g (1 lb) silverbeet, cooked
2 cloves garlic
2 teaspoons grated fresh ginger
2 green chillies, chopped
1 onion, chopped
2 tablespoons ghee
2 teaspoons ground cumin
1/2 teaspoon ground nutmeg
3 tablespoons plain yoghurt, extra
1/2 cup (125 ml/4 fl oz) cream

1 Heat the milk in a saucepan until just boiling. Reduce the heat to low, add the lemon juice and yoghurt and cook, stirring, until beginning to curdle. Remove from the heat and leave for 5 minutes for curds to form.
2 Pour into a colander lined with muslin and leave until most of the liquid has drained away. Gather the muslin together and squeeze as much moisture from the curd as possible. Return to the colander, place over a bowl and refrigerate for at least 3 hours, or until very firm and all the whey has drained away. Cut into 4 cm (1½ inch) cubes.
3 Squeeze out any excess moisture from the silverbeet and finely chop.
4 Finely chop the garlic, ginger, chilli and onion in a food processor.
5 Heat the ghee in a wok. Add the onion mixture and cook over medium heat for 5 minutes, or until the ghee begins to separate. Add the spices, extra yoghurt, 1 teaspoon salt and 1 cup (250 ml/8 fl oz) water and simmer for 5 minutes. Transfer to the food processor, add the silverbeet and process until smooth. Return to the wok, add the curd and cream and heat through for 10 minutes.

NUTRITION PER SERVE
Protein 20 g; Fat 42 g; Carbohydrate 34 g;
Dietary Fibre 1.2 g; Cholesterol 136 mg;
2457 kJ (587 cal)

Once the lemon juice and yoghurt are added to the milk it will begin to curdle.

Drain the curd mixture in a colander that has been lined with muslin.

Once the curd is firm and the whey has drained, cut the curd into bite-sized cubes.

Process the onion mixture with the silverbeet until it is smooth.

CHARGRILLED THAI-SPICED BABY OCTOPUS

Preparation time: 1 hour + marinating
Total cooking time: 20 minutes
Serves 6 as a starter

500 g (1 lb) baby octopus
2 tablespoons oil
3 cloves garlic, chopped
1 tablespoon green or pink
    peppercorns
2–4 small red chillies, finely chopped
1 tablespoon fish sauce

1 Use a small sharp knife to remove the octopus gut by either cutting off the head entirely or by slicing open the head and removing the gut.
2 Pick up the body and use your index finger to push up the beak. Remove the beak and discard. Clean the octopus thoroughly. Cut the head into two or three pieces. Place in a shallow dish.
3 Combine the octopus, oil, garlic, peppercorns and chilli in a bowl and marinate for 30 minutes. Heat a barbecue plate or chargrill pan until very hot. Cook three octopus at a time,

turning frequently, for 3 minutes or until they turn white. Do not overcook. Sprinkle the fish sauce over the top and serve immediately.

NUTRITION PER SERVE
Protein 15 g; Fat 8 g; Carbohydrate 0.5 g;
Dietary Fibre 0 g; Cholesterol 166 mg;
520 kJ (120 cal)

VARIATION: Also suitable for calamari. Wash the tubes, pat them dry and cut them into squares or long strips, then continue as for the octopus. Don't overcook or they will be tough.

Use a sharp knife to slice off the head of the octopus so you can remove the gut.

Use your index finger to push the beak up so you can remove and discard it.

Cook the octopus, turning frequently, until they turn white.

71

Skewers

LOW-FAT CHICKEN SKEWERS WITH MANGO SALSA

Preparation time: 20 minutes +
  4 hours marinating
Total cooking time: 20 minutes
Serves 4

4 chicken thigh fillets
1½ tablespoons soft brown sugar
1½ tablespoons lime juice
2 teaspoons green curry paste
18 kaffir lime leaves
2 stalks lemon grass

MANGO SALSA
1 small mango, finely diced
1 teaspoon grated lime rind
2 teaspoons lime juice
1 teaspoon soft brown sugar
½ teaspoon fish sauce

1 Cut the chicken fillets in half lengthways. Combine the brown sugar, lime juice, curry paste and two shredded kaffir lime leaves in a bowl. Add the chicken and mix well. Cover and refrigerate for at least 4 hours.
2 Trim the lemon grass to measure about 20 cm (8 inches), leaving the root end intact. Cut each lengthways into four pieces. Cut a slit in each of the remaining lime leaves and thread one onto each skewer. Cut two slits in the chicken and thread onto the lemon grass, followed by another lime leaf. Repeat with the remaining lime leaves, chicken and lemon grass. Pan-fry or barbecue until cooked through.
3 Gently stir together all the ingredients for the mango salsa and serve with the chicken skewers.

NUTRITION PER SERVE
Protein 25 g; Fat 2.5 g; Carbohydrate 15 g;
Dietary Fibre 1 g; Cholesterol 50 mg;
710 kJ (170 cal)

Cut each trimmed lemon grass stem lengthways into four pieces.

Thread a lime leaf, then the chicken and another lime leaf onto the lemon grass.

SALMON AND PRAWN KEBABS WITH CHINESE SPICES

Preparation time: 15 minutes +
  2 hours marinating
Total cooking time: 20 minutes
Serves 6

4 x 200 g (6^1/$_2$ oz) salmon fillets
36 raw prawns, peeled, deveined, tails
  intact
5 cm (2 inch) piece fresh ginger, finely
  shredded
^{2}/$_3$ cup (170 ml/2^3/$_4$ fl oz) Chinese rice
  wine
^{3}/$_4$ cup (185 ml/6 fl oz) kecap manis
^{1}/$_2$ teaspoon five-spice powder
200 g (6^1/$_2$ oz) fresh egg noodles
600 g (1^1/$_4$ lb) baby bok choy

1 Remove the skin and bones from
the salmon and cut into about
36 bite-sized cubes. Thread three
cubes of salmon alternately with three
prawns onto a skewer. Repeat with
the remaining ingredients to make
12 skewers. Lay the skewers in a
shallow non-metallic dish.
2 Mix together the ginger, rice wine,
kecap manis and five-spice powder.
Pour over the skewers, then cover and
marinate for at least 2 hours. Turn the
skewers over a few times to ensure
even coating.
3 Drain, reserving the marinade. Heat
a chargrill pan or barbecue flat plate
and brush with oil. Cook the skewers
in batches for 4–5 minutes each side,
or until cooked through.
4 Meanwhile, place the noodles in a
bowl and cover with boiling water.

Leave for 5 minutes, or until tender,
then drain and keep warm. Place the
reserved marinade in a saucepan and
bring to the boil. Reduce the heat to
simmer. Separate the bok choy leaves
and add to the marinade, stirring to
coat. Cook, covered, for 1–2 minutes,
or until the bok choy has just wilted.
5 To serve, divide the noodles among
six serving plates. Top with the bok
choy, then the kebabs. Spoon on the
marinade and serve immediately.

NUTRITION PER SERVE
Protein 50 g; Fat 15 g; Carbohydrate 24 g;
Dietary Fibre 5 g; Cholesterol 246 mg;
1856 kJ (440 cal)

Put the skewers in a shallow non-metallic dish
and pour over the marinade.

Cook the skewers on a chargrill pan or a
barbecue flat plate.

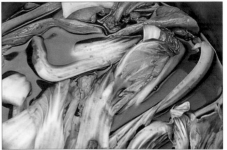
Separate the leaves of the bok choy and simmer
in the marinade until wilted.

CHICKEN TIKKA KEBABS

Preparation time: 10 minutes + 2 hours
    marinating
Total cooking time: 10 minutes
Serves 4

10 chicken thigh fillets, cubed
1 red onion, cut into wedges
3 tablespoons tikka paste

½ cup (125 ml/4 fl oz) coconut milk
2 tablespoons lemon juice

1 Thread two pieces of chicken and
a wedge of onion alternately along
eight skewers.
2 Combine the tikka paste, coconut
milk and lemon juice in a jar with a lid.
Season and shake well to combine.
Pour over the skewers and marinate
for at least 2 hours.

3 Place the skewers under a hot grill
and cook, basting, for 7–8 minutes, or
until the chicken is cooked through.

NUTRITION PER SERVE
Protein 50 g; Fat 13 g; Carbohydrate 4 g;
Dietary Fibre 1.5 g; Cholesterol 114 mg;
1457 kJ (350 cal)

NOTE: Any   can be
heat   uce.

Thread the chicken and wedges of onion
alternately on the skewers.

Mix together the tikka paste, coconut milk and
lemon juice and pour over the skewers.

Grill the skewers, basting, until the chicken is
cooked through.

PORK SKEWERS ON RICE NOODLE CAKES

Preparation time: 20 minutes +
  overnight marinating
Total cooking time: 30 minutes
Serves 4

1 kg (2 lb) pork fillet, cut into small
  cubes
8 spring onions, cut into short lengths
2 tablespoons rice wine vinegar
2 teaspoons chilli bean paste
3 tablespoons char siu sauce
400 g (13 oz) fresh flat rice noodles
1 cup (30 g/1 oz) fresh coriander
  leaves, chopped

3 spring onions, extra, sliced
1 tablespoon vegetable oil

1 Thread the pork and spring onion alternately onto eight skewers. Combine the vinegar, bean paste and char siu sauce in a shallow non-metallic dish. Add the skewers and turn to coat. Cover with plastic wrap and refrigerate overnight.
2 Drain the skewers, reserving the marinade. Chargrill or grill the skewers for 1–2 minutes on each side on very high heat until brown and cooked through. Remove and keep warm. Place the reserved marinade in a small saucepan and bring to the boil.
3 Separate the noodles, add the

coriander and extra spring onion and toss together. Divide into four portions. Heat the oil in a non-stick frying pan over medium heat. Place one portion of noodles in the pan, pressing down very firmly with a spatula to form a pancake. Cook on each side for 3–4 minutes, or until golden. Remove and keep warm. Repeat with the remaining noodles.
4 To serve, place each noodle cake on a serving plate and top with two skewers. Drizzle with the marinade.

NUTRITION PER SERVE
Protein 60 g; Fat 12 g; Carbohydrate 47 g;
Dietary Fibre 3 g; Cholesterol 238 mg;
2240 kJ (535 cal)

Thread the pork cubes and pieces of spring onion alternately onto each skewer.

Toss the coriander and spring onion through the flat rice noodles.

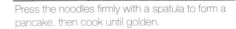
Press the noodles firmly with a spatula to form a pancake, then cook until golden.

SESAME CHICKEN SKEWERS

Preparation time: 10 minutes + 2 hours marinating
Total cooking time: 10 minutes
Serves 4

1/4 cup (60 ml/2 fl oz) oil
2 tablespoons soy sauce
2 tablespoons honey
1 tablespoon grated fresh ginger
1 tablespoon sesame oil
4 large chicken breast fillets, cut into small cubes
8 spring onions, cut into short lengths
1 tablespoon sesame seeds, toasted (see HINT)

1 To make the marinade, whisk together the oil, soy sauce, honey, ginger and sesame oil. Thread the chicken and spring onion alternately onto 12 skewers and place in a glass dish. Pour the marinade over the skewers, cover and refrigerate for at least 2 hours or overnight.

2 Put the skewers on a grill tray and place under a hot grill. Baste with the remaining marinade and cook, turning once, for 10 minutes, or until cooked through. Sprinkle with the sesame seeds to serve.

NUTRITION PER SERVE
Protein 55 g; Fat 25 g; Carbohydrate 13 g; Dietary Fibre 1 g; Cholesterol 120 mg; 2180 kJ (520 cal)

NOTE: These kebabs can also be barbecued on a flat plate.

HINT: To toast sesame seeds, place in a dry pan and shake over moderate heat until the seeds are golden.

Thread the pieces of chicken and spring onion alternately onto the skewers.

Once the skewers are cooked, sprinkle with the toasted sesame seeds.

SATAY LAMB

Preparation time: 10 minutes
Total cooking time: 20 minutes
Serves 4

750 g (1½ lb) lamb backstrap or
    loin fillet
2 tablespoons oil
2 onions, cut into thin wedges
3 cloves garlic, crushed
1 tablespoon red curry paste
1 cup (250 g/8 oz) crunchy peanut
    butter
1 cup (250 ml/8 fl oz) coconut milk
1 tablespoon kecap manis
2 tablespoons tomato sauce
fresh coriander, to garnish

1 Trim the lamb of any excess fat and sinew and cut into small cubes.
2 Heat the oil in a saucepan, add the onion and garlic and cook, stirring, over low heat for 4 minutes, or until the onion is soft. Add the curry paste and cook for 1 minute, then remove from the heat.
3 Add the peanut butter to the pan, return to the heat and stir in the coconut milk and 1 cup (250 ml/ 8 fl oz) water. Bring to the boil, stirring so the mixture does not stick. Add the kecap manis and tomato sauce, reduce the heat and simmer for 1 minute, or until thickened slightly.
4 Thread the meat onto 12 skewers, place on a lightly oiled grill tray and brush with the peanut mixture. Cook under a hot grill for 5 minutes each

side, or until tender, brushing with the peanut mixture during cooking.
5 Meanwhile, place the remaining peanut mixture in a small saucepan and stir over medium heat for 3–5 minutes, or until heated through. Serve the skewers, garnished with coriander with the sauce on the side.

NUTRITION PER SERVE
Protein 60 g; Fat 60 g; Carbohydrate 11 g; Dietary Fibre 8.5 g; Cholesterol 132 mg; 3509 kJ (838 cal)

NOTE: If you are using wooden skewers, soak them for 30 minutes prior to grilling to prevent them from burning.

Trim the lamb of any excess fat and sinew and cut into small cubes.

Simmer the peanut mixture for 1 minute, or until thickened slightly.

Cook the skewers under a hot grill, brushing with the peanut mixture.

SEEKH KEBABS

Preparation time: 40 minutes
Total cooking time: 12 minutes
Serves 4

pinch of ground cloves
pinch of ground nutmeg
1/2 teaspoon chilli powder
1 teaspoon ground cumin
2 teaspoons ground coriander
3 cloves garlic, finely chopped
5 cm (2 inch) piece of fresh ginger,
    grated
500 g (1 lb) lean beef mince
1 tablespoon oil
2 tablespoons lemon juice

ONION AND MINT RELISH
1 red onion, finely chopped
1 tablespoon white vinegar
1 tablespoon lemon juice
1 tablespoon chopped fresh mint

1 Soak 12 thick wooden skewers in cold water for 15 minutes. Dry-fry the cloves, nutmeg, chilli, cumin and coriander in a heavy-based frying pan, over low heat, for about 2 minutes, shaking the pan constantly. Transfer to a bowl with the garlic and ginger and set aside.

2 Knead the mince firmly using your fingertips and the base of your hand. The meat needs to be kneaded constantly for about 3 minutes, or until it becomes very soft and a little sticky. This process changes the texture of the meat when cooked, making it very soft and tender. Add the mince to the spice and garlic mixture and mix well, seasoning well.

3 Form tablespoons of the meat into small, round patty shapes. Wet your hands and press two portions of the meat around a skewer, leaving a gap of about 3 cm (1¼ inches) at the top of the skewer. Smooth the outside gently, place on baking paper and refrigerate while making the remaining kebabs.

4 To make the onion and mint relish, mix together the onion, vinegar and lemon juice and refrigerate for 10 minutes. Stir in the mint and season with pepper just before serving.

5 Grill the skewers or cook on an oiled barbecue flat plate for about 8 minutes, turning regularly and sprinkling with a little lemon juice. Serve with the relish.

NUTRITION PER SERVE
Protein 26 g; Fat 20 g; Carbohydrate 2 g;
Dietary Fibre 1 g; Cholesterol 80 mg;
1156 kJ (280 cal)

STORAGE: These kebabs freeze very well—simply defrost before grilling.

Finely chop the garlic and peel the fresh ginger and then grate.

Dry-fry the cloves, nutmeg, chilli, cumin and coriander in a heavy-based pan.

Press two rounds of meat around each wooden skewer, leaving space at the top of the skewer.

LEMON GRASS PRAWN SATAYS

Preparation time: 20 minutes + 1 hour
  refrigeration
Total cooking time: 15 minutes
Serves 6

1 tablespoon oil
1 clove garlic, crushed
1 tablespoon grated fresh ginger
1 tablespoon finely chopped lemon
  grass, white part only
1 onion, finely chopped
1 tablespoon tandoori curry paste
4 kaffir lime leaves, finely shredded
1 tablespoon coconut cream

2 teaspoons grated lime rind
600 g (1¼ lb) raw prawns, peeled and
  deveined
3 stalks lemon grass, cut into
  15 cm (6 inch) lengths

1 Heat the oil in a frying pan, add the garlic, ginger, lemon grass and onion and cook over medium heat for 3 minutes, or until golden.
2 Add the tandoori paste and kaffir lime leaves to the pan and cook for 5 minutes, or until the tandoori paste is fragrant. Allow to cool slightly. Transfer the mixture to a food processor, add the coconut cream, lime rind and prawns and process until finely minced. Divide the mixture into

six portions and shape around the lemon grass stems with wet hands, leaving about 3 cm (1¼ inches) uncovered at each end of the stems. The mixture is quite soft, so take care when handling it. Using wet hands will make the mixture easier to manage. Refrigerate for 1 hour.
3 Cook the satays under a preheated medium grill for 5 minutes, or until cooked through.

NUTRITION PER SERVE
Protein 20 g; Fat 5 g; Carbohydrate 2 g;
Dietary Fibre 0 g; Cholesterol 150 mg;
500 kJ (135 cal)

Add the tandoori paste and kaffir lime leaves to the pan and cook until fragrant.

Transfer the mixture to a food processor and add the coconut cream, lime zest and prawns.

Wet your hands to make it easier to shape the mixture around the stems.

TOFU KEBABS WITH MISO PESTO

Preparation time: 30 minutes +
  1 hour marinating
Total cooking time: 10 minutes
Serves 4

1 large red capsicum, cut into squares
12 button mushrooms, halved
6 pickling onions, quartered
3 zucchini, thickly sliced
450 g (14 oz) firm tofu, cut into small
  cubes
1/2 cup (125 ml/4 fl oz) olive oil
1/4 cup (60 ml/2 fl oz) soy sauce
2 cloves garlic, crushed
2 teaspoons grated fresh ginger

MISO PESTO
1/2 cup (90 g/3 oz) unsalted roasted
  peanuts
2 cups (60 g/2 oz) firmly packed fresh
  coriander leaves
2 tablespoons white miso paste
2 cloves garlic
100 ml (3 1/2 fl oz) olive oil

1 Soak 12 wooden skewers in cold
water for 10 minutes. Thread the
vegetable pieces and tofu alternately
onto the skewers, then place in a large
shallow non-metallic dish.
2 Combine the olive oil, soy sauce,
garlic and ginger, then pour half the
mixture over the kebabs. Cover with
plastic wrap and marinate for 1 hour.
3 To make the miso pesto, finely chop
the peanuts, coriander leaves, miso
paste and garlic in a food processor.
Slowly add the olive oil while the
machine is still running and blend to a
smooth paste.
4 Heat a chargrill pan or barbecue
grill plate and cook the kebabs,
turning and brushing often with the
remaining marinade, for 4–6 minutes,
or until the edges are slightly brown.
Serve with the miso pesto.

NUTRITION PER SERVE
Protein 8 g; Fat 64 g; Carbohydrate 10 g;
Dietary Fibre 4 g; Cholesterol 0 mg;
2698 kJ (645 cal)

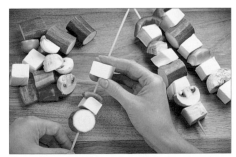

Thread the vegetable pieces and tofu cubes
alternately onto the skewers.

Mix the nuts, coriander leaves, miso and garlic
until finely chopped.

Brush the kebabs with the remaining marinade
during cooking.

MISO YAKITORI CHICKEN

Preparation time: 30 minutes
Total cooking time: 20 minutes
Serves 4

1 kg (2 lb) chicken thighs with skin
3 tablespoons yellow or red miso
   paste
2 tablespoons sugar
1/4 cup (60 ml/2 fl oz) sake
2 tablespoons mirin
1 cucumber
2 spring onions, cut into short
   lengths

1 Remove the bones from the chicken thighs. Meanwhile, soak 12 wooden skewers in cold water for at least 10 minutes. Place the miso, sugar, sake and mirin in a small saucepan over medium heat and cook, stirring well, for 2 minutes, or until the sauce is smooth and the sugar has dissolved.
2 Cut the chicken into bite-sized cubes. Seed the cucumber and cut into small batons. Thread the chicken, cucumber and spring onion alternately onto the skewers with three pieces of each per skewer.
3 Cook on a chargrill pan or barbecue grill plate over high heat, turning occasionally, for 10 minutes, or until the chicken is almost cooked. Brush with the miso sauce and continue cooking, then turn and brush the other side. Repeat once or twice until the chicken and vegetables are cooked. Serve immediately.

NUTRITION PER SERVE
Protein 58 g; Fat 6.5 g; Carbohydrate 9 g;
Dietary Fibre 0.5 g; Cholesterol 126 mg;
1377 kJ (329 cal)

Remove the bones from the chicken thighs with a sharp knife.

Remove the seeds from the centre of the cucumber, then cut into batons.

Brush the chicken and vegetables with the miso sauce during cooking.

SATAY CHICKEN

Preparation time: 40 minutes +
  30 minutes marinating
Total cooking time: 20 minutes
Serves 4

500 g (1 lb) chicken thigh fillets
1 onion, roughly chopped
2 stalks lemon grass, white part only,
  thinly sliced
4 cloves garlic
2 red chillies, chopped
2 teaspoons ground coriander
1 teaspoon ground cumin
1/2 teaspoon salt
1 tablespoon soy sauce
1/4 cup (60 ml/2 fl oz) oil
1 tablespoon soft brown sugar
cucumber slices and chopped roasted
  peanuts, to garnish

PEANUT SAUCE
1/2 cup (125 g/4 oz) crunchy peanut
  butter
1 cup (250 ml/8 fl oz) coconut milk
1–2 tablespoons sweet chilli sauce
1 tablespoon soy sauce
2 teaspoons lemon juice

1 Soak 20 wooden skewers in cold water for 30 minutes. Cut the chicken into 20 thick flat strips and thread onto the skewers.
2 Mix the onion, lemon grass, garlic, chilli, coriander, cumin, salt and soy sauce in a food processor until smooth, adding a little oil if necessary. Spread the mixture over the chicken, cover and refrigerate for 30 minutes.
3 To make the peanut sauce, stir all the ingredients and 1/2 cup (125 ml/ 4 fl oz) water over low heat, until the mixture boils. Remove from the heat. The sauce will thicken on standing.
4 Brush a very hot chargrill pan or barbecue flatplate with the remaining oil. Cook the skewers for 2–3 minutes on each side, sprinkling with a little oil and brown sugar. Serve with the peanut sauce, cucumber slices and chopped peanuts.

NUTRITION PER SERVE
Protein 40 g; Fat 46 g; Carbohydrate 14 g;
Dietary Fibre 5 g; Cholesterol 62 mg;
2590 kJ (620 cal)

Thread one thick chicken strip onto each skewer, flattening it out on the skewer.

Add a little oil to the paste to assist the processing if it is too firm.

The peanut sauce will thicken when it is left to stand.

During cooking, sprinkle the chicken with oil and brown sugar to give it a good flavour and colour.

THAI MEATBALLS

Preparation time: 25 minutes
Total cooking time: 10 minutes
Serves 4

350 g (11 oz) beef mince
3 French shallots, finely chopped
3 cloves garlic, chopped
2.5 cm (1 inch) piece of fresh ginger, grated
1 tablespoon green or pink peppercorns, crushed
2 teaspoons light soy sauce
2 teaspoons fish sauce

2 teaspoons soft brown sugar
1/2 cup (15 g/1/2 oz) fresh coriander leaves
lime wedges
1 cucumber, chopped
3 sliced red or green chillies

1 Chop the mince with a cleaver or a large knife until very fine. Mix together the mince, shallots, garlic, ginger, peppercorns, light soy sauce, fish sauce and brown sugar.
2 Form 2 teaspoons of the mixture at a time into balls. Thread the balls onto 8 wooden skewers, using three balls for each skewer.

3 Cook the skewers on an oiled hot chargrill pan or barbecue grill plate, turning frequently, for 7–8 minutes or until cooked through. Sprinkle with coriander. Serve with the lime wedges, cucumber and sliced chillies.

NUTRITION PER SERVE
Protein 20 g; Fat 10 g; Carbohydrate 3 g;
Dietary Fibre 0 g; Cholesterol 55 mg;
700 kJ (170 cal)

HINT: Soak the wooden skewers in water for at least thirty minutes before use, to help prevent them burning.

Use a large, sharp knife or a cleaver to chop the mince until very fine.

Form 2 teaspoonsful of mixture at a time into small compact balls.

Cook the skewered meatballs, turning frequently, for 7–8 minutes.

THAI SATAY PRAWNS

Preparation time: 30 minutes + 2 hours
   marinating
Total cooking time: 20 minutes
Makes 6 skewers

12 raw king prawns
1 clove garlic, crushed
1/3 cup (80 g/2¾ oz) smooth peanut
   butter
1 onion, grated
1 tablespoon fish sauce
1/2 teaspoon chilli flakes
1 teaspoon ground turmeric
5 fresh coriander roots, finely chopped
2/3 cup (170 ml/5½ fl oz) coconut milk

SATAY SAUCE
2 teaspoons oil
1 teaspoon Thai red curry paste
1 stalk lemon grass, white part only,
   finely chopped
2 teaspoons tamarind purée
1 cup (250 ml/8 fl oz) coconut milk
3 tablespoons smooth peanut butter
2 teaspoons sugar
2 teaspoons roasted unsalted
   peanuts, finely chopped

1 Soak six long wooden skewers in water for several hours to prevent them burning. Peel and devein the prawns, leaving the tails intact.
2 Using a mortar and pestle or blender, make a marinade by blending the garlic, peanut butter, onion, fish sauce, chilli flakes, turmeric, coriander roots and about 2 tablespoons of the coconut milk until smooth. Stir in the remaining coconut milk.
3 Coat the prawns in the marinade, keeping the tails out if possible. Cover and refrigerate for at least 2 hours. Thread two prawns onto each skewer.

Reserve the remaining marinade for the satay sauce, leaving a little to brush over the prawns during cooking.
4 To make the satay sauce, heat the oil in a small pan. Add the curry paste, lemon grass and tamarind and cook over high heat for 1 minute or until aromatic. Add the coconut milk, peanut butter and sugar, bring to the boil, reduce the heat and simmer, uncovered, for 2 minutes. Stir in the reserved marinade and boil for 2 minutes, or until thickened.
5 Chargrill or barbecue the prawns until cooked through, turning once

during cooking and brushing with the marinade. Serve immediately with the satay sauce, sprinkled with the chopped peanuts.

NUTRITION PER SKEWER
Protein 13 g; Fat 15 g; Carbohydrate 5 g;
Dietary Fibre 1 g; Cholesterol 21 mg;
800 kJ (200 cal)

HINT: The thickness of the sauce will depend on the peanut butter—if you prefer a more runny sauce, thin it with a little water. On standing, oil will rise to the surface of the sauce.

Peel the prawns, leaving the tails intact, and then remove the veins.

Add the coconut milk, peanut butter and sugar to the pan and bring to the boil.

During cooking, brush the prawns with the remaining marinade.

Salads

THAI BEEF SALAD

Preparation time: 35 minutes
Total cooking time: 10 minutes
Serves 4

3 cloves garlic, finely chopped
4 coriander roots, finely chopped
1/2 teaspoon black pepper
3 tablespoons oil
400 g (13 oz) piece rump or sirloin
  steak
1 small soft-leaved lettuce, leaves
  separated
200 g (61/2 oz) cherry tomatoes,
  halved
1 Lebanese cucumber, thickly sliced
4 spring onions, chopped
1/2 cup (15 g/1/2 oz) fresh coriander
  leaves

DRESSING
2 tablespoons fish sauce
2 tablespoons lime juice
1 tablespoon soy sauce
2 teaspoons chopped fresh red chillies
2 teaspoons soft brown sugar

1 Finely grind the chopped garlic,
coriander roots, black pepper and
2 tablespoons of the oil in a mortar
and pestle, food processor or blender.
Spread evenly over the steak.
2 Heat the remaining oil in a heavy-
based frying pan or wok over high
heat. Add the steak to the pan and
cook for about 4 minutes each side,
turning once only during the cooking
time. Remove and allow to cool.
3 Meanwhile, combine the lettuce,
cherry tomatoes, cucumber and
spring onions on a serving plate.
4 To make the dressing, stir together
the fish sauce, lime juice, soy sauce,
chopped red chillies and brown sugar
until the sugar has dissolved.
5 Cut the steak into thin strips.
Arrange over the salad and toss
together very gently. Drizzle with the
dressing and scatter the coriander over
the top. Serve immediately.

NUTRITION PER SERVE
Protein 25 g; Fat 18 g; Carbohydrate 6 g;
Dietary Fibre 0 g; Cholesterol 67 mg;
1160 kJ (280 cal)

HINT: Be careful that you don't
overcook the steak—it should be pink
and, therefore, succulent and tender.

NOTE: Ground herbs and spices are
used extensively for flavouring in
Asian cookery. Small amounts can be
ground with a mortar and pestle or a
clean coffee grinder. For larger
quantities, use a blender or food
processor. To help clean the bowl after
grinding spices, run some stale bread
through the processor.

Grind the garlic, coriander roots, black pepper
and oil in a mortar and pestle or processor.

When the steak has cooled, use a sharp knife to
cut it into thin strips.

COCONUT PRAWN SALAD

Preparation time: 35 minutes +
    30 minutes refrigeration
Total cooking time: 30 minutes
Serves 4

24 raw king prawns, peeled and
    deveined, tails left intact
plain flour, to coat
1 egg
1 tablespoon milk
1 cup (60 g/2 oz) shredded coconut
$^1/_2$ cup (30 g/1 oz) chopped fresh
    coriander leaves, plus
    1 tablespoon extra
$2^1/_2$ tablespoons oil
300 g (10 oz) Asian shallots, chopped
2 cloves garlic, finely chopped
2 teaspoons grated fresh ginger
1 red chilli, seeds and membrane
    removed, thinly sliced
1 teaspoon ground turmeric
270 ml (9 fl oz) coconut cream
2 kaffir lime leaves, thinly sliced
2 teaspoons lime juice
2 teaspoons palm sugar
3 teaspoons fish sauce
oil, for shallow-frying
150 g (5 oz) mixed lettuce leaves

1 Holding the prawns by their tails, coat in flour, then dip into the combined egg and milk and then into the combined coconut and coriander. Refrigerate for 30 minutes.
2 Heat the oil in a saucepan and cook the shallots, garlic, ginger, chilli and turmeric over medium heat for 3–5 minutes, or until fragrant. Add the coconut cream, lime leaves, lime juice, sugar and fish sauce. Bring to the boil, then reduce the heat and simmer for 2–3 minutes, or until thick.
3 Heat 2 cm (1 inch) oil in a frying pan and cook the prawns in batches for 3–5 minutes, or until golden. Drain on paper towels and season with salt.
4 Add the extra coriander to the dressing. Toss the lettuce and prawns together and drizzle with the dressing.

NUTRITION PER SERVE
Protein 7.5 g; Fat 47 g; Carbohydrate 12 g;
Dietary Fibre 5 g; Cholesterol 55 mg;
2060 kJ (490 cal)

Peel and devein the prawns, keeping the tails intact.

Dip the floured prawns into the egg, then in the coriander mixture.

Boil the dressing and then simmer until it becomes quite thick.

Cook the prawns in batches until golden, then drain on paper towels.

THAI-SPICED GRILLED PORK TENDERLOIN AND GREEN MANGO SALAD

Preparation time: 45 minutes +
  2 hours refrigeration
Total cooking time: 10 minutes
Serves 4

2 stalks lemon grass, white part only,
  thinly sliced
1 clove garlic
2 red Asian shallots
1 tablespoon coarsely chopped fresh
  ginger
1 red bird's-eye chilli, seeded
1 tablespoon fish sauce
1/2 cup (15 g/1/2 oz) fresh coriander
1 teaspoon grated lime rind
1 tablespoon lime juice
2 tablespoons oil
2 pork tenderloins, trimmed

DRESSING
1 large red chilli, seeded and finely
  chopped
2 cloves garlic, finely chopped
3 fresh coriander roots, finely chopped
11/4 tablespoons grated palm sugar
2 tablespoons fish sauce
1/4 cup (60 ml/2 fl oz) lime juice

SALAD
2 green mangoes or 1 small green
  papaya, peeled, pitted and cut into
  matchsticks
1 carrot, grated
1/2 cup (45 g/11/2 oz) bean sprouts
1/2 red onion, thinly sliced
3 tablespoons roughly chopped fresh
  mint
3 tablespoons roughly chopped fresh
  coriander leaves
3 tablespoons roughly chopped fresh
  Vietnamese mint

1 Place the lemon grass, garlic, shallots, ginger, chilli, fish sauce, coriander, lime rind, lime juice and oil in a blender or food processor and process to a coarse paste. Transfer to a non-metallic dish. Coat the pork in the marinade, cover and refrigerate for between 2 and 4 hours.
2 Mix together all the ingredients for the salad dressing. Combine all the salad ingredients in a large bowl.
3 Preheat a grill or chargrill pan and cook the pork over medium heat for 4–5 minutes each side, or until cooked through. Remove from the heat, rest for 5 minutes, then slice.
4 Toss the dressing and salad together. Season well. Arrange the sliced pork in a circle in the centre of each plate and top with salad.

NUTRITION PER SERVE
Protein 60 g; Fat 14 g; Carbohydrate 20 g;
Dietary Fibre 3 g; Cholesterol 122 mg;
1860 kJ (444 cal)

Mix the marinade ingredients to a coarse paste in a food processor or blender.

Cook the pork on a chargrill pan or grill until cooked through.

JAPANESE SCALLOP AND GINGER SALAD

Preparation time: 10 minutes
Total cooking time: 5 minutes
Serves 4

300 g (10 oz) fresh scallops, without roe
2 cups (100 g/3¹/₂ oz) baby English spinach leaves
1 small red capsicum, cut into very fine strips
50 g (1¹/₂ oz) bean sprouts

30 ml (1 fl oz) sake
1 tablespoon lime juice
2 teaspoons shaved palm sugar
1 teaspoon fish sauce

1 Remove any veins, membrane or hard white muscle from the scallops. Lightly brush a chargrill plate with oil. Cook the scallops in batches on the chargrill plate for 1 minute each side, or until cooked.
2 Divide the English spinach leaves, capsicum and bean sprouts among four serving plates. Arrange the scallops over the top.

3 To make the dressing, whisk together the sake, lime juice, palm sugar and fish sauce. Pour over the salad and serve immediately.

NUTRITION PER SERVE
Protein 10 g; Fat 0.5 g; Carbohydrate 3.5 g; Dietary Fibre 1.5 g; Cholesterol 25 mg; 274 kJ (65 cal)

NOTE: Sprinkle with toasted sesame seeds as a garnish.

Remove any veins, membrane or hard white muscle from the scallops.

Divide the spinach, capsicum and bean sprouts among the plates.

Whisk together the sake, lime juice, palm sugar and fish sauce.

CHILLI OCTOPUS SALAD

Preparation time: 15 minutes
Total cooking time: 5 minutes
Serves 4

1.5 kg (3 lb) baby octopus
1 cup (250 ml/8 fl oz) sweet chilli sauce
1/3 cup (80 ml/2³/4 fl oz) lime juice
1/3 cup (80 ml/2³/4 fl oz) fish sauce
1/3 cup (60 g/2 oz) soft brown sugar

oil, for chargrilling
200 g (6¹/2 oz) mixed salad leaves, to serve
lime wedges, to serve

1 Cut the head from the octopus and discard. With your index finger, push the hard beak up and out of the body. Rinse the octopus under cold water, drain and pat dry.
2 Mix together the sweet chilli sauce, lime juice, fish sauce and sugar.
3 Brush a chargrill plate or barbecue

with oil and heat to very hot. Cook the octopus, turning, for 3–4 minutes, or until they change colour. Brush with a quarter of the sauce during cooking. Do not overcook. Serve immediately on a bed of salad greens with the remaining sauce and the lime wedges.

NUTRITION PER SERVE
Protein 43 g; Fat 11 g; Carbohydrate 25 g; Dietary Fibre 2.5 g; Cholesterol 500 mg; 1543 kJ (370 cal)

Push the hard beak up and out of the body with your index finger.

Mix together the sweet chilli sauce, lime juice, fish sauce and sugar.

Cook the octopus, turning, until they change colour. Don't overcook or they'll become tough.

VIETNAMESE CHICKEN SALAD

Preparation time: 15 minutes
Total cooking time: 10 minutes
Serves 4

3 chicken breast fillets
1 red chilli, seeded and finely chopped
1/4 cup (60 ml/2 fl oz) lime juice
2 tablespoons soft brown sugar
1/4 cup (60 ml/2 fl oz) fish sauce
1/2 Chinese cabbage, shredded

2 carrots, grated
1 cup (50 g/1 1/2 oz) shredded fresh mint

1 Put the chicken in a saucepan, cover with water and bring to the boil, then reduce the heat and simmer for 10 minutes, or until cooked through.
2 While the chicken is cooking, mix together the chilli, lime juice, sugar and fish sauce. Remove the chicken from the water. Cool slightly, then shred into small pieces.
3 Combine the chicken, cabbage,

carrot, mint and dressing. Toss well and serve immediately.

NUTRITION PER SERVE
Protein 30 g; Fat 3 g; Carbohydrate 15 g;
Dietary Fibre 3.5 g; Cholesterol 62 mg;
900 kJ (215 cal)

STORAGE: Any leftovers can be used the next day in a stir-fry.

Poach the chicken in water for 10 minutes, or until cooked through.

Mix together the chilli, lime juice, sugar and fish sauce.

Toss together the chicken, cabbage, carrot, mint and dressing.

THAI PRAWN AND NOODLE SALAD

Preparation time: 25 minutes
Total cooking time: 2 minutes
Serves 4

DRESSING
2 tablespoons grated fresh ginger
2 tablespoons soy sauce
2 tablespoons sesame oil
1/3 cup (80 ml/2³/4 fl oz) red wine
    vinegar
1 tablespoon sweet chilli sauce

2 cloves garlic, crushed
1/3 cup (80 ml/2³/4 fl oz) kecap manis
500 g (1 lb) large cooked prawns
250 g (8 oz) dried instant egg noodles
5 spring onions, sliced diagonally
2 tablespoons chopped fresh
    coriander
1 red capsicum, diced
100 g (3¹/2 oz) snow peas, sliced
lime wedges, to serve

1 For the dressing, whisk together the fresh ginger, soy sauce, sesame oil, red wine vinegar, chilli sauce, garlic and kecap manis.

2 Peel and devein the prawns. Cut each prawn in half lengthways.
3 Cook the egg noodles in a large saucepan of boiling water for 2 minutes, or until tender, then drain thoroughly. Cool in a large bowl.
4 Add the dressing, prawns and remaining ingredients to the noodles and toss gently. Serve with the lime wedges.

NUTRITION PER SERVE
Protein 32 g; Fat 12 g; Carbohydrate 48 g;
Dietary Fibre 4 g; Cholesterol 176 mg;
1805 kJ (430 cal)

Whisk all the dressing ingredients together in a large bowl.

Cut each of the peeled, deveined prawns in half lengthways with a very sharp knife.

Toss the noodles, prawns, dressing, herbs and vegetables together.

GADO GADO

Preparation time: 30 minutes
Total cooking time: 35 minutes
Serves 4

6 new potatoes
2 carrots, cut into thick strips
250 g (8 oz) snake beans, cut into
    long lengths
2 tablespoons peanut oil
250 g (8 oz) firm tofu, cubed
100 g (3½ oz) baby English spinach
    leaves
2 Lebanese cucumbers, cut into
    batons
1 large red capsicum, cut into batons
100 g (3½ oz) bean sprouts
5 hard-boiled eggs

PEANUT SAUCE
1 tablespoon peanut oil
1 onion, finely chopped
²⁄₃ cup (150 g/5 oz) peanut butter
¼ cup (60 ml/2 fl oz) kecap manis
2 tablespoons ground coriander
2 teaspoons chilli sauce
¾ cup (185 ml/6 fl oz) coconut cream
1 teaspoon grated palm sugar
1 tablespoon lemon juice

1 Cook the potatoes in boiling water until tender. Drain and cool slightly. Cut into quarters. Cook the carrots and beans separately in boiling water until just tender. Plunge into iced water, then drain.
2 Heat the oil in a non-stick frying pan and cook the tofu in batches until crisp. Drain on paper towels.
3 To make the peanut sauce, heat the oil in a pan over low heat and cook the onion for 5 minutes, or until golden. Add the peanut butter, kecap manis, coriander, chilli sauce and coconut cream. Bring to the boil, reduce the heat and simmer for 5 minutes. Stir in the sugar and juice until dissolved.
4 Arrange the vegetables and tofu on a plate. Halve the eggs and place in the centre. Serve with the sauce.

NUTRITION PER SERVE
Protein 35 g; Fat 55 g; Carbohydrate 35 g;
Dietary Fibre 15 g; Cholesterol 265 mg;
3175 kJ (755 cal)

Cut the cucumbers and capsicum into even-sized batons.

Cook the snake beans quickly in a pan of boiling water then plunge into iced water.

Heat the oil and cook the tofu in batches until crisp and golden brown.

Add the peanut butter, kecap manis, coriander, chilli sauce and coconut cream to the pan.

JAPANESE SPINACH SALAD

Preparation time: 25 minutes
Total cooking time: 5 minutes
Serves 4

2 eggs
1 sheet nori, cut into matchsticks
100 g (3½ oz) baby English spinach
    leaves
1 small red onion, finely sliced
½ small daikon radish, finely sliced
2 Lebanese cucumbers, sliced
30 g (1 oz) pickled ginger, sliced
1 tablespoon toasted sesame seeds

DRESSING
⅓ cup (80 ml/2¾ fl oz) light olive oil
1 tablespoon rice vinegar
1 tablespoon light soy sauce

1 Preheat the grill to hot. Beat the eggs lightly in a small bowl, add 1 tablespoon water and the nori. Season well. Heat and grease a 20 cm (8 inch) omelette pan. Pour in the mixture to make a thin omelette. When lightly browned underneath, place under the grill to set the top, without colouring. Turn out onto a board and leave to cool. Cut the omelette into thin strips.
2 To make the dressing, whisk together the olive oil, vinegar and soy sauce until combined.
3 Toss together the spinach leaves, onion, daikon, cucumber, ginger, toasted sesame seeds, omelette strips and dressing in a large bowl.

NUTRITION PER SERVE
Protein 5 g; Fat 25 g; Carbohydrate 15 g;
Dietary Fibre 2 g; Cholesterol 90 mg;
1235 kJ (295 cal)

Peel the daikon radish and cut it into fine slices with a sharp knife.

Add 1 tablespoon water and the nori to the lightly beaten eggs.

Once the omelette has cooled, slice it into thin strips for adding to the salad.

BOK CHOY SALAD

Preparation time: 20 minutes
Total cooking time: 5 minutes
Serves 4

1 cup (250 ml/8 fl oz) chicken stock
1 small carrot, cut into matchsticks
4 baby bok choy
100 g (3¹/₂ oz) snow peas, thinly
    sliced
1 cup (90 g/3 oz) bean sprouts,
    trimmed
1 tablespoon chopped fresh coriander

SESAME DRESSING
¹/₃ cup (80 ml/2³/₄ fl oz) peanut oil
1 teaspoon sesame oil
1 tablespoon white vinegar
1 tablespoon sesame seeds, toasted
    (see HINT)
2 teaspoons grated fresh ginger
2 teaspoons honey, warmed
1 clove garlic, crushed

1 Pour the chicken stock into a frying pan and bring to the boil. Add the carrot and bok choy, cover and cook for 2 minutes. Drain the vegetables and leave to cool, then halve the bok choy lengthways.
2 To make the dressing, whisk together the oils, vinegar, sesame seeds, ginger, honey and garlic. Season with salt and pepper, to taste.
3 Place the cooled carrot strips and halved bok choy in a large serving dish and arrange the snow peas, bean sprouts and chopped coriander on top. Drizzle with the sesame dressing.

NUTRITION PER SERVE
Protein 7 g; Fat 20 g; Carbohydrate 10 g;
Dietary Fibre 4 g; Cholesterol 0 mg;
1110 kJ (265 cal)

HINT: To toast the sesame seeds, place in a dry pan and shake gently over medium heat until the seeds smell fragrant and begin to turn a pale golden colour. Turn the seeds out onto a plate and leave to cool.

Cut the carrots into matchsticks for quick and even cooking.

Remove and discard the scraggly ends from the bean sprouts.

Using a large sharp knife, halve the bok choy lengthways.

INDIAN-STYLE LAMB COUSCOUS SALAD

Preparation time: 25 minutes
Total cooking time: 35 minutes
Serves 4–6

250 g (8 oz) lamb backstrap (tender eye of the lamb loin)
1 tablespoon mild curry powder
2 tablespoons pepitas (pumpkin seeds)
2 tablespoons sesame seeds
2 teaspoons cumin seeds
2 teaspoons coriander seeds
1 tablespoon oil
2 tablespoons lemon juice
1 onion, chopped
1 carrot, chopped
125 g (4 oz) orange sweet potato, cubed
1 clove garlic, finely chopped
2 teaspoons oil, extra
1 cup (185 g/6 oz) couscous
1/4 cup (50 g/1³/4 oz) raisins

1 Sprinkle the lamb with the combined curry powder and a pinch of salt, then turn to coat well. Cover with plastic wrap and refrigerate while preparing the salad.
2 Place the pepitas and sesame seeds in a dry frying pan and cook, stirring, over medium-high heat until the seeds begin to brown. Add the cumin and coriander seeds and continue stirring until the pepitas are puffed and begin to pop. Remove from the heat and allow to cool.
3 Heat the oil in a pan, add the lamb and cook over medium-high heat for 5–8 minutes, or until browned and tender. Remove from the pan, drizzle with half the lemon juice and leave to cool to room temperature. Turn the meat occasionally to coat in the lemon juice while cooling. To the same pan, add the onion, carrot and sweet potato and stir over high heat until the onion is translucent. Reduce the heat to medium, add 1/4 cup (60 ml/2 fl oz) water, cover and cook for about 3 minutes, or until the vegetables are tender. Stir in the chopped garlic and remaining lemon juice.
4 Pour 1 cup (250 ml/8 fl oz) boiling water into a heatproof bowl and add the extra oil. Add the couscous and stir until combined. Leave for about 2 minutes, or until the water has been absorbed. Fluff gently with a fork to separate the grains. Add the vegetable mixture, raisins and most of the toasted nuts and seeds, reserving some to sprinkle over the top, and toss. Spoon onto a serving plate. Slice the lamb thinly and arrange over the salad. Drizzle with any leftover lemon juice and sprinkle with the reserved nuts and seeds.

NUTRITION PER SERVE (6)
Protein 15 g; Fat 10 g; Carbohydrate 30 g; Dietary Fibre 3 g; Cholesterol 30 mg; 1135 kJ (270 cal)

Sprinkle the lamb backstrap with the combined curry powder and salt.

Fry the seeds in a dry frying pan until the pepitas puff up.

When the water has been absorbed, fluff the couscous gently with a fork.

TANDOORI CHICKEN SALAD

Preparation time: 20 minutes +
  overnight marinating
Total cooking time: 15 minutes
Serves 4

4 chicken breast fillets
2–3 tablespoons tandoori paste
200 g (6^1/$_2$ oz) plain thick yoghurt
1 tablespoon lemon juice
^{1}/$_2$ cup (15 g/^{1}/$_2$ oz) fresh coriander
  leaves
^{1}/$_2$ cup (60 g/2 oz) slivered almonds,
  toasted
snow pea sprouts, to serve

CUCUMBER AND YOGHURT
  DRESSING
1 Lebanese cucumber, grated
200 g (6^1/$_2$ oz) plain thick yoghurt
1 tablespoon chopped fresh mint
2 teaspoons lemon juice

1 Cut the chicken breast fillets into thick strips. Combine the tandoori paste, yoghurt and lemon juice in a large bowl, add the chicken strips and toss to coat well. Refrigerate and leave to marinate overnight.
2 To make the dressing, put the grated cucumber in a medium bowl. Add the yoghurt, chopped mint and lemon juice, and stir until well combined. Refrigerate until needed.
3 Heat a large non-stick frying pan, add the marinated chicken in batches and cook, turning frequently, until cooked through. Cool and place in a large bowl. Add the coriander leaves and toasted almonds, and toss until well combined. Serve on a bed of snow pea sprouts, with the dressing served separately.

NUTRITION PER SERVE
Protein 35 g; Fat 15 g; Carbohydrate 7 g;
Dietary Fibre 2 g; Cholesterol 70 mg;
1230 kJ (290 cal)

NOTE: The quality of the tandoori paste used will determine the flavour and look of the chicken. There are many good-quality home-made varieties available from supermarkets and delicatessens.

Combine the tandoori paste, yoghurt and lemon juice to make a marinade.

Using a metal grater, coarsely grate the Lebanese cucumber for the dressing.

Cook the marinated chicken in a large frying pan in batches, turning frequently.

DUCK AND INDIAN SPICED RICE SALAD WITH SWEET GINGER DRESSING

Preparation time: 30 minutes
Total cooking time: 1 hour
Serves 4–6

DRESSING
1/3 cup (80 ml/2³/4 fl oz) oil
1 teaspoon walnut oil
1 teaspoon grated orange rind
1 tablespoon orange juice
1 tablespoon finely chopped
    preserved ginger
1 teaspoon sambal oelek
1 teaspoon white wine vinegar

100 g (3¹/2 oz) wild rice
oil, for cooking
50 g (1³/4 oz) pecans
1/2 teaspoon ground cumin
1/2 teaspoon garam masala
1/4 teaspoon cayenne pepper
75 g (2¹/2 oz) long-grain white rice
1 celery stick, finely sliced
20 yellow pear tomatoes, cut in half
    lengthways
20 g (³/4 oz) French spinach or small
    English spinach leaves
4 spring onions, thinly sliced
450 g (14 oz) Chinese barbecued
    duck, with skin, cut into pieces
    (see NOTE)
strips of orange rind, to garnish

1 To make the dressing, mix the ingredients together thoroughly. Season with salt and black pepper.
2 Rinse the wild rice under cold water and add to 300 ml (10 fl oz) of simmering water. Cook, covered, for 45 minutes, or until the grains puff open. Drain off any excess water.
3 Meanwhile, heat 2 teaspoons oil in a large frying pan. Add the pecans and cook, stirring, until golden. Remove from the pan and allow to cool. Coarsely chop the nuts. Add the cumin, garam masala, cayenne pepper and a pinch of salt to the pan, and cook for 1 minute, or until aromatic. Add the pecans and toss to coat.
4 Add the white rice to a pan of boiling water and simmer until tender. Drain and mix with the wild rice and pecans in a large, shallow bowl. Add the celery, tomato, spinach and spring onion. Add half of the dressing and

toss well. Arrange the pieces of duck on top with the skin uppermost. Drizzle with the remaining dressing and garnish with the orange rind.

NUTRITION PER SERVE (6)
Protein 20 g; Fat 40 g; Carbohydrate 30 g; Dietary Fibre 6 g; Cholesterol 90 mg; 2325 kJ (555 cal)

NOTE: Chinese barbecued duck can be purchased from any Chinatown, or from your local Chinese restaurant.

Finely slice the celery stick, and halve the pear tomatoes lengthways.

Cook the wild rice, covered, until the grains puff open.

Return the chopped pecans to the pan and toss until well coated with the spices.

BASMATI RICE, CASHEW AND PEA SALAD

Preparation time: 30 minutes +
    30 minutes standing
Total cooking time: 20 minutes
Serves 6

40 g (1¼ oz) butter or ghee
½ teaspoon turmeric
300 g (10 oz) basmati rice
½ teaspoon salt
200 g (6½ oz) fresh or frozen peas,
    thawed
¼ cup (60 ml/2 fl oz) peanut oil
1 teaspoon yellow mustard seeds
1 teaspoon cumin seeds
¼ cup (30 g/1 oz) currants
1 clove garlic, crushed
1–2 small green chillies, finely
    chopped
1 teaspoon Madras curry powder
100 ml (3½ fl oz) coconut cream
50 g (1¾ oz) glacé ginger, cut into
    thin strips
¼ small red onion, finely chopped
1 tablespoon chopped fresh mint
    leaves
1 tablespoon chopped fresh coriander
½ cup (30 g/1 oz) shredded coconut
100 g (3½ oz) roasted cashew nuts,
    coarsely chopped
2 teaspoons shredded coconut, to
    garnish

1 Melt the butter or ghee in a heavy-based pan and stir in the turmeric. Add the rice and salt, and stir for 10–15 seconds, then pour in 1½ cups (375 ml/12 fl oz) of water. Stir over high heat until boiling, then reduce the heat until gently simmering. Simmer, tightly covered, and cook for 13 minutes without removing the lid. Remove the pan from the heat and leave for 10 minutes without removing the lid, then fluff gently with a fork. Add the peas, transfer to a large bowl and allow to cool.

2 Heat 2 teaspoons of the oil in a pan and stir in the mustard and cumin seeds. When the mustard seeds start to pop, add the currants, garlic, chilli and curry powder. Stir to combine, but do not brown. Stir in the coconut cream, remove from the heat and transfer to the bowl of rice and peas.

3 Add the ginger, onion, herbs and the remaining oil. Toss well, and set aside for at least 30 minutes. Just before serving, toss through the coconut and cashew nuts. Garnish with the shredded coconut.

NUTRITION PER SERVE
Protein 9 g; Fat 30 g; Carbohydrate 55 g;
Dietary Fibre 6 g; Cholesterol 15 mg;
2110 kJ (500 cal)

NOTE: Rice salads often improve if made in advance. This dish may be prepared up to 24 hours in advance, but add the cashew nuts and coconut just before serving to keep them crisp.

Cut the glacé ginger into thin strips and chop the red onion and mint.

Add the rice and salt to the melted butter and turmeric in the pan.

Add the currants, garlic, chilli and curry powder to the mustard and cumin seeds.

THAI NOODLE SALAD

Preparation time: 25 minutes
Total cooking time: 5 minutes
Serves 4

DRESSING
2 tablespoons grated fresh ginger
2 tablespoons soy sauce
2 tablespoons sesame oil
1/3 cup (80 ml/2³/4 fl oz) red wine
    vinegar
3–4 teaspoons sweet chilli sauce
2 cloves garlic, crushed
1/3 cup (80 ml/2³/4 fl oz) kecap manis
    (see NOTE)

250 g (8 oz) fine instant noodles
5 spring onions, sliced
2 tablespoons chopped fresh
    coriander
1 red capsicum, chopped
100 g (3¹/2 oz) snow peas, sliced
500 g (1 lb) cooked king prawns,
    peeled, halved and deveined

1 To make the dressing, put the
ingredients in a large bowl and whisk
with a fork to combine.
2 Cook the noodles in a large pan of
boiling water for 2 minutes and drain
well. Add to the dressing and toss to
combine. Leave to cool.
3 Add the remaining ingredients to
the noodles and toss gently. Serve at
room temperature.

NUTRITION PER SERVE
Protein 35 g; Fat 15 g; Carbohydrate 60 g;
Dietary Fibre 3 g; Cholesterol 235 mg;
2275 kJ (540 cal)

NOTE: Kecap manis (sweet soy sauce)
is available from Asian food stores.

Peel and finely grate the fresh ginger on the fine
side of the grater.

Add the kecap manis to the other ingredients and
mix to combine.

Add the noodles to a large pan of boiling water
and cook until tender.

SPICY INDIAN LENTIL SALAD

Preparation time: 30 minutes
Total cooking time: 1 hour 10 minutes
Serves 6

1 cup (220 g/7 oz) brown rice
1 cup (185 g/6 oz) brown lentils
1 teaspoon turmeric
1 teaspoon ground cinnamon
6 cardamom pods
3 star anise
2 bay leaves
1/2 cup (60 ml/2 fl oz) sunflower oil
1 tablespoon lemon juice
250 g (8 oz) broccoli florets
2 carrots, cut into matchsticks
1 onion, finely chopped
2 cloves garlic, crushed
1 red capsicum, finely chopped
1 teaspoon garam masala
1 teaspoon ground coriander
1 1/2 cups (235 g/7 1/2 oz) fresh or
   frozen peas, thawed

MINT AND YOGHURT DRESSING
1 cup (250 g/8 oz) plain yoghurt
1 tablespoon lemon juice
1 tablespoon finely chopped fresh
   mint
1 teaspoon cumin seeds

1 Put 3 cups (750 ml/24 fl oz) water with the rice, lentils, turmeric, cinnamon, cardamom, star anise and bay leaves in a pan. Stir to combine and bring to the boil. Reduce the heat, cover and simmer gently for 50–60 minutes, or until the liquid is absorbed. Remove the whole spices and discard. Transfer the mixture to a large bowl. Whisk 2 tablespoons of the oil with the lemon juice and fork through the rice mixture.

2 Boil, steam or microwave the broccoli and carrots until tender. Drain and refresh in cold water.
3 Heat the remaining oil in a large pan and add the onion, garlic and capsicum. Stir-fry for 2–3 minutes, then add the garam masala and coriander, and stir-fry for a further 1–2 minutes. Add the vegetables and toss to coat in the spice mixture. Add to the rice mixture and fork through to combine. Cover and refrigerate.

4 To make the dressing, mix the yoghurt, lemon juice, mint and cumin seeds together, and season with salt and pepper. Spoon the salad into individual serving bowls or onto a platter and serve with the dressing.

NUTRITION PER SERVE
Protein 20 g; Fat 15 g; Carbohydrate 50 g; Dietary Fibre 10 g; Cholesterol 7 mg; 1605 kJ (380 cal)

Add the cardamom pods, star anise and bay leaves to the pan.

Add the vegetables and toss to coat with the spice mixture.

Mix the yoghurt, lemon juice, mint and cumin seeds together.

MISO TOFU STICKS WITH CUCUMBER AND WAKAME SALAD

Preparation time: 30 minutes +
    20 minutes standing
Total cooking time: 15 minutes
Serves 4

3 Lebanese cucumbers, thinly sliced
20 g (3/4 oz) dried wakame
500 g (1 lb) silken firm tofu, well
    drained
3 tablespoons shiro miso
1 tablespoon mirin
1 tablespoon sugar
1 tablespoon rice vinegar
1 egg yolk
100 g (3 1/2 oz) bean sprouts,
    blanched
2 tablespoons sesame seeds, toasted

DRESSING
3 tablespoons rice vinegar
1/4 teaspoon soy sauce
1 1/2 tablespoons sugar
1 tablespoon mirin

1 Sprinkle the cucumber generously with salt and leave for 20 minutes, or until very soft, then rinse and drain. To rehydrate the wakame, place it in a colander in the sink and leave it under cold running water for 10 minutes, then drain well.

2 Place the tofu in a colander, weigh down with a plate and leave to drain.

3 Place the shiro miso, mirin, sugar, rice vinegar and 2 tablespoons water in a saucepan and stir over low heat for 1 minute, or until the sugar dissolves. Remove from the heat, then add the egg yolk and whisk until glossy. Cool slightly.

4 Cut the tofu into thick sticks and place on a non-stick baking tray. Brush the miso mixture over the tofu and cook under a hot grill for 6 minutes each side, or until light golden on both sides.

5 To make the dressing, place all the ingredients and 1/2 teaspoon salt in a bowl and whisk together well.

6 To assemble, place the cucumber in the centre of a plate, top with the sprouts and wakame, drizzle with the dressing, top with tofu and serve sprinkled with the sesame seeds.

NUTRITION PER SERVE
Protein 10 g; Fat 7 g; Carbohydrate 8 g;
Dietary Fibre 2.5 g; Cholesterol 0 mg;
710 kJ (180 cal)

Once the cucumber is very soft, rinse the salt off under running water.

Place the wakame in a colander and leave it under cold running water.

Brush the miso mixture over the tofu sticks and grill under golden.

VIETNAMESE SALAD

Preparation time: 30 minutes +
  10 minutes standing + 30 minutes
  refrigeration
Total cooking time: Nil
Serves 4–6

200 g (6¹/₂ oz) dried rice vermicelli
1 cup (140 g/4¹/₂ oz) crushed peanuts
¹/₂ cup (10 g/¹/₄ oz) fresh Vietnamese
  mint leaves, torn
¹/₂ cup (15 g/¹/₂ oz) firmly packed
  fresh coriander leaves
¹/₂ red onion, cut into thin wedges
1 green mango, cut into matchsticks

1 Lebanese cucumber, halved
  lengthways and thinly sliced on the
  diagonal

LEMON GRASS DRESSING
¹/₂ cup (125 ml/4 fl oz) lime juice
1 tablespoon shaved palm sugar
¹/₄ cup (60 ml/2 fl oz) seasoned rice
  vinegar
2 stems lemon grass, finely chopped
2 red chillies, seeded and finely
  chopped
3 kaffir lime leaves, shredded

1 Place the rice vermicelli in a bowl
and cover with boiling water. Leave for
10 minutes, or until soft, then drain,

rinse under cold water and cut into
short lengths.
2 Place the vermicelli, three-quarters
of the peanuts, the mint, coriander,
onion, mango and cucumber in a large
bowl and toss together.
3 To make the dressing, place all the
ingredients in a jar with a lid and
shake together.
4 Toss the salad and dressing and
refrigerate for 30 minutes. Sprinkle
with the remaining nuts to serve.

NUTRITION PER SERVE (6)
Protein 6.5 g; Fat 13 g; Carbohydrate 19 g;
Dietary Fibre 3 g; Cholesterol 0 mg;
926 kJ (221 cal)

Cut the green mango into short thin strips the
size and shape of matchsticks.

Using scissors, cut the rice vermicelli into shorter,
more manageable lengths.

Put the salad ingredients in a bowl and toss well,
reserving some of the peanuts to garnish.

HOKKIEN NOODLE SALAD

Preparation time: 20 minutes
Total cooking time: Nil
Serves 8

900 g (1³/₄ lb) Hokkien noodles
6 spring onions, sliced diagonally
1 large red capsicum, thinly sliced
200 g (6¹/₂ oz) snow peas, sliced
1 carrot, sliced diagonally
60 g (2 oz) fresh mint, chopped
60 g (2 oz) fresh coriander, chopped
100 g (3¹/₂ oz) roasted cashew nuts

SESAME DRESSING
2 teaspoons sesame oil
1 tablespoon peanut oil
2 tablespoons lime juice
2 tablespoons kecap manis (see NOTE)
3 tablespoons sweet chilli sauce

1 Gently separate the noodles and place in a large bowl, cover with boiling water and leave for 2 minutes. Rinse and drain.
2 Put the noodles in a large bowl, and add spring onions, capsicum, snow peas, carrot, mint and coriander. Toss together well.

3 To make the dressing, whisk together the oils, lime juice, kecap manis and sweet chilli sauce. Pour the dressing over the salad and toss again. Sprinkle the cashew nuts over the top and serve immediately.

NUTRITION PER SERVE
Protein 10 g; Fat 9 g; Carbohydrate 35 g; Dietary Fibre 4.5 g; Cholesterol 0 mg; 1115 kJ (265 cal)

NOTE: If you can't find kecap manis, you can use soy sauce sweetened with a little soft brown sugar.

Top and tail the snow peas, then finely slice lengthways with a sharp knife.

Separate the noodles, then put them in a large bowl and cover with boiling water.

Whisk together the oils, lime juice, kecap manis and sweet chilli sauce.

SICHUAN CHICKEN AND NOODLE SALAD

Preparation time: 20 minutes
Total cooking time: 40 minutes
Serves 4

5 cm (2 inch) piece of fresh ginger,
    thinly sliced
5 spring onions
2 chicken breasts, with bone and skin
1 teaspoon Sichuan peppercorns (or
    whole black peppercorns)
250 g (8 oz) Shanghai noodles
1 teaspoon sesame oil
1 tablespoon light soy sauce
2 Lebanese cucumbers, cut in half
    lengthways and thinly sliced
1¹/₂ tablespoons lime juice
¹/₂ cup (15 g/¹/₂ oz) fresh coriander
    leaves
lime wedges, to serve

1 Bring a large saucepan of water to
the boil. Add the ginger, 2 spring
onions, thinly sliced, and 2 teaspoons
salt and simmer for 10 minutes. Add
the chicken and simmer gently for
15–20 minutes. Remove the chicken
from the pan. When cool enough to
handle, remove the skin and bones,
then finely shred the flesh—there
should be about 300 g (10 oz) of
shredded chicken. Place in a bowl and
cover with plastic wrap. Refrigerate
until ready to use.
2 Heat the peppercorns and
1 teaspoon salt in a small non-stick
frying pan over medium-high heat.
Dry roast, stirring constantly, for
5 minutes, or until the salt begins to
darken. Remove from the heat and
cool. When cool, grind the salt and
pepper mixture in a spice grinder or
mortar and pestle, until very fine.

3 Cook the noodles in a saucepan of
boiling water for 4–5 minutes, or until
tender. Drain well and rinse under
cold water. Place the noodles in a
large bowl and toss with the sesame
oil and soy sauce.
4 Sprinkle the salt and pepper
mixture on the chicken and toss well,
covering as much of the chicken as
possible with the spice mixture. Thinly
slice the remaining spring onions, then
add to the chicken mixture with the

cucumber and toss well. Add the
chicken mixture and lime juice to
the noodles and toss together. Top
with the coriander and serve with
lime wedges.

NUTRITION PER SERVE
Protein 28 g; Fat 5 g; Carbohydrate 34 g;
Dietary Fibre 2 g; Cholesterol 77 mg;
1255 kJ (300 Cal)

Remove the skin and bones from the chicken
breasts and shred the flesh.

Toss the Shanghai noodles, sesame oil and soy
sauce in a large bowl.

Add the cucumber and spring onion to the
seasoned chicken and toss well.

LOW-FAT TANDOORI LAMB SALAD

Preparation time: 20 minutes +
    overnight marinating
Total cooking time: 15 minutes
Serves 4

1 cup (250 g/8 oz) low-fat plain
    yoghurt
2 cloves garlic, crushed
2 teaspoons grated fresh ginger
2 teaspoons ground turmeric
2 teaspoons garam masala
1/4 teaspoon paprika

2 teaspoons ground coriander
red food colouring, optional
500 g (1 lb) lean lamb fillets
4 tablespoons lemon juice
1 1/2 teaspoons chopped fresh
    coriander
1 teaspoon chopped fresh mint
150 g (5 oz) mixed salad leaves
1 large mango, cut into strips
2 cucumbers, cut into matchsticks

1 Mix the yoghurt, garlic, ginger and
spices in a bowl, add a little colouring
and toss with the lamb to thoroughly
coat. Cover and refrigerate overnight.
2 Grill the lamb on a foil-lined baking

tray under high heat for 7 minutes
each side, or until the marinade starts
to brown. Set aside for 5 minutes
before serving.
3 Mix the lemon juice, coriander and
mint, then season. Toss with the salad
leaves, mango and cucumber, then
arrange on plates. Slice the lamb and
serve over the salad.

NUTRITION PER SERVE
Protein 30 g; Fat 6.5 g; Carbohydrate 8 g;
Dietary Fibre 2 g; Cholesterol 90 mg;
965 kJ (230 cal)

Coat the lamb with the marinade, cover and
refrigerate overnight.

Cut the mango flesh into long, thin strips, using a
sharp knife.

Turn the lamb after about 7 minutes and cook
until the marinade starts to brown.

Noodles & Rice

PHAD THAI

Preparation time: 25 minutes
Total cooking time: 10–15 minutes
Serves 4

250 g (8 oz) thick rice stick noodles
2 tablespoons oil
3 cloves garlic, chopped
2 teaspoons chopped red chillies
150 g (5 oz) pork, thinly sliced
100 g (3¹/₂ oz) peeled raw prawns,
    chopped
¹/₂ bunch garlic chives, chopped
2 tablespoons fish sauce
2 tablespoons lime juice
2 teaspoons soft brown sugar
2 eggs, beaten
1 cup (90 g/3 oz) bean sprouts
sprigs of fresh coriander
3 tablespoons chopped roasted
    peanuts

1 Soak the rice stick noodles in warm water for 10 minutes or until they are soft. Drain and set aside. Heat the oil to very hot in a wok or large frying pan, then add the garlic, chillies and pork and stir-fry for 2 minutes.
2 Add the prawn meat to the wok. Stir-fry for 3 minutes. Add the garlic chives and drained noodles to the wok, cover and cook for another minute.
3 Add the fish sauce, lime juice, sugar and eggs to the wok. Toss well until heated through.
4 Sprinkle with bean sprouts, coriander and chopped peanuts. Traditionally served with crisp fried onion, soft brown sugar and more chopped peanuts on the side.

NUTRITION PER SERVE
Protein 20 g; Fat 10 g; Carbohydrate 10 g;
Dietary Fibre 2 g; Cholesterol 140 mg;
890 kJ (210 cal)

After stir-frying the pork for 2 minutes, stir in the prawn meat.

Toss the ingredients, using tongs or two wooden spoons, until heated through.

SOBA NOODLES WITH TEMPURA PRAWNS IN DASHI BROTH

Preparation time: 20 minutes
Total cooking time: 15 minutes
Serves 4 as a starter

200 g (6¹/₂ oz) dried soba noodles
1 spring onion, sliced on the diagonal
60 g (2 oz) daikon, cut into thin
　　strips
1 teaspoon dashi granules
¹/₄ cup (60 ml/2 fl oz) Japanese soy
　　sauce
2 tablespoons mirin
¹/₂ teaspoon caster sugar
2 spring onions, sliced thinly on the
　　diagonal, extra
2 teaspoons black sesame seeds
pickled ginger, to garnish

TEMPURA PRAWNS
12 raw king prawns
oil, for deep-frying
1 cup (125 g/4 oz) tempura flour
1 cup (250 ml/8 fl oz) iced water

1 Bring a large saucepan of water to the boil and cook the noodles for 5 minutes, or until just tender. Drain, then add the spring onion and daikon, toss well and keep warm.
2 To make the broth, place the dashi granules, soy sauce, mirin, sugar and 2 cups (500 ml/16 fl oz) water in a saucepan and bring to the boil. Reduce the heat and simmer for 2–3 minutes. Remove from the heat, cover and keep warm.
3 To make the tempura prawns, peel and devein the prawns, keeping the tails intact. Make four incisions in the underside of each prawn.
4 Fill a wok or deep heavy-based saucepan one-third full of oil and heat until a cube of bread dropped into the oil browns in 15 seconds. Combine the tempura flour with the iced water and mix briefly with chopsticks or a fork— the batter should still be lumpy. Dip each prawn into the batter, leaving the tail uncoated. Deep-fry in batches for about 30 seconds, or until crispy and cooked through. Drain well on crumpled paper towels.

5 Divide the noodles among four bowls and cover with broth, then top with the extra spring onion. Stand three prawns on top and sprinkle with sesame seeds. Garnish with pickled ginger and serve immediately.

NUTRITION PER SERVE
Protein 23 g; Fat 12 g; Carbohydrate 54 g; Dietary Fibre 5 g; Cholesterol 94 mg; 1757 kJ (420 cal)

Make four incisions in the underside of each prawn.

Briefly mix the tempura flour and iced water with chopsticks.

Cook the prawns until crisp, lightly golden and cooked through.

CORIANDER NOODLES WITH TUNA

Preparation time: 15 minutes
Total cooking time: 10 minutes
Serves 4

1/4 cup (60 ml/2 fl oz) lime juice
2 tablespoons fish sauce
2 tablespoons sweet chilli sauce
2 teaspoons grated palm sugar
1 teaspoon sesame oil
1 clove garlic, finely chopped
1 tablespoon virgin olive oil
4 tuna steaks, at room temperature
200 g (6½ oz) dried thin wheat
    noodles
6 spring onions, thinly sliced

3/4 cup (30 g/1 oz) chopped fresh
    coriander leaves
lime wedges, to garnish

1 To make the dressing, mix together the lime juice, fish sauce, chilli sauce, sugar, sesame oil and garlic.
2 Heat the olive oil in a chargrill pan. Add the tuna steaks and cook over high heat for 2 minutes each side, or until cooked to your liking. Transfer the steaks to a warm plate, cover and keep warm.
3 Place the noodles in a large saucepan of lightly salted, rapidly boiling water and return to the boil. Cook for 4 minutes, or until the noodles are tender. Drain well. Add half the dressing and half the spring

onion and coriander to the noodles and gently toss together.
4 Either cut the tuna into even cubes or slice it. Arrange the noodles on plates and top with the tuna. Mix the remaining dressing with the spring onion and coriander and drizzle over the tuna. Garnish with lime wedges.

NUTRITION PER SERVE
Protein 32 g; Fat 10 g; Carbohydrate 5 g;
Dietary Fibre 1 g; Cholesterol 105 mg;
1030 kJ (245 cal)

NOTE: If you prefer, serve the tuna steaks whole. If serving whole, they would look better served with the noodles on the side.

Cook the tuna steaks in a chargrill pan until cooked to your liking.

Cook the noodles in lightly salted water for 4 minutes or until tender.

Combine the remaining dressing with the spring onion and coriander.

NOODLE CAKES WITH CHINESE ROASTED PORK AND CUCUMBER SALAD

Preparation time: 45 minutes
Total cooking time: 25 minutes
Serves 4

500 g (1 lb) thin fresh rice noodles, at
     room temperature
2 Lebanese cucumbers, halved
     lengthways and thinly sliced
2 tablespoons chopped fresh
     coriander leaves
1 tablespoon lime juice
1 tablespoon fish sauce
2 teaspoons caster sugar
1/4 cup (60 ml/2 fl oz) oil
1 red capsicum, thinly sliced
3 cloves garlic, finely chopped
1 tablespoon white vinegar
1/4 cup (60 ml/2 fl oz) black bean
     sauce
1/3 cup (80 ml/2³/4 fl oz) chicken stock
1 tablespoon soft brown sugar
300 g (10 oz) Chinese barbecued
     pork, sliced

1 Pour boiling water over the noodles and leave for 5 minutes, or until softened. Drain, then gently separate.
2 To make the cucumber salad, toss the cucumber, coriander, lime juice, fish sauce and caster sugar together in a large bowl and leave until needed.
3 Heat 1 tablespoon of the oil in a large non-stick frying pan. Place four 10 cm (4 inch) rings in the frying pan. Fill as firmly as possible with the noodles and press down with the back of a spoon. Cook over medium heat for 10 minutes, or until crisp, pressing the noodles down occasionally. Turn over and repeat on the other side, adding another tablespoon of the oil if

necessary. Cover and keep warm.
4 Meanwhile, heat 1 tablespoon of the remaining oil in a wok, add the capsicum and stir-fry over high heat for 2 minutes, or until softened slightly. Add the garlic to the wok and toss for 1 minute, or until softened, then add the vinegar, black bean sauce, stock and sugar. Stir until the sugar has dissolved, then simmer for 2 minutes, or until the sauce thickens

slightly. Add the Chinese barbecued pork and stir to coat with the sauce.
5 To serve, place a noodle cake on each plate and top with some of the barbecued pork. Arrange the salad around the noodle cake and serve.

NUTRITION PER SERVE
Protein 34 g; Fat 28 g; Carbohydrate 100 g;
Dietary Fibre 7 g; Cholesterol 70 mg;
3360 kJ (805 cal)

Soak the noodles in boiling water until they are soft, then gently separate them.

Press the noodles down into the rings with the back of a spoon.

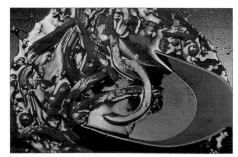

Simmer until the sugar dissolves and the sauce slightly thickens.

SWEET CHILLI CHICKEN NOODLES

Preparation time: 10 minutes
Total cooking time: 10 minutes
Serves 4–6

375 g (12 oz) Hokkien noodles
4 chicken thigh fillets, cut into small
   pieces
1–2 tablespoons sweet chilli sauce
2 teaspoons fish sauce
1 tablespoon oil
100 g (3$\frac{1}{2}$ oz) baby sweet corn,
   halved lengthways
150 g (5 oz) sugar snap peas, topped
   and tailed
1 tablespoon lime juice

1 Place the noodles in a large bowl, cover with boiling water and gently break apart with a fork. Leave for 5 minutes, then drain.
2 Combine the chicken, sweet chilli sauce and fish sauce in a bowl.
3 Heat a wok or frying pan over high heat, add the oil and swirl to coat. Add the chicken pieces and stir-fry for 3–5 minutes, or until cooked through. Then add the corn and sugar snap peas and stir-fry for 2 minutes. Add the noodles and lime juice and serve.

NUTRITION PER SERVE (6)
Protein 30 g; Fat 6.5 g; Carbohydrate 50 g;
Dietary Fibre 4 g; Cholesterol 53 mg;
1593 kJ (380 cal)

Cover the noodles with boiling water and gently break apart with a fork.

Put the chicken in a bowl with the sweet chilli and fish sauces.

Stir-fry the chicken until cooked through before adding the other ingredients.

UDON NOODLES

Preparation time: 15 minutes
Total cooking time: 10 minutes
Serves 4

500 g (1 lb) fresh udon noodles
1 tablespoon oil
6 spring onions, cut into short lengths
3 cloves garlic, crushed
1 tablespoon grated fresh ginger
2 carrots, cut into short lengths
150 g (5 oz) snow peas, cut in half on the diagonal
100 g (3¹/₂ oz) bean sprouts

500 g (1 lb) choy sum, cut into short lengths
2 tablespoons Japanese soy sauce
2 tablespoons mirin
2 tablespoons kecap manis
2 sheets roasted nori, cut into thin strips

1 Bring a saucepan of water to the boil, add the noodles and cook for 5 minutes, or until tender and not clumped together. Drain and rinse under hot water.

2 Heat the oil in a wok until hot, then add the spring onion, garlic and ginger. Stir-fry over high heat for 1–2 minutes, or until soft. Add the carrot, snow peas and 1 tablespoon water, toss well, cover and cook for 1–2 minutes, or until the vegetables are just tender.

3 Add the noodles, bean sprouts, choy sum, soy sauce, mirin and kecap manis, then toss until the choy sum is wilted and coated with the sauce. Stir in the nori just before serving.

NUTRITION PER SERVE
Protein 25 g; Fat 7.5 g; Carbohydrate 95 g; Dietary Fibre 13 g; Cholesterol 22 mg; 2330 kJ (557 cal)

Cut the roasted nori sheets into very thin strips. It is available from Asian speciality shops.

Cook the udon noodles until they are tender and not clumped together.

Stir-fry the greens, noodles and sauces until the choy sum is wilted and coated with sauce.

VEGETARIAN PHAD THAI

Preparation time: 20 minutes
Total cooking time: 15 minutes
Serves 4

400 g (13 oz) flat rice-stick noodles
2 tablespoons peanut oil
2 eggs, lightly beaten
1 onion, cut into thin wedges
2 cloves garlic, crushed
1 small red capsicum, thinly sliced
100 g (3¹/2 oz) fried tofu, cut into thin
    strips
6 spring onions, thinly sliced
¹/2 cup (30 g/1 oz) chopped fresh
    coriander leaves

¹/4 cup (60 ml/2 fl oz) soy sauce
2 tablespoons lime juice
1 tablespoon soft brown sugar
2 teaspoons sambal oelek
1 cup (90 g/3 oz) bean sprouts
3 tablespoons chopped roasted
    unsalted peanuts

1 Cook the noodles in a saucepan of boiling water for 5–10 minutes, or until tender. Drain and set aside.
2 Heat a wok over high heat and add enough peanut oil to coat the bottom and side. When smoking, add the egg and swirl to form a thin omelette. Cook for 30 seconds, or until just set. Roll up, remove and thinly slice.
3 Heat the remaining oil in the wok.

Add the onion, garlic and capsicum and cook over high heat for 2–3 minutes, or until the onion softens. Add the noodles, tossing well. Stir in the omelette, tofu, spring onion and half the coriander.
4 Pour in the combined soy sauce, lime juice, sugar and sambal oelek, then toss to coat the noodles. Sprinkle with the bean sprouts and top with roasted peanuts and the remaining coriander. Serve immediately.

NUTRITION PER SERVE
Protein 13 g; Fat 21 g; Carbohydrate 34 g;
Dietary Fibre 5 g; Cholesterol 90 mg;
1565 kJ (375 cal)

Buy fried tofu (rather than the silken variety) and cut into thin strips.

Cook the egg, swirling the wok, to make a thin omelette, then roll up and thinly slice.

Stir in the omelette, tofu, spring onion and fresh coriander.

SAFFRON RICE

Preparation time: 10 minutes +
  30 minutes soaking
Total cooking time: 25 minutes
Serves 6

2 cups (400 g/13 oz) basmati rice
30 g (1 oz) butter
3 bay leaves
1/4 teaspoon saffron threads (see
  NOTE)
2 cups (500 ml/16 fl oz) boiling
  vegetable stock

1 Wash the basmati rice thoroughly,
cover with cold water and soak for
30 minutes. Drain.
2 Heat the butter gently in a frying
pan until it melts. Add the bay leaves
and washed rice, and cook, stirring,
for 6 minutes, or until all the moisture

has evaporated.
3 Meanwhile, soak the saffron in
2 tablespoons hot water for a few
minutes. Add the saffron, and its
soaking liquid, to the rice with the
vegetable stock, 1 1/2 cups (375 ml/
12 fl oz) boiling water and salt to taste.
Bring to the boil, then reduce the heat
and cook, covered, for 12–15 minutes,
or until all the water is absorbed and
the rice is cooked.

Cook the bay leaves and rice in the butter until all
the moisture has evaporated.

NUTRITION PER SERVE
Protein 5 g; Fat 4 g; Carbohydrate 53 g;
Dietary Fibre 1.5 g; Cholesterol 10 mg;
1115 kJ (266 cal)

NOTE: Saffron threads are the dried
stigmas of the crocus flower. The
powdered form is generally inferior to
the threads, which are expensive but
only needed in tiny quantities.

Soak the saffron threads in 2 tablespoons hot
water before adding to the rice.

SEASONED RICE AND LENTILS

Preparation time: 15 minutes
Total cooking time: 25 minutes
Serves 6

1¹/₂ cups (300 g/10 oz) basmati rice
1¹/₂ cups (300 g/10 oz) split mung beans (mung lentils)
2 tablespoons oil
1 onion, sliced
3 bay leaves
1 teaspoon cumin seeds
2 pieces cassia bark
1 tablespoon cardamom seeds
6 cloves
¹/₄ teaspoon black peppercorns

1 Wash the rice and lentils, then drain and set aside.
2 Heat the oil in a frying pan, add the onion, bay leaves and spices, and cook over low heat for 5 minutes, or until the onion is softened and the spices are fragrant. Add the rice and lentils, and cook, stirring, for 2 minutes. Pour in 1.25 litres water and salt to taste. Bring to the boil, then reduce the heat and cook, covered, over low heat for 15 minutes. Stir gently to avoid breaking the grains and cook, uncovered, over low heat for 3 minutes, or until all the moisture has evaporated.

NUTRITION PER SERVE
Protein 6 g; Fat 10 g; Carbohydrate 44 g;
Dietary Fibre 3 g; Cholesterol 0 mg;
1217 kJ (290 cal)

NOTE: To avoid serving with the whole spices left intact, tie the spices in a piece of muslin and add it to the pan along with the boiling water. Discard when the dish is cooked.

Cook the onion and spices together until the onion is soft and the spices fragrant.

Stir gently until all the excess moisture has evaporated.

117

SESAME CHICKEN AND SHANGHAI NOODLES

Preparation time: 20 minutes
Total cooking time: 15 minutes
Serves 4

600 g (1¼ lb) Shanghai noodles
1 tablespoon olive oil
1 tablespoon fresh ginger, cut into matchsticks
1 long red chilli, seeded and finely chopped
500 g (1 lb) chicken breast fillets, thinly sliced
2 cloves garlic, crushed
¼ cup (60 ml/2 fl oz) salt-reduced soy sauce
3 teaspoons sesame oil
700 g (1 lb 7 oz) baby bok choy, sliced lengthways into eighths
2 tablespoons sesame seeds, toasted

1 Cook the noodles in a saucepan of boiling water for 4–5 minutes, or until tender. Drain and rinse under cold water. Drain again.
2 Heat the oil in a wok and swirl to coat. Add the ginger and chilli and stir-fry for 1 minute. Add the chicken and stir-fry for a further 3–5 minutes, or until browned and almost cooked.
3 Add the garlic and cook for a further 1 minute. Pour in the soy sauce and sesame oil and toss to coat. Add the bok choy and noodles and stir-fry until the bok choy is tender and the noodles are warmed through. Place in individual serving bowls, sprinkle with sesame seeds and serve.

NUTRITION PER SERVE
Protein 45 g; Fat 19 g; Carbohydrate 80 g; Dietary Fibre 6 g; Cholesterol 102 mg; 2850 kJ (680 cal)

Cut each baby bok choy into eighths with a sharp knife.

Cook the noodles until tender, drain and rinse, then drain again.

Stir-fry the chicken in the ginger and chilli mixture until browned and almost cooked.

SPICY NOODLES WITH PORK AND TOFU

Preparation time: 20 minutes
Total cooking time: 15 minutes
Serves 4

250 g (8 oz) Hokkien noodles
1 tablespoon oil
500 g (1 lb) pork fillet, thinly sliced
2 cloves garlic, crushed
2.5 cm (1 inch) piece of fresh ginger,
    cut into matchsticks
100 g (3¹/₂ oz) snow peas, sliced
100 g (3¹/₂ oz) fresh shiitake
    mushrooms, sliced
¹/₂ teaspoon five-spice powder

2 tablespoons hoisin sauce
2 tablespoons soy sauce
¹/₄ cup (60 ml/2 fl oz) vegetable stock
200 g (6¹/₂ oz) fried tofu, sliced
100 g (3¹/₂ oz) soy bean sprouts
fried red Asian shallot flakes, to
    garnish

1 Cook the noodles in a large
saucepan of boiling water for
2–3 minutes, or until tender. Drain.
2 Heat a wok over high heat, add half
the oil and swirl to coat. Add the pork
in two batches and stir-fry for
2 minutes each batch, or until
browned. Remove from the wok.
3 Add a little more oil if necessary,
then add the garlic and ginger and stir-

fry for 30 seconds, or until fragrant.
Add the snow peas, mushrooms and
five-spice powder and cook for a
further 1 minute. Pour in the hoisin
sauce, soy sauce and stock and cook,
stirring constantly, for 1–2 minutes.
Add the tofu, soy bean sprouts,
noodles and pork and toss to
warm through.
4 Serve immediately, garnished with
the fried shallot flakes.

NUTRITION PER SERVE
Protein 45 g; Fat 16 g; Carbohydrate 55 g;
Dietary Fibre 10 g; Cholesterol 75 mg;
2293 kJ (548 cal)

Use a sharp knife to slice the pork fillets as thinly
as you can.

Stir-fry the pork slices in batches until they are
browned all over.

Add the hoisin and soy sauces and stock and
cook for a further 1–2 minutes.

MEE GROB

Preparation time: 30 minutes +
  20 minutes drying
Total cooking time: 15 minutes
Serves 4

100 g (3½ oz) dried rice vermicelli
2 cups (500 ml/16 fl oz) oil
100 g (3½ oz) tofu, cut into strips
2 cloves garlic, finely chopped
4 cm (1½ inch) piece of fresh ginger,
  finely grated
150 g (5 oz) chicken or pork mince
100 g (3½ oz) peeled raw prawns,
  roughly chopped
2 tablespoons fish sauce
1 tablespoon white vinegar
2 tablespoons soft brown sugar
2 tablespoons chilli sauce
1 teaspoon finely chopped red chillies
2 small pieces pickled garlic, chopped
40 g (1¼ oz) garlic chives, chopped
1 cup (30 g/1 oz) fresh coriander
  leaves

1 Soak the rice vermicelli in boiling water for 1 minute. Drain and allow to dry for about 20 minutes.
2 Heat the oil in a wok and stir-fry the tofu in two batches for 1 minute, or until crisp. Drain on paper towels.
3 Add the completely dry vermicelli to the wok in several batches, cooking for 10 seconds, or until puffed and crisp. Remove from the oil immediately to prevent the vermicelli absorbing too much. Drain on paper towels and allow to cool.
4 Drain all but 1 tablespoon of the oil and reheat the wok. Add the garlic, ginger, mince and the prawn meat and stir-fry for 3 minutes. Add the fish sauce, vinegar, sugar, chilli sauce and chilli and stir until boiling.
5 Just before serving, return the noodles and tofu to the wok and mix in thoroughly. Toss the pickled garlic, garlic chives and coriander leaves through. Serve immediately to prevent the noodles from becoming soggy.

NUTRITION PER SERVE
Protein 20 g; Fat 65 g; Carbohydrate 35 g;
Dietary Fibre 3 g; Cholesterol 65 mg;
3275 kJ (780 cal)

Soak the rice vermicelli in boiling water for 1 minute to soften.

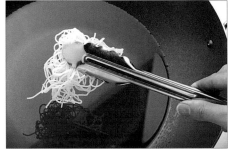

Add the vermicelli in batches to the hot oil and cook for 10 seconds.

When puffed and crisp, remove the vermicelli from the oil and drain.

Stir-fry the garlic, ginger, mince and prawn meat for 3 minutes.

PRAWN AND PEA NOODLE BASKETS

Preparation time: 40 minutes
Total cooking time: 25 minutes
Serves 4

oil, for deep-frying
200 g (6¹/₂ oz) fresh egg noodles
700 g (1 lb 7 oz) raw prawns, peeled
    and deveined
2 spring onions, chopped
1 clove garlic, crushed
¹/₂ teaspoon finely grated fresh ginger
¹/₂ teaspoon sesame oil
¹/₂ teaspoon fish sauce
100 g (3¹/₂ oz) peas, cooked
3 tablespoons sliced water chestnuts
1 tablespoon fresh mint
2 teaspoons chopped fresh chives
80 g (2³/₄ oz) snow pea sprouts

1 Half-fill a deep-fryer or large pan with oil and heat to 180°C (350°F). Before the oil is too hot, dip in 2 wire baskets, one slightly smaller than the other, then shake dry. Drop a noodle into the oil: if the oil bubbles and the noodle turns golden in 8–10 seconds, the oil is hot enough.
2 Separate the noodles and divide into four bundles. Arrange the first batch inside the large basket and press the smaller basket inside to mould the noodles. Holding the handles firmly, ease the baskets into the oil, keeping the noodles under. Gently twist the top basket to help stop sticking, tipping from side to side, and cook the noodles to an even golden brown. Drain on paper towels. Repeat with the other noodles.
3 Heat 2 tablespoons of oil in a wok. Stir-fry the prawns, spring onion, garlic and ginger over high heat for 2 minutes, or until the prawns turn pink. Stir in the sesame oil, fish sauce, peas and water chestnuts. Remove from the heat, season and mix in the mint, chives and snow pea sprouts.
4 Pile the prawn and pea mixture into the noodle baskets and serve at once.

NUTRITION PER SERVE:
Protein 40 g; Fat 15 g; Carbohydrate 15 g;
Dietary Fibre 3 g; Cholesterol 260 mg;
1575 kJ (375 cal)

Loosely separate the noodles and divide them into bundles.

Arrange the first bundle of noodles inside the larger basket.

Fit the baskets together, hold firmly, then gently lower them into the oil.

Stir-fry the prawns over high heat until they just turn pink.

THAI FRIED RICE WITH DRIED SHRIMP

Preparation time: 25 minutes +
 overnight refrigeration of rice
Total cooking time: 20 minutes
Serves 4

3 tablespoons oil
1 egg, beaten with 2 teaspoons water
2 cloves garlic, chopped
3 spring onions, chopped
1/2 cup (45 g/1 1/2 oz) dried shrimp,
 roughly chopped
4 cups (750 g/1 1/2 lb) cold cooked
 rice (see NOTE)

1 tablespoon fish sauce
2 teaspoons light soy sauce
1 cup (30 g/1 oz) fresh coriander
 leaves
1/4 pineapple, cut into pieces
1 cucumber, cut into pieces
chilli sauce, for serving

1 Heat 1 tablespoon of oil in a wok or
large frying pan. Pour in the egg and
swirl the wok until set. Cut into
quarters, flip each quarter and cook
the other side. Remove from the wok
and cut into thin strips.
2 Add the remaining oil, reheat the
wok and add the garlic, spring onions
and shrimp. Stir-fry for 2 minutes. Add

the rice to the wok and stir-fry for
5 minutes over high heat, tossing
constantly until heated through.
3 Add the sauces, coriander and
omelette strips. Toss well. Arrange the
rice on a serving platter. Serve with the
combined pineapple and cucumber,
and chilli sauce on the side.

NUTRITION PER SERVE
Protein 12 g; Fat 15 g; Carbohydrate 60 g;
Dietary Fibre 3 g; Cholesterol 100 mg;
1800 kJ (430 cal)

NOTE: Rice should be refrigerated
overnight before making fried rice to
let the grains dry out and separate.

Cut the omelette into quarters to make it easy to
turn over and cook the other side.

Stir-fry the garlic, spring onions and shrimp for
2 minutes.

Just before serving, add the sauces, coriander
leaves and omelette strips to the wok.

FRIED RICE WITH CORIANDER AND BASIL

Preparation time: 20 minutes +
  overnight standing
Total cooking time: 20 minutes
Serves 4

2 tablespoons oil
2.5 cm (1 inch) piece of pork fat,
  chopped
4 cloves garlic, chopped
2 tablespoons grated fresh ginger
2 teaspoons chopped red chillies
2 chicken thigh fillets, diced
100 g (3¹/₂ oz) pork loin, diced
2¹/₂ cups (470 g/15 oz) cold cooked
  jasmine rice (see NOTE)
1 tablespoon fish sauce
2 teaspoons light soy sauce
2 spring onions, chopped
1 cup (30 g/1 oz) fresh Thai basil
  leaves, chopped
¹/₂ cup (15 g/¹/₂ oz) fresh coriander
  leaves, chopped

1 Heat the oil to very hot in a wok. Stir-fry the pork fat, garlic, ginger and chillies for 2 minutes.
2 Add the diced chicken and pork to the wok and stir-fry for 3 minutes or until the meat changes colour. Break up any lumps in the rice; add to the wok and toss well to warm through. Add the sauces and toss through with the spring onions and herbs.

NUTRITION PER SERVE
Protein 40 g; Fat 14 g; Carbohydrate 100 g;
Dietary Fibre 3 g; Cholesterol 70 mg;
2900 kJ (690 cal)

NOTE: Rice should be refrigerated overnight before making fried rice to let the grains dry out and separate.

Cut the pork loin into small dice with a sharp knife. You can use any lean cut of pork.

Add the pork fat, garlic, ginger and chillies to the wok and stir with a wooden spoon.

Break up any lumps in the cold rice. Add to the wok and toss to heat through.

SESAME TOFU RICE

Preparation time: 20 minutes +
  overnight refrigeration of rice +
  30 minutes marinating
Total cooking time: 10 minutes
Serves 4

300 g (10 oz) firm tofu
2 teaspoons sesame oil
2 tablespoons soy sauce
1 tablespoon sesame seeds
2 tablespoons oil
3 zucchini, sliced
150 g (5 oz) button mushrooms,
  halved or quartered
1 large red capsicum, cut into squares
2 cloves garlic, crushed
3 cups (550 g/1 lb 2 oz) cold cooked
  brown rice (see NOTE)
1–2 tablespoons soy sauce, extra

1 Drain the tofu and pat dry with
paper towels. Cut into cubes, place in
a glass or ceramic bowl and add the
sesame oil and soy sauce. Stir well and
leave in the fridge to marinate for
30 minutes, stirring occasionally.
2 Heat the wok until very hot, add the
sesame seeds and dry-fry until lightly
golden. Tip onto a plate to cool.
3 Reheat the wok, add the oil and
swirl it around to coat the side.
Remove the tofu from the dish with a
slotted spoon and reserve the
marinade. Stir-fry the tofu over high
heat, turning occasionally, for about
3 minutes, or until browned. Remove
from the wok and set aside.
4 Add the vegetables and garlic, and
cook, stirring often, until they are just
tender. Add the rice and tofu, and stir-
fry until heated through.
5 Add the toasted sesame seeds, the
reserved marinade and extra soy sauce

to taste. Toss to coat the tofu and
vegetables, then serve immediately.

NUTRITION PER SERVE
Protein 15 g; Fat 20 g; Carbohydrate 50 g;
Dietary Fibre 5.5 g; Cholesterol 0 mg;
1815 kJ (435 cal)

NOTE: Rice should be refrigerated
overnight before making fried rice to
let the grains dry out and separate.

Dry-fry the sesame seeds until they are lightly
golden brown.

SICHUAN PEPPER CHICKEN NOODLES

Preparation time: 25 minutes + 2 hours
    marinating
Total cooking time: 20 minutes
Serves 4

3 teaspoons Sichuan pepper
500 g (1 lb) chicken thigh fillets, cut
    into strips
2 tablespoons soy sauce
1 clove garlic, crushed
1 teaspoon grated fresh ginger
3 teaspoons cornflour
100 g (3¹/₂ oz) dried thin egg noodles
oil, for cooking
1 onion, sliced
1 yellow capsicum, cut into thin strips
1 red capsicum, cut into thin strips
100 g (3¹/₂ oz) sugar snap peas
¹/₄ cup (60 ml/2 fl oz) chicken stock

1 Heat the wok until very hot and dry-fry the Sichuan pepper for 30 seconds. Remove from the wok and crush with a mortar and pestle or in a spice mill or small food processor.
2 Combine the chicken pieces with the soy sauce, garlic, ginger, cornflour and Szechwan pepper in a non-metallic bowl. Cover and refrigerate for 2 hours.
3 Bring a large pan of water to the boil, add the egg noodles and cook for 5 minutes, or until tender. Drain, then drizzle with a little oil and toss it through the noodles to prevent them from sticking together. Set aside.
4 Heat the wok until very hot, add 1 tablespoon of the oil and swirl it around to coat the side. Stir-fry the chicken in batches over medium-high heat for 5 minutes, or until golden brown and cooked. Add more oil

when necessary. Remove from the wok and set aside.
5 Reheat the wok, add 1 tablespoon of the oil and stir-fry the onion, capsicum and sugar snap peas over high heat for 2–3 minutes, or until the vegetables are tender. Add the chicken stock and bring to the boil.

6 Return the chicken and egg noodles to the wok and toss over high heat until well combined.

NUTRITION PER SERVE
Protein 35 g; Fat 15 g; Carbohydrate 25 g;
Dietary Fibre 3 g; Cholesterol 65 mg;
1515 kJ (360 cal)

Heat the wok until very hot, then dry-fry the Sichuan pepper.

Crush the Sichuan pepper with a mortar and pestle or food processor.

Toss the oil through the noodles to prevent them sticking together.

SINGAPORE NOODLES

Preparation time: 20 minutes
Total cooking time: 10 minutes
Serves 4–6

150 g (5 oz) dried rice vermicelli
oil, for cooking
250 g (8 oz) Chinese barbecued pork,
   cut into small pieces
250 g (8 oz) peeled raw prawns, cut
   into small pieces
2 tablespoons Madras curry powder
2 cloves garlic, crushed
1 onion, thinly sliced
100 g (3½ oz) shiitake mushrooms,
   thinly sliced

100 g (3½ oz) green beans, thinly
   sliced on the diagonal
1 tablespoon soy sauce
4 spring onions, thinly sliced on the
   diagonal

1 Place the vermicelli in a large bowl, cover with boiling water and soak for 5 minutes. Drain well and spread out on a clean tea towel to dry.
2 Heat the wok until very hot, add 1 tablespoon of the oil and swirl it around to coat the side. Stir-fry the Chinese barbecued pork and the prawn pieces in batches over high heat. Remove from the wok.
3 Reheat the wok, add 2 tablespoons of the oil and stir-fry the curry powder

and garlic for 1–2 minutes, or until fragrant. Add the onion and mushrooms, and stir-fry over medium heat for 2–3 minutes, or until the onion and mushrooms are soft.
4 Return the pork and prawns to the wok, add the beans and 2 teaspoons water, and toss to combine. Add the drained noodles, soy sauce and spring onion. Toss well and serve.

NUTRITION PER SERVE (6)
Protein 10 g; Fat 7.5 g; Carbohydrate 25 g;
Dietary Fibre 3 g; Cholesterol 60 mg;
905 kJ (215 cal)

Cut the barbecued pork into slices, then into small pieces.

Cover the vermicelli with boiling water in a heatproof bowl and leave to soak.

Stir-fry the curry powder and garlic in the oil until they are fragrant.

NASI GORENG

Preparation time: 25 minutes
Total cooking time: 15 minutes
Serves 4–6

5–8 long red chillies, seeded and
     chopped
2 teaspoons shrimp paste
8 cloves garlic, finely chopped
oil, for cooking
2 eggs, lightly beaten
350 g (12 oz) chicken thigh fillets, cut
     into thin strips
200 g (6½ oz) peeled raw prawns,
     deveined
8 cups (1.5 kg/3 lb) cold cooked rice
     (see NOTE)
⅓ cup (80 ml/2¾ fl oz) kecap manis
⅓ cup (80 ml/2¾ fl oz) soy sauce
2 small Lebanese cucumbers, finely
     chopped
1 large tomato, finely chopped
lime wedges, to serve

1 Mix the chilli, shrimp paste and
garlic to a paste in a food processor.
2 Heat the wok until very hot, add
1 tablespoon of the oil and swirl it
around to coat the side. Add the
beaten eggs and push the egg up the
edges of the wok to form a large
omelette. Cook for 1 minute over
medium heat, or until the egg is set,
then flip it over and cook the other
side for 1 minute. Remove from the
wok and cool before slicing into strips.
3 Reheat the wok, add 1 tablespoon
of the oil and stir-fry the chicken and
half the chilli paste over high heat until
the chicken is just cooked. Remove the
chicken from the wok.
4 Reheat the wok, add 1 tablespoon
of the oil and stir-fry the prawns and
the remaining chilli paste until cooked.

Remove from the wok and set aside.
5 Reheat the wok, add 1 tablespoon
of the oil and the rice, and toss over
medium heat for 4–5 minutes to heat
through. Add the kecap manis and soy
sauce and toss constantly until all of
the rice is coated in the sauces. Return
the chicken and prawns to the wok,
and toss to heat through. Season well.
Transfer to a serving bowl and top
with the omelette strips, cucumber and
tomato. Serve with the lime wedges.

NUTRITION PER SERVE (6)
Protein 30 g; Fat 10 g; Carbohydrate 70 g;
Dietary Fibre 3.5 g; Cholesterol 140 mg;
2105 kJ (505 cal)

NOTE: Rice should be refrigerated
overnight before making fried rice to
let the grains dry out and separate.

Remove the seeds from the chillies and finely
chop the flesh.

Slit the peeled prawns down the backs to remove
the vein.

Process the chilli, shrimp paste and garlic until a
paste forms.

NOODLES WITH CHICKEN AND FRESH BLACK BEANS

Preparation time: 15 minutes
Total cooking time: 15 minutes
Serves 2–3

2 teaspoons salted black beans
oil, for cooking
2 teaspoons sesame oil
500 g (1 lb) chicken thigh fillets, cut
    into thin strips
3 cloves garlic, very thinly sliced
4 spring onions, chopped
1 teaspoon sugar
1 red capsicum, sliced

100 g (3¹/₂ oz) green beans, cut into
    short pieces
300 g (10 oz) Hokkien noodles
2 tablespoons oyster sauce
1 tablespoon soy sauce

1 Rinse the black beans in running water. Drain and roughly chop.
2 Heat the wok until very hot, add 1 tablespoon of oil and the sesame oil and swirl it around to coat the side. Stir-fry the chicken in three batches, until well browned, tossing regularly. Remove from the wok and set aside.
3 Reheat the wok, add 1 tablespoon of the oil and stir-fry the garlic and spring onion for 1 minute. Add the

black beans, sugar, capsicum and beans and cook for 1 minute. Sprinkle with 2 tablespoons of water, cover and steam for 2 minutes.
4 Gently separate the noodles and add to the wok with the chicken, oyster sauce and soy sauce, and toss well. Cook, covered, for about 2 minutes, or until the noodles are just softened.

NUTRITION PER SERVE (3)
Protein 50 g; Fat 20 g; Carbohydrate 50 g;
Dietary Fibre 2 g; Cholesterol 85 mg;
2490 kJ (595 cal)

Cut the chicken thigh fillets into thin strips, removing any excess fat.

Roughly chop the rinsed and drained salted black beans.

Add the black beans, sugar and capsicum to the wok and cook for a minute.

NOODLES WITH FRIED TOFU

Preparation time: 10 minutes
Total cooking time: 5 minutes
Serves 4

100 g (3¹/² oz) deep-fried tofu puffs (see NOTE)
2 tablespoons oil
1 onion, sliced
1 red capsicum, cut into squares
3 cloves garlic, crushed
2 teaspoons grated fresh ginger
³/⁴ cup (120 g/4 oz) small chunks fresh pineapple

500 g (1 lb) thin Hokkien noodles, separated
¹/⁴ cup (60 ml/2 fl oz) pineapple juice
¹/⁴ cup (60 ml/2 fl oz) hoisin sauce
¹/⁴ cup (15 g/¹/² oz) roughly chopped fresh coriander

1 Slice the tofu puffs into three, then cut each slice into two or three pieces.
2 Heat the wok until very hot, add the oil and stir-fry the onion and capsicum for 1–2 minutes, or until beginning to soften. Add the garlic and ginger, stir-fry for 1 minute, then add the tofu and stir-fry for 2 minutes.
3 Add the pineapple chunks and noodles and toss until the mixture is combined and heated through. Add the pineapple juice, hoisin sauce and chopped coriander and toss to combine. Serve immediately.

NUTRITION PER SERVE
Protein 10 g; Fat 15 g; Carbohydrate 65 g; Dietary Fibre 3.5 g; Cholesterol 0 mg; 1830 kJ (435 cal)

NOTE: Deep-fried tofu puffs are available from the refrigerated section in Asian grocery stores and some supermarkets. They have a very different texture to ordinary tofu.

Use your fingers to gently separate the Hokkien noodles before cooking.

Slice the deep-fried tofu puffs into three, then cut into pieces.

Stir-fry the onion and capsicum until they are beginning to soften.

CURRIED CHICKEN NOODLES

Preparation time: 20 minutes
Total cooking time: 10 minutes
Serves 4

100 g (3½ oz) dried rice vermicelli
oil, for cooking
500 g (1 lb) chicken breast fillets, cut
    into thin strips
2 cloves garlic, crushed
1 teaspoon grated fresh ginger
2 teaspoons Asian-style curry powder
1 red onion, sliced

1 red capsicum, cut into thin strips
2 carrots, cut into matchsticks
2 zucchini, cut into matchsticks
1 tablespoon soy sauce

1 Place the vermicelli in a large bowl, cover with boiling water and soak for 5 minutes. Drain well and place on a tea towel to dry.
2 Heat the wok until very hot, add 1 tablespoon of the oil and swirl it around to coat the side. Stir-fry the chicken in batches over high heat until browned and tender. Remove all the chicken and drain on paper towels.
3 Reheat the wok, add 1 tablespoon

of the oil and stir-fry the garlic, ginger, curry powder and onion for 1–2 minutes, or until fragrant. Add the capsicum, carrot and zucchini to the wok, and stir-fry until well coated in the spices. Add 1 tablespoon water and stir-fry for 1 minute.
4 Add the drained noodles and chicken to the wok. Add the soy sauce and toss well. Season with salt before serving.

NUTRITION PER SERVE
Protein 30 g; Fat 15 g; Carbohydrate 25 g;
Dietary Fibre 4 g; Cholesterol 60 mg;
1495 kJ (355 cal)

Trim any excess fat from the chicken and cut the chicken into thin strips.

Cut the carrot into strips, the size and shape of matchsticks.

Soak the dried rice vermicelli in boiling water for 5 minutes.

SOBA NOODLES WITH SALMON AND MISO

Preparation time: 20 minutes
Total cooking time: 15 minutes
Serves 6

300 g (10 oz) soba noodles
1 tablespoon soy bean oil
3 teaspoons white miso paste
100 ml (3 1/2 fl oz) honey
1 1/2 tablespoons sesame oil
6 salmon fillets, skin and bones
    removed
1 teaspoon chopped garlic
1 tablespoon grated fresh ginger
1 carrot, cut into matchsticks
6 small spring onions, thinly sliced
1 cup (60 g/2 oz) soy bean sprouts
1/3 cup (80 ml/2 3/4 fl oz) rice vinegar
3 tablespoons light soy sauce
1 teaspoon sesame oil, extra
1 tablespoon toasted sesame seeds
mustard cress, to serve

1 Preheat the oven to moderate 180°C (350°F/Gas 4). Fill a large pan three-quarters full with water and bring to the boil. Add the soba noodles and return to the boil. Cook for 1 minute, then add 1 cup (250 ml/8 fl oz) cold water. Boil for 1–2 minutes, then add another 1 cup (250 ml/8 fl oz) water. Boil for 2 minutes, or until tender, then drain and toss with 1/2 teaspoon of the soy bean oil.

2 Whisk together the miso, honey, sesame oil and 1 tablespoon water to form a paste. Brush over the salmon, then sear in a hot chargrill or frying pan for 30 seconds on each side. Brush the salmon with the remaining paste and place on a baking tray. Bake for 6 minutes, then cover and leave to rest in a warm place.

3 Heat the remaining soy bean oil in a wok. Add the garlic, ginger, carrot, spring onion and sprouts and stir-fry for 1 minute—the vegetables should not brown, but remain crisp and bright. Add the noodles, rice vinegar, soy sauce and extra sesame oil and stir-fry quickly to heat through.

4 Divide the noodles among six serving plates, top with a portion of salmon and sprinkle with the sesame seeds. Garnish with the mustard cress before serving.

NUTRITION PER SERVE
Protein 8 g; Fat 9.5 g; Carbohydrate 56 g;
Dietary Fibre 2.5 g; Cholesterol 9 mg;
1423 kJ (340 cal)

Place the cooked soba noodles in a large bowl and toss with the soy bean oil.

Whisk together the miso, honey, sesame oil and water to make a paste.

Stir-fry the vegetables, without browning, until they are crisp and bright.

131

RICE STICKS WITH CHICKEN AND GREENS

Preparation time: 25 minutes
Total cooking time: 10 minutes
Serves 4

6 baby bok choy
8 stems Chinese broccoli
150 g (5 oz) dried rice stick noodles
2 tablespoons oil
375 g (12 oz) chicken breast fillets or
     tenderloins, cut into thin strips
2–3 cloves garlic, crushed
5 cm (2 inch) piece of fresh ginger,
     grated
6 spring onions, cut into short pieces
1 tablespoon sherry
1 cup (90 g/3 oz) bean sprouts

SAUCE
2 teaspoons cornflour
2 tablespoons soy sauce
2 tablespoons oyster sauce
2 teaspoons soft brown sugar
1 teaspoon sesame oil

1 Remove any tough outer leaves from the bok choy and Chinese broccoli. Cut into 4 cm (1¹/₂ inch) pieces across the leaves, including the stems. Wash well, then drain and dry thoroughly.
2 Place the rice stick noodles in a large heatproof bowl and cover with boiling water. Soak for 5–8 minutes, or until softened. Rinse, then drain. Cut into short lengths using scissors.
3 Meanwhile, to make the sauce, combine the cornflour and soy sauce in a small bowl. Mix to a smooth paste, then stir in the oyster sauce, brown sugar, sesame oil and ¹/₂ cup (125 ml/4 fl oz) water.
4 Heat the wok until very hot, add the oil and swirl it around to coat the side. Stir-fry the chicken strips, garlic, ginger and spring onion in batches over high heat for 3–4 minutes, or until the chicken is cooked. Remove from the wok and set aside.
5 Add the chopped bok choy, Chinese broccoli and sherry to the wok, cover and steam for 2 minutes, or until the vegetables are wilted. Remove from the wok and set aside. Add the sauce to the wok and stir until

the sauce is glossy and slightly thickened. Return the chicken, vegetables, noodles and bean sprouts to the wok and heat through. Serve at once.

NUTRITION PER SERVE
Protein 30 g; Fat 15 g; Carbohydrate 50 g;
Dietary Fibre 4 g; Cholesterol 45 mg;
1855 kJ (445 cal)

Cut the bok choy and Chinese broccoli into pieces across the leaves.

Cut the soaked noodles into short lengths to make them more manageable.

CHILLI NOODLES WITH NUTS

Preparation time: 20 minutes
Total cooking time: 12 minutes
Serves 4

1¹/₂ tablespoons oil
1 tablespoon sesame oil
2–3 small red chillies, finely chopped
1 large onion, cut into thin wedges
4 cloves garlic, cut into paper-thin
  slices
1 red capsicum, cut into strips
1 green capsicum, cut into strips
2 large carrots, cut into thick
  matchsticks
100 g (3¹/₂ oz) green beans

2 celery sticks, cut into matchsticks
2 teaspoons honey
500 g (1 lb) Hokkien noodles, gently
  separated
100 g (3¹/₂ oz) dry-roasted peanuts
100 g (3¹/₂ oz) honey-roasted
  cashews
¹/₄ cup (30 g/1 oz) chopped fresh
  garlic chives, or 4 spring onions,
  chopped
sweet chilli sauce and sesame oil, to
  serve

1 Heat the wok over low heat, add the oils and swirl them around to coat the side. When the oil is warm, add the chilli and heat until very hot.
2 Add the onion and garlic and stir-fry for 1 minute, or until the onion just softens. Add the capsicum, carrot and beans and stir-fry for 1 minute. Add the celery, honey and 1 tablespoon water and season with salt and pepper. Toss well, then cover and cook for 1–2 minutes, or until the vegetables are brightly coloured and just tender.
3 Add the noodles and nuts and toss well. Cook, covered, for 1–2 minutes, or until the noodles are heated through. Stir in the garlic chives and serve, drizzled with the sweet chilli sauce and sesame oil.

NUTRITION PER SERVE
Protein 20 g; Fat 45 g; Carbohydrate 75 g;
Dietary Fibre 7 g; Cholesterol 0 mg;
3330 kJ (795 cal)

Peel the cloves of garlic, then cut them into paper-thin slices.

Remove the seeds from the capsicum and cut the flesh into strips.

Heat the chopped chilli in the oil until the oil is very hot.

NOODLES WITH BARBECUED PORK AND GREENS

Preparation time: 20 minutes
Total cooking time: 25 minutes
Serves 4

250 g (8 oz) fresh thick egg noodles
1 tablespoon oil
1 tablespoon sesame oil
250 g (8 oz) Chinese barbecued pork, cut into small cubes (see NOTE)
1 large onion, very thinly sliced
2 cloves garlic, finely chopped
400 g (13 oz) green vegetables (beans, broccoli, celery), cut into bite-sized pieces
2 tablespoons hoisin sauce

1 tablespoon kecap manis
100 g (3½ oz) snow peas
3 baby bok choy, leaves separated
230 g (7½ oz) can water chestnuts, sliced

1 Two-thirds fill a pan with water and bring to the boil. Add the noodles and cook for about 3 minutes, or until just tender. Drain well.
2 Heat the wok until very hot, add the oils and swirl them around to coat the side. Stir-fry the pork over medium heat for 2 minutes, or until crisp. Drain on paper towels.
3 Reheat the wok, add the onion and garlic and stir-fry over very high heat for about 1 minute, or until just softened. Add the vegetables and cook, tossing regularly, for 2 minutes,

or until just softened. Stir in the hoisin sauce, kecap manis, snow peas, bok choy, water chestnuts and 1 tablespoon of water. Cook for 2 minutes, covered. Add the noodles and stir-fried pork, and toss gently to combine. Serve immediately.

NUTRITION PER SERVE
Protein 10 g; Fat 20 g; Carbohydrate 60 g; Dietary Fibre 10 g; Cholesterol 0 mg; 3910 kJ (930 cal)

NOTES: Chinese barbecued pork is also known as *char siu*. You can buy it at Chinese barbecue shops.

You can use Asian greens instead of beans, broccoli and celery.

Cut the barbecued pork into strips, then into small cubes.

Trim the base of the baby bok choy, then cut them into quarters lengthways.

Drain the can of water chestnuts and then slice them.

CHICKEN CHOW MEIN

Preparation time: 25 minutes + 1 hour
   marinating
Total cooking time: 20 minutes
Serves 4–6

1 tablespoon cornflour
2 tablespoons soy sauce
1 tablespoon oyster sauce
2 teaspoons sugar
500 g (1 lb) chicken thigh fillets, cut
   into small cubes
oil, for cooking
2 onions, thinly sliced
2 cloves garlic, finely chopped
1 tablespoon finely chopped fresh
   ginger
1 green capsicum, cubed
2 celery sticks, diagonally sliced
8 spring onions, cut into short pieces
100 g (3½ oz) mushrooms, thinly
   sliced
½ cup (80 g/2¾ oz) water chestnuts,
   thinly sliced
2 teaspoons cornflour, extra
1 tablespoon sherry
½ cup (125 ml/4 fl oz) chicken stock

1 tablespoon soy sauce, extra
90 g (3 oz) Chinese cabbage, finely
   shredded
200 g (6½ oz) ready-made fried
   noodles

1 Mix together the cornflour, soy
sauce, oyster sauce and sugar in a
non-metallic dish. Add the chicken,
cover and refrigerate for 1 hour.
2 Heat the wok until very hot, add
1 tablespoon of the oil and swirl it
around to coat the side. Stir-fry the
chicken in two batches over high heat
for 4–5 minutes, or until cooked. Add
oil between batches. Remove all the
chicken from the wok and set it aside.
3 Reheat the wok, add 1 tablespoon
of the oil and stir-fry the onion over
medium-high heat for 3–4 minutes, or
until the onion is slightly softened.
Add the garlic, ginger, capsicum,
celery, spring onion, mushrooms and
water chestnuts to the wok. Stir-fry
over high heat for 3–4 minutes.
4 Combine the extra cornflour with
the sherry, chicken stock and soy
sauce. Add to the wok and bring to the
boil. Simmer for 1–2 minutes, or until

the sauce thickens slightly. Stir in the
cabbage and cook, covered, for
1–2 minutes, or until the cabbage is
just wilted. Return the chicken to the
wok and toss until heated through.
Season with salt and pepper. Arrange
the noodles around the edge of a large
platter and spoon the chicken mixture
into the centre. Serve immediately.

NUTRITION PER SERVE (6)
Protein 25 g; Fat 8.5 g; Carbohydrate 20 g;
Dietary Fibre 4 g; Cholesterol 55 mg;
1110 kJ (265 cal)

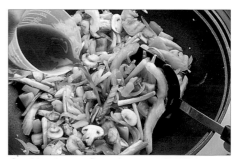

Combine the cornflour, sherry, stock and soy
sauce, and pour into the wok.

Sushi & Sashimi

Ingredients for these Japanese delicacies are available from speciality stores. Shoyu is a soy sauce, lighter and sweeter than the Chinese one. Wasabi has a fierce flavour, rather like horseradish, and comes in paste or powder form. Nori is dried seaweed, sold in sheets.

SUSHI RICE

Put 2$^{1}/_{2}$ cups (500 g/1 lb) white short-grain rice in a fine colander and rinse under cold water until the water runs clear. Drain and leave in the colander for 1 hour. Transfer to a large saucepan, add 3 cups (750 ml/12 fl oz) water, bring to the boil and cook, without stirring, for 5–10 minutes, or until tunnels form on the surface. Reduce the heat to low, cover and cook for 12–15 minutes, or until tender. Remove from the heat and set aside for 15 minutes. Put 5 tablespoons rice vinegar, 1 tablespoon mirin, 2 teaspoons salt and 2 tablespoons sugar in a bowl and stir until the sugar dissolves. Spread the rice over a flat non-metallic tray and stir the dressing through. Spread out and cool just to body temperature. Cover with a damp tea towel. To prevent the rice sticking to your hands, dip your fingers in a bowl of warm water with a few drops of rice vinegar added.

SASHIMI

Remove any skin from 500 g (1 lb) good-quality, very fresh fish such as tuna, salmon or kingfish. Freeze until firm enough to cut into slices about 5 mm ($^{1}/_{4}$ inch) thick. Serve with wasabi and shoyu. Serves 4–6.

SALMON AND CUCUMBER ROLLS

Cut a 200 g (6$^{1}/_{2}$ oz) fillet of sashimi salmon on an angle into paper-thin slices. Halve a Lebanese cucumber lengthways, remove the seeds and cut into thin strips. Top each salmon slice with a few cucumber strips, roll up and tie with chives. Serve with ginger, shoyu and wasabi. Makes about 24.

TUNA/SALMON NORI ROLLS

Cut 5 sheets of nori in half lengthways. Cut 200 g (6$^{1}/_{2}$ oz) sashimi tuna or salmon into thin strips. Place a piece of nori on a bamboo mat, shiny-side-down, and spread 4 tablespoons cooked sushi rice over it, leaving a narrow border along one end. Make a slight indentation along the centre, then dab a small amount of wasabi paste along the ridge. Top with fish. Roll the mat to enclose the filling, pressing to form a firm roll. Slice into six pieces. You will need 4 cups (800 g/1 lb 10 oz) sushi rice altogether. Makes 60 rolls.

INSIDE-OUT ROLLS

Place a nori sheet on a bamboo mat and spread with 1 cm ($^{1}/_{2}$ inch) sushi rice, leaving a small border at one end. Cover with a sheet of plastic wrap larger than the nori. In one quick motion, turn the whole thing over, then place it back on the mat, so the plastic is under the rice and the nori on top. Spread a little wasabi paste on the nori, along the short end, 4 cm (1$^{1}/_{2}$ inches) from the edge. Lay thin strips of Lebanese cucumber and avocado and a little fresh crab meat on top of the wasabi, then roll from this end, using the plastic as a guide. Wrap in plastic, then roll up in the mat, to form a firm roll. Unroll and discard the plastic. Roll in flying fish roe or toasted black sesame seeds. Trim the ends with a very sharp knife, then cut into six. Repeat to make another seven rolls. You will need 6 cups (1.2 kg/2 lb 7 oz) cooked sushi rice and 200 g (6$^{1}/_{2}$ oz) crab meat altogether. Serve with shoyu. Makes 48 rolls.

PRAWN AND TUNA NIGIRI

Peel and butterfly 10 cooked prawns. Trim 250 g (8 oz) tuna into a rectangle, then cut into thin slices, wiping the knife after each slice. Form a tablespoon of sushi rice into an oval the same length and width as the fish. Place one tuna slice flat on your hand, then spread wasabi paste over the centre. Place the rice on the fish and cup your palm. Press the rice onto the fish, firmly pushing with a slight upward motion to make a neat shape. Turn over and repeat the shaping process, finishing with the fish on top. You will need 2 cups (400 g/13 oz) sushi rice. Makes 16–20 pieces.

PRAWN/CRAB CALIFORNIA ROLLS

Place a sheet of nori on a bamboo mat, shiny-side-down. Spread $^{3}/_{4}$ cup (150 g/5 oz) sushi rice in the middle of the sheet, leaving a 2 cm ($^{3}/_{4}$ inch) border along the end nearest you. Make a slight indentation along the centre of the rice to hold the filling, then spread a small line of Japanese mayonnaise along the ridge. Spread 1 tablespoon flying fish roe over the mayonnaise and top with a couple of cooked, peeled, halved prawns or chopped crab stick. Roll the mat over to enclose the filling, then roll, pressing to form a firm roll. Slice into six. Make three more rolls. You will need 3 cups (600 g/1$^{1}/_{4}$ lb) sushi rice altogether. Makes 24 rolls.

Clockwise, from top left: Inside-out rolls; Prawn/crab California rolls; Sashimi; Salmon and cucumber rolls; Tuna/salmon nori rolls; Prawn and tuna nigiri.

ASIAN RISOTTO CAKES WITH SCALLOPS

Preparation time: 35 minutes +
  3 hours refrigeration
Total cooking time: 40 minutes
Serves 4 as a starter

2 cups (500 ml/16 fl oz) vegetable
  stock
2 tablespoons mirin
1 stalk lemon grass, white part only,
  bruised
2 kaffir lime leaves
3 fresh coriander roots
2 tablespoons fish sauce
1 tablespoon butter
2–3 tablespoons peanut oil
3 red Asian shallots, thinly sliced
4 spring onions, chopped
3 cloves garlic, chopped
2 tablespoons finely chopped fresh
  ginger
1¼ teaspoons white pepper
²/₃ cup (150 g/5 oz) arborio rice
2 tablespoons toasted unsalted
  chopped peanuts
1 cup (60 g/2 oz) chopped fresh
  coriander leaves
2 cloves garlic, chopped, extra
1 teaspoon finely chopped fresh
  ginger, extra
¼ cup (60 ml/2 fl oz) lime juice
1–2 teaspoons grated palm sugar
vegetable oil, for pan-frying
plain flour, to dust
1 tablespoon vegetable oil, extra
16 large white scallops without roe,
  beards removed
lime wedges, to serve

1 Heat the stock, mirin, lemon grass, lime leaves, coriander roots, half the fish sauce and 1 cup (250 ml/8 fl oz) water in a saucepan and maintain at a low simmer.
2 Heat the butter and 1 tablespoon of the peanut oil in a large saucepan over medium heat until bubbling. Add the shallots, spring onion, garlic, ginger and 1 teaspoon of the white pepper and cook for 2–3 minutes, or until fragrant and the onion is soft. Stir in the rice and toss until well coated.
3 Add ½ cup (125 ml/4 fl oz) of the stock (avoid the lemon grass and coriander roots). Stir constantly over

medium heat until nearly all the liquid is absorbed. Continue adding the stock ½ cup at a time, stirring constantly, for 20–25 minutes, or until all the stock is absorbed and the rice is tender and creamy. Remove from the heat, cool, then cover and refrigerate for 3 hours, or until cold.
4 To make the pesto, finely chop the peanuts, coriander, extra garlic and ginger and the remaining pepper in a blender or food processor. With the motor running, slowly add the lime juice, sugar and remaining fish sauce and peanut oil and process until smooth—you may not need all the oil.
5 Divide the risotto into four balls,

then mould into patties. Cover and refrigerate for 10 minutes. Heat the oil in a large frying pan over medium heat. Dust the patties with flour and cook in batches for 2 minutes each side, or until crisp. Drain on paper towels. Cover and keep warm.
6 Heat the extra oil in a clean frying pan over high heat. Cook the scallops in batches for 1 minute each side. Serve with the risotto cakes, pesto and lime wedges.

NUTRITION PER SERVE
Protein 12 g; Fat 32 g; Carbohydrate 36 g;
Dietary Fibre 2 g; Cholesterol 30 mg;
1987 kJ (475 cal)

Stir the rice until the stock is absorbed and the rice is tender and creamy.

Cook the flour-dusted patties until they are crisp and golden.

SHIITAKE MUSHROOM AND PEARL BARLEY PILAF

Preparation time: 20 minutes +
  overnight soaking
Total cooking time: 45 minutes
Serves 4

1½ cups (330 g/11 oz) pearl barley
3 dried shiitake mushrooms
2½ cups (625 ml/21 fl oz) vegetable
  or chicken stock
½ cup (125 ml/4 fl oz) dry sherry
2 tablespoons olive oil
1 large onion, finely chopped
3 cloves garlic, crushed
2 tablespoons grated fresh ginger
1 teaspoon Sichuan peppercorns,
  crushed
500 g (1 lb) mixed fresh Asian
  mushrooms (oyster, Swiss brown,
  enoki)
500 g (1 lb) choy sum, cut into short
  lengths
3 teaspoons kecap manis
1 teaspoon sesame oil

1 Soak the barley in enough cold water to cover for at least 6 hours or preferably overnight. Drain.
2 Soak the shiitake mushrooms in enough boiling water to cover for 15 minutes. Strain, reserving ½ cup (125 ml/4 fl oz) of the liquid. Discard the tough stalks and slice the caps.
3 Heat the stock and sherry in a pan and maintain at a low simmer.
4 Heat the oil in a large pan over medium heat. Add the onion and cook for 4–5 minutes, or until softened. Add the garlic, ginger and peppercorns and cook for 1 minute. Slice the Asian mushrooms, reserving the enoki for later. Increase the heat and add the mushrooms. Cook for 5 minutes, or

until the mushrooms have softened. Add the barley, shiitake mushrooms, the reserved soaking liquid and the hot stock. Stir well to combine. Bring to the boil, then reduce the heat to low and simmer, covered, for 35 minutes, or until the liquid evaporates.
5 Steam the choy sum until just

wilted. Add to the barley mixture with the enoki mushrooms. Stir in the kecap manis and sesame oil.

NUTRITION PER SERVE
Protein 15 g; Fat 13 g; Carbohydrate 52 g;
Dietary Fibre 14.5 g; Cholesterol 0 mg;
1725 kJ (410 cal)

Once the shiitake mushrooms have been soaked, finely slice the caps.

Stir the barley, shiitake mushrooms, soaking liquid and stock until combined.

Steam the lengths of choy sum until the leaves have just wilted.

RICE CAKES WITH CHINESE ROAST DUCK

Preparation time: 15 minutes +
2 hours refrigeration
Total cooking time: 20 minutes
Serves 4

1 kg (2 lb) Chinese barbecued duck
2 cloves garlic, crushed
200 ml (6¹/₂ fl oz) orange juice
2 tablespoons soy sauce
4 tablespoons chopped fresh
   coriander
2 cups (500 ml/16 fl oz) chicken stock
1¹/₄ cups (250 g/8 oz) quick-cooking
   brown rice

1 Remove the meat from the duck, cut into large slices and place in a large non-metallic bowl. Whisk together the garlic, orange juice, soy sauce and 2 tablespoons coriander and pour over the duck. Toss to coat, cover and refrigerate for 2 hours.
2 Place the chicken stock in a saucepan and bring to the boil. Add the rice, then reduce the heat and simmer rapidly until tunnels appear. Reduce the heat to very low, cover and cook for 10–12 minutes, or until tender. Stir in the remaining coriander. Divide the rice among four ¹/₂ cup (125 ml/4 fl oz) ramekins. Keep warm.
3 Drain the duck, reserving the marinade. Heat a large frying pan, add the duck and stir until warmed

through. Heat the marinade until boiling in a separate pan. To serve, turn the timbales out onto four serving plates and arrange the duck over the top. Spoon on some reserved marinade and garnish with a few coriander leaves.

NUTRITION PER SERVE
Protein 66 g; Fat 26 g; Carbohydrate 55 g; Dietary Fibre 3 g; Cholesterol 350 mg; 3007 kJ (718 cal)

NOTE: For something special, try peeling and segmenting 2 oranges and arrange the segments around the bottom of the timbales. Sprinkle with some toasted black sesame seeds.

You can buy barbecued duck in any Chinatown. Cut the meat into large slices.

Cook the rice until it is tender and then stir in the remaining coriander.

Drain the duck, reserving the marinade, and then heat through in a frying pan.

KEDGEREE

Preparation time: 20 minutes
Total cooking time: 30 minutes
Serves 4

600 g (1¹/4 lb) smoked haddock
50 g (1¹/2 oz) butter
1 onion, finely chopped
2 teaspoons curry powder
1 teaspoon ground cumin
1 teaspoon ground coriander
2 teaspoons seeded and finely sliced
    green chilli
1 cup (200 g/6¹/2 oz) basmati rice
2³/4 cups (660 ml/22 fl oz) chicken or
    fish stock
1 cinnamon stick
¹/3 cup (80 ml/2³/4 fl oz) cream
2 hard-boiled eggs, finely chopped
2 tablespoons chopped fresh parsley
2 tablespoons chopped fresh
    coriander

1 Poach the haddock in batches in a large shallow pan, skin-side up: cover with boiling water and simmer very gently for about 10 minutes. The fish is cooked when the flesh can be flaked easily with a fork. Drain and pat dry with paper towels. Remove the skin and flake into bite-size chunks.
2 Heat the butter in a large saucepan and add the onion. Cook until golden, then add the curry powder, cumin, coriander and chilli. Cook, stirring, for 1 minute. Add the rice, stir well, then pour in the stock and add the cinnamon. Cover tightly and simmer over gentle heat for about 12 minutes, or until the rice is tender.
3 Remove the cinnamon and gently stir in the haddock. Fold through the cream, chopped egg and the herbs. Season and serve immediately.

NUTRITION PER SERVE
Protein 45 g; Fat 25 g; Carbohydrate 45 g;
Dietary Fibre 2 g; Cholesterol 255 mg;
2355 kJ (560 cal)

When the fish is cooked, the flesh will flake easily when tested with a fork.

Add the rice to the onion, curry powder, cumin, coriander and chilli and stir well.

Fold through the cream, chopped egg, parsley and coriander.

SAVOURY RICE AND EGGS

Preparation time: 20 minutes
Total cooking time: 12 minutes
Serves 4

2 tablespoons ghee or oil
1 onion, finely chopped
1/2 red capsicum, finely chopped
10 spring onions, thinly sliced
2–3 small red chillies, seeded and
    finely chopped
2–3 cloves garlic, finely chopped
1 tablespoon grated fresh ginger
125 g (4 oz) Chinese barbecued pork,
    finely chopped
6 eggs, lightly beaten

4 cups (750 g/1 1/2 lb) cold cooked
    jasmine rice (see NOTES)
1–2 teaspoons seasoning sauce
1/3 cup (20 g/3/4 oz) chopped fresh
    coriander
onion flakes, to garnish (see NOTES)

1 Heat the wok until very hot, add the
ghee and swirl it around to coat the
side. Stir-fry the onion, capsicum,
spring onion, chilli, garlic and
ginger over medium-high heat for
2–3 minutes, or until the vegetables
are cooked but not brown. Add the
barbecued pork and toss to combine.
2 Reduce the heat, then pour in the
beaten eggs. Season well with salt and
pepper. Gently stir the egg mixture

until it is creamy and almost set. Add
the rice and gently stir-fry to
incorporate all the ingredients and
heat the mixture through.
3 Sprinkle with seasoning sauce and
stir in the coriander. Serve sprinkled
with onion flakes.

NUTRITION PER SERVE
Protein 15 g; Fat 20 g; Carbohydrate 60 g;
Dietary Fibre 3.5 g; Cholesterol 295 mg;
2105 kJ (500 cal)

NOTES: Rice should be refrigerated
overnight before making fried rice to
let the grains dry out and separate.
    Buy onion flakes from Asian
grocery stores and most supermarkets.

Cut the barbecued pork into slices and then
chop it finely.

Add the barbecued pork to the onion mixture and
toss to combine.

Add the egg, season well and stir gently until the
mixture is creamy.

WHEAT NOODLES WITH GINGER CHICKEN

Preparation time: 20 minutes + soaking
Total cooking time: 10 minutes
Serves 4

4 dried Chinese mushrooms
2 teaspoons cornflour
2 tablespoons soy sauce
2 tablespoons oyster sauce
1 tablespoon mirin or sweet sherry
200 g (6¹/₂ oz) dried wheat noodles
1 teaspoon sesame oil
oil, for cooking
2–3 cloves garlic, crushed
8 cm (3 inch) piece of fresh ginger, cut
    into matchsticks
375 g (12 oz) chicken breast fillets or
    tenderloins, cut into thin strips
1 red onion, cut into thin wedges
6 spring onions, cut into short lengths
185 g (6 oz) small field mushrooms,
    thickly sliced
1 cup (90 g/3 oz) bean sprouts
¹/₃ cup (20 g/³/₄ oz) chopped fresh
    mint

1 Place the dried mushrooms in a small bowl and cover with hot water. Leave to soak for 10 minutes, or until softened. Drain and squeeze dry, then discard the tough stems and chop the mushroom caps finely.
2 Combine the cornflour with ¹/₄ cup (60 ml/2 fl oz) water and mix to a fine paste. Add the soy sauce, oyster sauce and mirin.
3 Cook the noodles in a large pan of boiling salted water for 1–2 minutes, or according to the manufacturer's instructions. Drain and set aside.
4 Heat the wok until very hot, add the sesame oil and 1 tablespoon of the oil, and swirl it around to coat the side. Stir-fry the garlic, ginger and chicken strips in batches over high heat for 2–3 minutes, or until the chicken has cooked through. Remove from the wok and set aside.
5 Reheat the wok, add 1 tablespoon of the oil and stir-fry the red onion and spring onion for 1–2 minutes, or until softened. Add the dried and field mushrooms, then stir-fry the mixture for 1–2 minutes, or until tender. Remove from the wok and set aside.

6 Add the soy sauce mixture to the wok and stir for 1–2 minutes, or until the sauce is well heated and slightly thickened. Return the chicken and vegetables to the wok with the bean sprouts, noodles and chopped mint. Stir until the noodles are well coated with the sauce. Serve at once.

NUTRITION PER SERVE
Protein 30 g; Fat 9 g; Carbohydrate 45 g;
Dietary Fibre 6 g; Cholesterol 45 mg;
1650 kJ (395 cal)

Cover the dried mushrooms with hot water and leave to soak.

Cook the noodles in a large pan of boiling salted water for a couple of minutes.

COCONUT RICE

Preparation time: 35 minutes +
  40 minutes standing
Total cooking time: 15 minutes
Serves 6

2 cups (400 g/13 oz) long-grain white
  rice
1 pandan leaf, knotted (see NOTE)
3/4 cup (185 ml/6 fl oz) coconut cream

1 Rinse the rice and cover with 1 litre water. Set aside for 30 minutes. Drain. Bring 3 cups (750 ml/24 fl oz) water to the boil. Add the rice, pandan leaf and salt to taste. Reduce the heat and cook, covered, for 12 minutes, or until the rice is just cooked.
2 Remove from heat and add the coconut cream. Stir gently, cover and leave for 10 minutes or until the rice has absorbed the coconut cream. Discard the leaf before serving.

NUTRITION PER SERVE
Protein 5 g; Fat 6.5 g; Carbohydrate 54 g;
Dietary Fibre 2 g; Cholesterol 0 mg;
1240 kJ (295 cal)

NOTE: Pandan leaves, also known as pandanus or screw pine leaves, are used both to wrap food and to flavour rice or curries. They are available in Asian grocery stores.

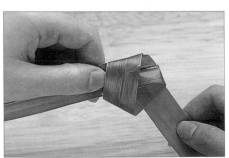

Gently tie the pandan leaf in a knot, being careful not to tear it.

Place the pandan leaf in the saucepan with the rice, water and salt.

Once the rice has absorbed all the coconut cream, discard the pandan leaf.

CHINESE FRIED RICE

Preparation time: 15 minutes
Total cooking time: 10 minutes
Serves 4

2 tablespoons peanut oil
2 eggs, lightly beaten and seasoned
2 teaspoons lard, optional
1 onion, cut into wedges
250 g (8 oz) ham, cut into thin strips
4 cups (750 g/1¹/₂ lb) cold cooked
    rice (see NOTE)
3 tablespoons frozen peas
2 tablespoons soy sauce
4 spring onions, cut into short lengths
250 g (8 oz) cooked small prawns,
    peeled

1 Heat 1 tablespoon of the peanut oil in a wok or large frying pan and add the eggs, pulling the set egg towards the centre and tilting the wok to let the unset egg run to the edges.
2 When it is almost set, break up the egg into large pieces to resemble scrambled eggs. Transfer to a plate.
3 Heat the remaining oil and lard in the wok, swirling to coat the base and side. Add the onion and stir-fry over high heat until clear and softened. Add the ham and stir-fry for 1 minute. Add the rice and peas and stir-fry for 3 minutes until the rice is heated through. Add the eggs, soy sauce, spring onion and prawns. Heat through and serve.

NUTRITION PER SERVE
Protein 32 g; Fat 20 g; Carbohydrate 56 g;
Dietary Fibre 3 g; Cholesterol 222 mg;
2200 kJ (525 cal)

NOTE: Rice should be refrigerated overnight before making fried rice to let the grains dry out and separate.

VARIATION: This dish is traditionally served as a snack or course in its own right rather than as an accompaniment to other dishes. You can include barbecued pork, *lap cheong* (Chinese sausage) or bacon instead of ham.

Cut the ham into thin strips and the onion into wedges for cooking.

Once the egg is almost set, break it up into large pieces, a little like scrambled egg.

Add the eggs, soy sauce, spring onion and cooked prawns to the wok.

Stir-fries
& Pan-fries

CHICKEN AND CASHEW STIR-FRY

Preparation time: 30 minutes
Total cooking time: 20 minutes
Serves 4–6

oil, for cooking
750 g (1¹/₂ lb) chicken thigh fillets, cut
    into strips
2 egg whites, lightly beaten
¹/₂ cup (60 g/2 oz) cornflour
2 onions, thinly sliced
1 red capsicum, thinly sliced
200 g (6¹/₂ oz) broccoli, cut into bite-
    sized pieces
2 tablespoons soy sauce
2 tablespoons sherry
1 tablespoon oyster sauce
¹/₃ cup (50 g/1³/₄ oz) roasted cashews
4 spring onions, diagonally sliced

1 Heat the wok until very hot, add
1 tablespoon of the oil and swirl it
around to coat the side. Dip about a
quarter of the chicken strips into
the egg white and then into the
cornflour. Add to the wok and stir-fry
for 3–5 minutes, or until the chicken is
golden brown and just cooked. Drain

on paper towels and repeat with the
remaining chicken, reheating the wok
and adding a little more oil each time.
2 Reheat the wok, add 1 tablespoon
of the oil and stir-fry the onion,
capsicum and broccoli over medium
heat for 4–5 minutes, or until the
vegetables have softened slightly.
Increase the heat to high and add the
soy sauce, sherry and oyster sauce.
Toss the vegetables well in the sauce
and bring to the boil.
3 Return the chicken to the wok and
toss over high heat for 1–2 minutes to
heat the chicken and make sure it is
entirely cooked through. Season well
with salt and freshly cracked pepper.
Toss the cashews and spring onion
through the chicken mixture, and
serve immediately.

NUTRITION PER SERVE (6)
Protein 35 g; Fat 15 g; Carbohydrate 15 g;
Dietary Fibre 3 g; Cholesterol 60 mg;
1375 kJ (330 cal)

NOTE: When choosing chicken, buy
free range if you can as it has a better
flavour and texture. Yellowish flesh
indicates the chicken has been grain
fed but it is not necessarily free range.

Dip the chicken strips into the egg white, then
into the cornflour.

Stir-fry the chicken in batches until it is golden
brown and just cooked.

SWEET AND SOUR PORK

Preparation time: 25 minutes +
  30 minutes marinating
Total cooking time: 20 minutes
Serves 4

500 g (1 lb) pork fillet, cut into thick
    slices
2 tablespoons cornflour
1 tablespoon sherry
1 tablespoon soy sauce
1 tablespoon sugar
oil, for cooking
1 large onion, thinly sliced
1 green capsicum, cut into cubes
2 small carrots, thinly sliced
1 small Lebanese cucumber, seeded
    and chopped
5 spring onions, cut into short lengths
440 g (14 oz) can pineapple pieces in
    natural juice, drained and juice
    reserved
1/4 cup (60 ml/2 fl oz) white vinegar
1/2 teaspoon salt

1 Place the pork in a shallow glass or
ceramic bowl. Combine the cornflour
with the sherry, soy sauce and half the
sugar, and pour into the bowl. Cover
and refrigerate for 30 minutes.
2 Drain the pork, reserving the
marinade. Heat the wok until very hot,
add 2 tablespoons of the oil and swirl
to coat the side. Stir-fry half the pork
over high heat for 4–5 minutes, or until
the pork is golden brown and just
cooked. Remove from the wok, add
more oil if necessary and repeat with
the remaining pork. Remove all the
pork from the wok.
3 Reheat the wok, add 1 tablespoon
of the oil and stir-fry the onion over
high heat for 3–4 minutes, or until
slightly softened. Add the capsicum

and carrot, and cook for 3–4 minutes,
or until tender. Stir in the marinade,
cucumber, spring onion, pineapple,
vinegar, salt, remaining sugar and
1/3 cup (80 ml/2 3/4 fl oz) of the juice.
4 Bring to the boil and simmer for
2–3 minutes, or until the sauce has

thickened slightly. Return the pork to
the wok and toss to heat through.

NUTRITION PER SERVE
Protein 25 g; Fat 12 g; Carbohydrate 25 g;
Dietary Fibre 4 g; Cholesterol 50 mg;
1325 kJ (315 cal)

Peel the carrots, if necessary, and cut them into
thin diagonal slices.

Halve the cucumber lengthways and scoop out
the seeds using a teaspoon.

Stir-fry the pork until it is golden brown and just
cooked, then remove from the wok.

MONGOLIAN LAMB

Preparation time: 15 minutes
Total cooking time: 12 minutes
Serves 4

oil, for cooking
500 g (1 lb) lamb backstrap (tender eye of the lamb loin), cut into thin strips
2 cloves garlic, crushed
4 spring onions, thickly sliced
2 tablespoons soy sauce
1/3 cup (80 ml/2³/4 fl oz) dry sherry
2 tablespoons sweet chilli sauce
2 teaspoons sesame seeds, toasted

1 Heat the wok until very hot, add 1 tablespoon of the oil and swirl it around to coat the side. Stir-fry the lamb strips in batches over high heat. Remove all the lamb from the wok.
2 Reheat the wok, add 1 tablespoon of oil and stir-fry the garlic and spring onion for 2 minutes. Remove from the wok and set aside. Add the soy sauce, sherry and sweet chilli sauce to the wok. Bring to the boil, reduce the heat and simmer for 3–4 minutes, or until the sauce thickens slightly.
3 Return the meat, with any juices, and the spring onion to the wok, and toss to coat. Serve sprinkled with the toasted sesame seeds.

NUTRITION PER SERVE
Protein 30 g; Fat 20 g; Carbohydrate 7 g;
Dietary Fibre 1.5 g; Cholesterol 80 mg;
1445 kJ (345 cal)

Slice the lamb backstrap into thin strips with a sharp knife.

Stir-fry the lamb strips in batches over high heat and then remove from the wok.

Add the soy sauce, sherry and sweet chilli sauce to the wok, and bring to the boil.

HONEY CHICKEN

Preparation time: 15 minutes
Total cooking time: 25 minutes
Serves 4

oil, for cooking
500 g (1 lb) chicken thigh fillets, cut
    into cubes
1 egg white, lightly beaten
1/3 cup (40 g/1 1/4 oz) cornflour
2 onions, thinly sliced
1 green capsicum, cubed
2 carrots, cut into batons
100 g (3 1/2 oz) snow peas, sliced
1/4 cup (90 g/3 oz) honey
2 tablespoons toasted almonds

1 Heat the wok until very hot, add
1 1/2 tablespoons of the oil and swirl it
around to coat the side. Dip half of the
chicken into the egg white, then lightly
dust with the cornflour. Stir-fry over
high heat for 4–5 minutes, or until the
chicken is golden brown and just
cooked. Remove from the wok and
drain on paper towels. Repeat with the
remaining chicken, then remove all
the chicken from the wok.
2 Reheat the wok, add 1 tablespoon
of the oil and stir-fry the sliced onion
over high heat for 3–4 minutes, or until
slightly softened. Add the capsicum
and carrot, and cook, tossing
constantly, for 3–4 minutes, or until
tender. Stir in the snow peas and cook

for 2 minutes.
3 Increase the heat, add the honey
and toss the vegetables until well
coated. Return the chicken to the wok
and toss until it is heated through and
is well coated in the honey. Remove
from the heat and season well with salt
and pepper. Serve immediately,
sprinkled with the almonds.

NUTRITION PER SERVE
Protein 35 g; Fat 20 g; Carbohydrate 35 g;
Dietary Fibre 4 g; Cholesterol 60 mg;
1815 kJ (435 cal)

Trim the excess fat from the chicken and cut the
chicken into cubes.

Dip the chicken into the egg white, then lightly
dust with the cornflour.

Stir-fry the chicken pieces until golden brown and
just cooked.

CHICKEN STIR-FRY WITH SNOW PEA SPROUTS

Preparation time: 15 minutes
Total cooking time: 15 minutes
Serves 4

2 tablespoons oil
1 onion, finely sliced
3 kaffir lime leaves, shredded
3 chicken breast fillets, diced
1 red capsicum, sliced
1/4 cup (60 ml/2 fl oz) lime juice
100 ml (3 1/2 fl oz) soy sauce
100 g (3 1/2 oz) snow pea sprouts
2 tablespoons chopped fresh
    coriander leaves

1 Heat a wok or frying pan over medium heat, add the oil and swirl to coat. Add the onion and kaffir lime leaves and stir-fry for 3–5 minutes, or until the onion begins to soften. Add the chicken and cook for a further 4 minutes. Add the capsicum and continue to cook for 2–3 minutes.
2 Stir in the lime juice and soy sauce and cook for 1–2 minutes, or until the sauce reduces slightly. Add the sprouts and coriander and cook until the sprouts have wilted slightly.

NUTRITION PER SERVE
Protein 45 g; Fat 15 g; Carbohydrate 5.5 g;
Dietary Fibre 2 g; Cholesterol 90 mg;
1375 kJ (330 cal)

VARIATION: Use the chicken, soy sauce and lime juice as a base and add fresh asparagus, or mint and basil instead of coriander.

Cook the chicken for 4 minutes and then add the capsicum to the wok.

Add the snow pea sprouts and coriander and cook until the sprouts wilt slightly.

151

SALMON WITH ASIAN GREENS AND CHILLI JAM

Preparation time: 20 minutes
Total cooking time: 1 hour
Serves 4

CHILLI JAM
2¹/₂ tablespoons vegetable oil
1 large onion, thinly sliced
6 red bird's-eye chillies, seeded
    and thinly sliced
2 teaspoons grated fresh ginger
³/₄ cup (185 ml/6 fl oz) white wine
    vinegar
³/₄ cup (150 g/5 oz) soft brown sugar
2 teaspoons lime juice

1 tablespoon peanut oil
1 red capsicum, thinly sliced
500 g (1 lb) baby bok choy, quartered
1 clove garlic, finely chopped
1 tablespoon soy sauce
1 teaspoon sugar
1 tablespoon oil
4 salmon cutlets

1 To make the chilli jam, heat the oil in a saucepan and add the onion, chilli and ginger. Cook over medium heat for 3–4 minutes, or until the onion is soft. Add the remaining ingredients and ¹/₄ cup (60 ml/2 fl oz) water and stir until the sugar dissolves. Bring to the boil, then reduce the heat and simmer for 35–40 minutes, or until thick and pulpy (it will thicken as it cools). Cool slightly and mix until smooth in a food processor. Cool.
2 Heat the peanut oil in a frying pan, add the capsicum and cook over medium heat for 2 minutes, or until softened slightly, then add the bok

choy and cook for 1 minute, or until wilted. Add the garlic and cook until fragrant. Reduce the heat, add the soy sauce and sugar and warm gently. Remove from the heat and keep warm.
3 Heat the oil in a frying pan, season the salmon and cook over medium heat for 2 minutes each side, or until cooked to your liking—do not overcook or the flesh will dry out. Serve with the vegetables and jam.

NUTRITION PER SERVE
Protein 50 g; Fat 27 g; Carbohydrate 40 g; Dietary Fibre 6.5 g; Cholesterol 140 mg; 2513 kJ (600 cal)

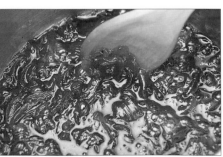

Simmer the chilli jam until it thickens and becomes pulpy.

Cook the seasoned salmon cutlets, taking care not to overcook or the flesh will be dry.

TERIYAKI PORK WITH SOYA BEANS

Preparation time: 20 minutes +
  2 hours refrigeration + 10 minutes
  resting
Total cooking time: 30 minutes
Serves 4

1¹/₂ tablespoons soy sauce
3 teaspoons grated fresh ginger
1 clove garlic, crushed
¹/₄ cup (60 ml/2 fl oz) peanut oil
¹/₄ cup (60 ml/2 fl oz) dry sherry
750 g (1¹/₂ lb) pork fillet
2 tablespoons honey
300 g (10 oz) frozen soya beans
4 baby bok choy, sliced in half
  lengthways
3 teaspoons sesame oil
2 teaspoons finely chopped fresh
  ginger, extra
1 clove garlic, crushed, extra
sesame seeds, toasted, to garnish

1 Place the soy sauce, ginger, garlic and 2 tablespoons each of the peanut oil and sherry in a large shallow non-metallic dish and mix well. Add the pork and toss gently to coat well. Cover and refrigerate for 2 hours, turning the meat occasionally. Preheat the oven to moderate 180°C (350°F/Gas 4).

2 Remove the pork and drain well, reserving the marinade. Pat the pork dry with paper towels. Heat the remaining peanut oil in a large frying pan and cook the pork over medium heat for 5–6 minutes, or until browned all over. Transfer to a baking tray and roast for 10–15 minutes. Cover with foil and rest for 10 minutes.

3 Put the reserved marinade, honey, the remaining sherry and ¹/₃ cup

(80 ml/2³/₄ fl oz) water in a small pan and bring to the boil. Reduce the heat and simmer for 3–4 minutes, or until reduced to a glaze. Keep the glaze hot.

4 Cook the soya beans in a large covered saucepan of lightly salted boiling water for 1 minute, then add the bok choy and cook for a further 2 minutes. Drain. Heat the sesame oil in the same saucepan, add the extra ginger and garlic and heat for

30 seconds. Return the soya beans and bok choy to the pan and toss gently.

5 Slice the pork and serve over the vegetables. Spoon the glaze over the pork, sprinkle with sesame seeds and serve immediately.

NUTRITION PER SERVE
Protein 48 g; Fat 25 g; Carbohydrate 6.5 g;
Dietary Fibre 5 g; Cholesterol 86 mg;
1899 kJ (455 cal)

Cook the pork fillets until they are browned all over.

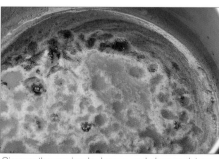

Simmer the marinade, honey and sherry mixture until reduced to a glaze.

Toss together the soya beans, bok choy, ginger and garlic.

153

FIVE-SPICE BEEF WITH ASIAN MUSHROOMS

Preparation time: 20 minutes +
    10 minutes resting
Total cooking time: 30 minutes
Serves 4

1/4 cup (60 ml/2 fl oz) soy sauce
1/4 cup (60 ml/2 fl oz) mirin
1/4 cup (60 ml/2 fl oz) sake
2 tablespoons soft brown sugar
3 teaspoons five-spice powder
1 teaspoon sea salt flakes
4 fillet steaks
600 g (1 1/4 lb) orange sweet potato,
    chopped
1 tablespoon butter
1/3 cup (90 g/3 oz) sour cream
2 cloves garlic, crushed
1 teaspoon ground ginger
1 tablespoon peanut oil
2 teaspoons butter, for pan-frying,
    extra
1 teaspoon grated fresh ginger
1 clove garlic, crushed, extra
100 g (3 1/2 oz) shiitake mushrooms,
    sliced
100 g (3 1/2 oz) shimeji mushrooms,
    pulled apart
100 g (3 1/2 oz) enoki mushrooms
toasted sesame seeds, to serve

1 Place the soy sauce, mirin, sake and sugar in a small saucepan and boil over high heat for 5 minutes, or until reduced and thickened slightly. Remove from the heat and cover.
2 Rub the combined five-spice powder and sea salt into the steaks.
3 Boil the orange sweet potato for 12 minutes, or until soft. Drain well, then add the butter, sour cream, garlic and ground ginger and mash together until smooth and creamy. Season, cover and keep warm.
4 Heat the oil in a large frying pan over high heat. When very hot, cook the steaks for 4–5 minutes each side for medium–rare, or until done to your liking. Remove from the pan, cover with foil and rest for 10 minutes.
5 Melt the extra butter in a frying pan over medium heat until just sizzling,

then stir in the ginger and extra garlic. Add the shiitake and shimeji mushrooms and stir for 3 minutes, or until wilted. Add the enoki, remove from the heat, cover and keep warm. Reheat the sauce and sweet potato and serve with the steaks. Top with the mushrooms and sesame seeds.

NUTRITION PER SERVE
Protein 47 g; Fat 28 g; Carbohydrate 13 g;
Dietary Fibre 2.5 g; Cholesterol 180 mg;
2105 kJ (505 cal)

Boil the sauce over high heat until it has reduced and thickened slightly.

Cook the shiitake and shimeji mushrooms until they are wilted, then add the enoki.

TERIYAKI TUNA WITH WASABI MAYONNAISE AND PICKLED GINGER

Preparation time: 10 minutes +
  10 minutes marinating
Total cooking time: 10 minutes
Serves 4

1/2 cup (125 ml/4 fl oz) teriyaki
  marinade
1/2 teaspoon five-spice powder
1 tablespoon grated fresh ginger

3 tuna steaks, each cut into 4 strips
2 tablespoons peanut oil
1/4 cup (60 g/2 oz) mayonnaise
1 teaspoon wasabi paste
2 tablespoons pickled ginger, to serve

1 Combine the teriyaki marinade, five-spice powder and ginger. Place the tuna in a non-metallic dish, pour over the marinade, cover and leave to marinate for 10 minutes. Drain and discard the marinade.
2 Heat the oil in a large non-stick frying pan. Add the tuna, in batches if

necessary, and cook over high heat for 1–2 minutes each side, or until cooked to your liking. The time will vary depending on the thickness of the fish.
3 Mix together the mayonnaise and wasabi paste. Serve the tuna steaks with wasabi mayonnaise and a little pickled ginger.

NUTRITION PER SERVE
Protein 27 g; Fat 17 g; Carbohydrate 4 g;
Dietary Fibre 0 g; Cholesterol 50 mg;
1196 kJ (284 cal)

Marinate the tuna in a non-metallic dish, so that the acidic marinade doesn't react with the dish.

Cook the tuna, in batches if necessary, over high heat until cooked to your liking.

Mix together the mayonnaise and wasabi paste to make a hot dressing.

HOISIN PORK WITH STIR-FRIED GREENS AND GINGERED RICE

Preparation time: 15 minutes +
  10 minutes standing
Total cooking time: 35 minutes
Serves 4

1¹/4 cups (250 g/8 oz) jasmine rice
500 g (1 lb) pork fillets, thinly sliced
1 tablespoon caster sugar
2 tablespoons oil
¹/2 cup (125 ml/4 fl oz) white wine
  vinegar
1 cup (250 ml/8 fl oz) hoisin sauce
2 tablespoons stem ginger in syrup,
  chopped (see NOTE)
1.25 kg (2¹/2 lb) mixed Asian greens
  (bok choy, choy sum or spinach)

1 Rinse the rice and place in a large saucepan. Add 1³/4 cups (435 ml/ 14 fl oz) water and bring to the boil. Cover, reduce the heat to very low and cook for 10 minutes. Remove from the heat and leave to stand, covered, for 10 minutes. Meanwhile, place the pork in a bowl and sprinkle with the sugar. Toss to coat. Heat a wok over high heat, add 1 tablespoon oil and swirl to coat. Add the pork in batches and stir-fry for 3 minutes, or until brown. Remove all the pork from the wok. Add the vinegar to the wok and boil for 3–5 minutes, or until reduced by two-thirds. Reduce the heat, add the hoisin sauce and 1 tablespoon ginger, and simmer for 5 minutes.

2 Reheat the wok over high heat, add the remaining oil and swirl to coat. Add the greens and stir-fry for 3 minutes, or until crisp and cooked. Stir the remaining ginger through the rice, then press into four round teacups or small Asian bowls, smoothing the surface. Unmould the rice onto four serving plates, arrange the pork and greens on the side and drizzle the sauce over the top.

NUTRITION PER SERVE
Protein 50 g; Fat 17 g; Carbohydrate 177 g;
Dietary Fibre 20 g; Cholesterol 60 mg;
4523 kJ (1080 cal)

NOTE: Stem ginger is available from Asian food stores. Substitute glacé ginger if it is unavailable.

Sprinkle the pork with sugar and then stir-fry until it is brown.

Press the gingered rice into teacups or small Asian bowls to give it a neat shape.

SATAY CHICKEN WITH MANGO

Preparation time: 10 minutes
Total cooking time: 15 minutes
Serves 4

$^{1}/_{3}$ cup (80 ml/2$^{3}/_{4}$ fl oz) ready-made
   satay sauce
$^{1}/_{2}$ cup (125 ml/4 fl oz) coconut cream
$^{1}/_{2}$ cup (125 ml/4 fl oz) chicken stock
2 teaspoons soy sauce
4 chicken breast fillets, cut into strips
plain flour, for coating
2 tablespoons oil
1 large ripe mango, sliced

1 Whisk together the satay sauce, coconut cream, stock and soy sauce.
2 Lightly coat the chicken with flour. Heat the oil in a large deep frying pan and cook the chicken over medium heat for 4–5 minutes, or until golden brown. Remove from the pan.
3 Add the satay sauce mixture to the pan and bring to the boil. Boil for 3–5 minutes, or until the sauce is reduced by half. Return the chicken to the pan and heat through for 1 minute. Serve the chicken over steamed rice, topped with mango slices.

NUTRITION PER SERVE
Protein 30 g; Fat 25 g; Carbohydrate 17 g;
Dietary Fibre 2 g; Cholesterol 70 mg;
1710 kJ (410 cal)

Whisk together the satay sauce, coconut cream, chicken stock and soy sauce.

Lightly coat the chicken with flour and then cook in a frying pan until golden brown.

Return the chicken to the sauce and heat through for 1 minute.

CORIANDER AND LIME CHICKEN

Preparation time: 10 minutes
Total cooking time: 15 minutes
Serves 4

2/3 cup (170 ml/5 1/2 fl oz) coconut cream
1/2 cup (125 ml/4 fl oz) chicken stock
1 1/2 tablespoons lime juice
2 teaspoons grated fresh ginger
4 chicken breast fillets, cut into strips

plain flour, for coating
2 tablespoons oil
2 tablespoons chopped fresh coriander leaves, plus extra to garnish

1 Whisk together the coconut cream, stock, lime juice and ginger. Lightly coat the chicken with flour.
2 Heat the oil in a frying pan and cook the chicken over medium heat for 4–5 minutes, or until golden brown. Remove from the pan and keep warm. Add the coconut cream

mixture to the pan and bring to the boil. Cook for 5 minutes, or until reduced by half and thickened slightly.
3 Return the chicken to the pan, add the coriander and simmer for 1 minute to heat the chicken through. Garnish with coriander leaves.

NUTRITION PER SERVE
Protein 50 g; Fat 20 g; Carbohydrate 13 g; Dietary Fibre 1 g; Cholesterol 110 mg; 1785 kJ (425 cal)

Whisk together the coconut cream, stock, lime juice and ginger.

Boil the coconut cream, stock, lime juice and ginger until reduced and thickened.

Return the chicken to the pan, add the coriander and simmer to heat through.

ASIAN GREENS WITH TERIYAKI TOFU DRESSING

Preparation time: 15 minutes
Total cooking time: 20 minutes
Serves 6

650 g (1 lb 5 oz) baby bok choy
500 g (1 lb) choy sum
440 g (14 oz) snake beans, topped and tailed
1/4 cup (60 ml/2 fl oz) oil
1 onion, thinly sliced
1/3 cup (60 g/2 oz) soft brown sugar
1/2 teaspoon ground chilli
2 tablespoons grated fresh ginger
1 cup (250 ml/8 fl oz) teriyaki sauce
1 tablespoon sesame oil
600 g (1 1/4 lb) silken firm tofu, drained

1 Cut the the baby bok choy and choy sum widthways into thirds. Cut the beans into 10 cm (4 inch) lengths.
2 Heat a wok over high heat, add 1 tablespoon of the oil and swirl to coat the side. Cook the onion in batches for 3–5 minutes, or until crisp. Remove with a slotted spoon and drain on paper towels.
3 Heat 1 tablespoon of the oil in the wok, add half the greens and stir-fry for 2–3 minutes, or until wilted.

Remove and keep warm. Repeat with the remaining oil and greens. Remove. Drain any liquid from the wok.
4 Add the combined sugar, chilli, ginger and teriyaki sauce to the wok and bring to the boil. Simmer for 1 minute. Add the sesame oil and tofu and simmer for 2 minutes, turning once—the tofu will break up. Divide the greens among serving plates, then top with the dressing. Sprinkle with the fried onion.

NUTRITION PER SERVE
Protein 19 g; Fat 11 g; Carbohydrate 20 g; Dietary Fibre 11 g; Cholesterol 1 mg; 1093 kJ (260 cal)

Cut the baby bok choy and choy sum widthways into thirds.

Cook the combined greens in two batches until the leaves are wilted.

Turn the tofu with an egg-flip halfway through cooking—it will break up.

SESAME-COATED TUNA WITH CORIANDER SALSA

Preparation time: 15 minutes +
15 minutes refrigeration
Total cooking time: 10 minutes
Serves 4

4 tuna steaks
3/4 cup (120 g/4 oz) sesame seeds
100 g (3 1/2 oz) baby rocket leaves

CORIANDER SALSA
2 tomatoes, seeded and diced
1 large clove garlic, crushed

2 tablespoons finely chopped fresh
coriander leaves
2 tablespoons virgin olive oil, plus
extra for shallow-frying
1 tablespoon lime juice

1 Cut each tuna steak into three pieces. Place the sesame seeds on a sheet of baking paper. Roll the tuna in the sesame seeds to coat. Refrigerate for 15 minutes.
2 To make the salsa, mix together the tomato, garlic, coriander, oil and lime juice. Cover and refrigerate.
3 Fill a heavy-based frying pan to 1.5 cm (5/8 inch) deep with the extra

oil and place over high heat. Add the tuna in two batches and cook for 2 minutes each side (it should be pink in the centre). Remove and drain on paper towels. Divide the rocket among four serving plates, top with the tuna and serve with the salsa.

NUTRITION PER SERVE
Protein 26 g; Fat 36 g; Carbohydrate 2 g;
Dietary Fibre 2 g; Cholesterol 45 mg;
1696 kJ (403 cal)

Put the sesame seeds on baking paper and roll the tuna in the seeds to coat.

Mix together the tomato, garlic, coriander, oil and lime juice to make a salsa.

Shallow-fry the tuna for 2 minutes on each side, or until it is cooked but still pink in the centre.

TEMPEH STIR-FRY

Preparation time: 15 minutes
Total cooking time: 15 minutes
Serves 4

1 teaspoon sesame oil
1 tablespoon peanut oil
2 cloves garlic, crushed
1 tablespoon grated fresh ginger
1 red chilli, finely sliced
4 spring onions, sliced on the diagonal
300 g (10 oz) tempeh, diced
500 g (1 lb) baby bok choy leaves

800 g (1 lb 10 oz) Chinese broccoli,
    chopped
1/2 cup (125 ml/4 fl oz) mushroom
    oyster sauce
2 tablespoons rice vinegar
2 tablespoons fresh coriander leaves
3 tablespoons toasted cashew nuts

1 Heat the oils in a wok over high
heat, add the garlic, ginger, chilli
and spring onion and cook for
1–2 minutes, or until the onion is soft.
Add the tempeh and cook for
5 minutes, or until golden. Remove
and keep warm.

2 Add half the greens and 1 tablespoon water to the wok and cook,
covered, for 3–4 minutes, or until
wilted. Remove and repeat with the
remaining greens and more water.
3 Return the greens and tempeh to
the wok, add the sauce and vinegar
and warm through. Top with the
coriander and nuts. Serve with rice.

NUTRITION PER SERVE
Protein 23 g; Fat 15 g; Carbohydrate 12 g;
Dietary Fibre 15 g; Cholesterol 0 mg;
2220 kJ (529 cal)

Stir-fry the garlic, ginger, chilli and spring onion for
1–2 minutes.

Add the tempeh to the wok and stir-fry for
5 minutes, or until golden.

Add the greens to the wok in two batches and
cook until wilted.

BEEF AND HOKKIEN NOODLE STIR-FRY

Preparation time: 15 minutes +
   10 minutes soaking
Total cooking time: 15 minutes
Serves 4

350 g (11 oz) beef fillet, partially frozen
   (see HINT)
100 g (3¹/₂ oz) snow peas
600 g (1¹/₄ lb) fresh Hokkien noodles
2 tablespoons peanut oil
1 large onion, cut into thin wedges
1 large carrot, sliced thinly on the
   diagonal
1 red capsicum, cut into thin strips
2 cloves garlic, crushed
1 teaspoon grated fresh ginger
200 g (6¹/₂ oz) fresh shiitake
   mushrooms, sliced
¹/₄ cup (60 ml/2 fl oz) oyster sauce
2 tablespoons light soy sauce
1 tablespoon soft brown sugar
¹/₂ teaspoon five-spice powder

1 Cut the steak into thin slices. Top and tail the snow peas and slice in half diagonally. Soak the noodles in a large bowl of boiling water for 10 minutes.
2 Heat a wok to very hot, add half the peanut oil and stir-fry the steak in batches until brown. Remove.
3 Heat the remaining peanut oil in the wok until very hot and stir-fry the onion, carrot and capsicum for 2–3 minutes, or until tender. Add the garlic, ginger, snow peas and shiitake mushrooms and cook for another minute. Return the steak to the wok.
4 Separate the noodles with a fork, then drain. Add to the wok, tossing well. Combine the oyster sauce with the soy sauce, brown sugar, five-spice powder and 1 tablespoon water and pour over the noodles. Toss until warmed through.

NUTRITION PER SERVE
Protein 38 g; Fat 10 g; Carbohydrate 92 g;
Dietary Fibre 7 g; Cholesterol 78 mg;
2555 kJ (610 cal)

HINT: Partially freezing the meat will firm it up and make it easier to slice thinly.

Cut the partially frozen beef fillet into thin slices with a sharp knife.

Add the garlic, ginger, snow peas and shiitake mushrooms and cook for another minute.

TUNA IN KAFFIR LIME SAUCE

Preparation time: 5 minutes
Total cooking time: 15 minutes
Serves 4

1¹/₂ cups (375 ml/12 fl oz) cream
1¹/₂ cups (375 ml/12 fl oz) fish stock
12 kaffir lime leaves, finely sliced
2 tablespoons peanut oil
4 small tuna steaks, cubed
1 kg (2 lb) baby bok choy, halved

1 Place the cream, fish stock and lime leaves in a small saucepan over low heat. Boil for 15 minutes, stirring occasionally, or until the sauce has reduced and thickened. Keep warm.
2 Meanwhile, heat a wok until very hot, add the oil and swirl to coat the sides. Add the tuna, in batches if necessary, and stir-fry for 2 minutes, or until seared on all sides but not cooked through. Remove the tuna.
3 Add the bok choy to the wok and stir-fry over high heat for 1–2 minutes, or until the leaves are just starting to

wilt. Add 1–2 teaspoons water, if necessary, to assist wilting.
4 Place the bok choy and tuna on a serving plate and pour on the sauce. Serve with lime wedges.

NUTRITION PER SERVE
Protein 68 g; Fat 55 g; Carbohydrate 6 g; Dietary Fibre 20 g; Cholesterol 276 mg; 3300 kJ (788 cal)

Place the cream, fish stock and lime leaves in a saucepan and simmer.

Quickly stir-fry the tuna until just seared on all sides but not cooked through.

Add the bok choy to the wok and stir-fry until just starting to wilt.

FISH FILLETS IN CRISP BATTER WITH SHIITAKE MUSHROOM SAUCE

Preparation time: 15 minutes +
    15 minutes soaking
Total cooking time: 15 minutes
Serves 4

SHIITAKE MUSHROOM SAUCE
60 g (2 oz) dried shiitake mushrooms
2 tablespoons peanut oil
2 cloves garlic, chopped
2 teaspoons chopped fresh ginger
1 small red chilli, seeded and sliced
3 spring onions, sliced diagonally
2 tablespoons oyster sauce
2 tablespoons soy sauce
2 tablespoons Chinese wine
2 teaspoons sugar

BATTER
1/2 cup (60 g/2 oz) plain flour
1/2 cup (60 g/2 oz) cornflour
1 teaspoon baking powder
1 1/2 teaspoons salt

4 x 200 g (6 1/2 oz) flounder or sole
    fillets
plain flour, for dusting
oil, for deep-frying

1 Soak the shiitake mushrooms in boiling water for 10 minutes, or until soft. Drain, remove the tough stalks and thinly slice the caps. Heat the oil in a frying pan or wok and cook the garlic, ginger and chilli over low heat for 1 minute, or until aromatic. Add the mushrooms and spring onion and cook for 1 minute over medium heat. Mix together the oyster and soy sauces, wine, sugar and 1/4 cup (60 ml/2 fl oz) water. Add to the pan and cook, stirring, for 1–2 minutes.
2 Sift all the dry ingredients for the batter into a bowl and make a well. Add 3/4 cup (185 ml/6 fl oz) chilled water and whisk together. Dry the fish with paper towels and dust with flour.
3 Fill a wok one-third full of oil and heat to 180°C (350°F), or until a cube of bread browns in 15 seconds. Dip the fish in batter, drain the excess and cook in batches for 5–6 minutes, or until golden. Drain on paper towels and serve with the sauce.

NUTRITION PER SERVE
Protein 44 g; Fat 20 g; Carbohydrate 42 g;
Dietary Fibre 3 g; Cholesterol 131 mg;
2185 kJ (520 cal)

NOTE: If the sauce is left to stand for too long, the mushrooms will soak up the liquid—simply add a little more water and reheat.

You can use 100 g (3 1/2 oz) fresh shiitake mushrooms, if preferred.

Add the oyster and soy sauces, wine, sugar and water and cook for a couple of minutes.

Deep-fry the battered fish in batches until it is golden and flakes when tested with a fork.

CALAMARI IN BLACK BEAN AND CHILLI SAUCE

Preparation time: 20 minutes
Total cooking time: 10 minutes
Serves 4

4 squid hoods
2 tablespoons oil
1 onion, cut into wedges
1 red capsicum, sliced
120 g (4 oz) baby corn, halved
3 spring onions, cut into short lengths

BLACK BEAN SAUCE
3 teaspoons cornflour
2 tablespoons canned salted black
    beans, rinsed (see NOTE)
2 small red chillies, seeded and
    chopped
2 cloves garlic, finely chopped
2 teaspoons grated fresh ginger
2 tablespoons oyster sauce
2 teaspoons soy sauce
1 teaspoon sugar

1 Open out the squid hoods. Lightly score a diamond pattern over the inside surface of each, then cut into 5 cm (2 inch) squares.

2 For the sauce, mix the cornflour with ¹/₂ cup (125 ml/4 fl oz) water. Mash the black beans with a fork. Add the chilli, garlic, ginger, oyster and soy sauces, sugar and the cornflour mixture and stir well.

3 Heat the oil in a wok or frying pan and stir-fry the onion for 1 minute over high heat. Add the capsicum and corn and cook for another 2 minutes.

4 Add the squid to the wok and stir for 1–2 minutes, until it curls up. Add the sauce and bring to the boil, stirring until the sauce thickens. Stir in the spring onion.

NUTRITION PER SERVE
Protein 12 g; Fat 11 g; Carbohydrate 13 g;
Dietary Fibre 3.5 g; Cholesterol 100 mg;
800 kJ (190 cal)

VARIATION: Instead of squid, you can use fish, cuttlefish, prawns or octopus.

NOTE: Black beans are available in cans in Asian food stores.

Score a shallow diamond pattern over the inside surface of each hood.

The squid are cooked when they start to curl up. Don't overcook them or they'll be tough.

Add the sauce, bring to the boil and stir constantly until the sauce thickens.

165

CHILLI CRAB

Preparation time: 20 minutes
Total cooking time: 15 minutes
Serves 4

1 kg (2 lb) raw blue swimmer crabs
2 tablespoons peanut oil
2 cloves garlic, finely chopped
2 teaspoons finely chopped fresh
    ginger
2 small red chillies, seeded and sliced
    (see NOTE)
2 tablespoons hoisin sauce
1/2 cup (125 ml/4 fl oz) tomato sauce
1/4 cup (60 ml/2 fl oz) sweet chilli
    sauce
1 tablespoon fish sauce
1/2 teaspoon sesame oil
4 spring onions, finely sliced, to
    garnish, optional

1 Pull back the apron and remove the top shell from each crab. Remove the intestines and grey feathery gills. Segment each crab into four pieces. Crack the claws open with a crab cracker to allow the flavours to enter the crab meat and also to make it easier to eat the crab.
2 Heat a wok until very hot, add the oil and swirl to coat. Add the garlic, ginger and chilli and stir-fry for 1–2 minutes.
3 Add the crab pieces and stir-fry for 5–7 minutes, or until the meat turns white. Stir in the hoisin, tomato, sweet chilli and fish sauces, the sesame oil and 1/4 cup (60 ml/2 fl oz) water. Bring to the boil, then reduce the heat and simmer, covered, for 6 minutes, or until the crab flesh is cooked through and flakes easily. Garnish with spring onion and serve with finger bowls.

NUTRITION PER SERVE
Protein 17 g; Fat 12 g; Carbohydrate 19 g;
Dietary Fibre 3 g; Cholesterol 105 mg;
1045 kJ (250 cal)

VARIATION: You can use any variety of raw crab meat for this recipe, or use prawns instead.

NOTE: If you prefer a hotter sauce, leave the seeds and membrane in the chillies.

Pull the apron back from the crabs and remove the top shell from each.

Pull out and discard the intestines and grey feathery gills.

Use a sharp, strong knife to cut each crab into four pieces.

After adding the sauces, oil and water, cook until the crab flesh flakes easily.

DEEP-FRIED SNAPPER WITH THAI SAUCE

Preparation time: 20 minutes
Total cooking time: 25 minutes
Serves 4

SAUCE
2 tablespoons chilli jam (see NOTE)
2 kaffir lime leaves, finely shredded
2 tablespoons fish sauce
1 teaspoon sesame oil
2 stems lemon grass, white part only, finely chopped
1 tablespoon finely grated fresh ginger
1 clove garlic, crushed
2 tablespoons shaved palm sugar
2 tablespoons lime juice
1/3 cup (80 ml/2³/4 fl oz) rice wine vinegar
1 tablespoon chopped fresh coriander roots

4 x 350 g (11 oz) whole snapper or bream, cleaned and scaled
cornflour, for dusting
oil, for deep-frying
fresh coriander sprigs and spring onions, to garnish

1 Stir the sauce ingredients together with 2 tablespoons water in a small saucepan over medium heat. Bring to the boil and cook for 2 minutes, or until the sauce is reduced and slightly caramelised. Keep warm.
2 Score a shallow diamond pattern on both sides of each fish. Pat dry with paper towels and lightly coat in the cornflour, shaking off any excess.
3 Fill a wok or a deep heavy-based saucepan one-third full of oil and heat to 180°C (350°F), or until a cube of bread dropped into the oil browns in 15 seconds. Cook each fish for 5 minutes, or until golden brown and cooked through. You may need to turn the fish with tongs or a long-handled spoon. Drain on crumpled paper towels and season. Serve immediately with the sauce. Garnish with coriander and raw or grilled spring onions.

NUTRITION PER SERVE
Protein 58 g; Fat 26 g; Carbohydrate 18 g; Dietary Fibre 1.5 g; Cholesterol 215 mg; 2240 kJ (535 cal)

NOTE: Chilli jam is available from Asian speciality stores.

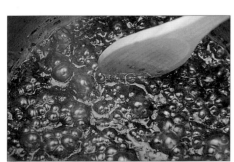
Cook the sauce ingredients until reduced and slightly caramelised.

Cut a shallow diamond pattern into both sides of each fish with a sharp knife.

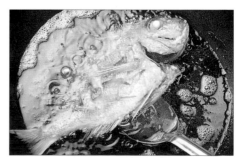
Fry the fish until cooked through, then remove with a slotted spoon.

TOFU WITH ASIAN GREENS AND SHIITAKE MUSHROOMS

Preparation time: 15 minutes
Total cooking time: 20 minutes
Serves 4

1/3 cup (80 ml/2 3/4 fl oz) vegetable oil
1 clove garlic, chopped
1 teaspoon grated fresh ginger
60 g (2 oz) shiitake mushrooms, sliced
2 teaspoons dashi powder
3 tablespoons mushroom soy sauce
3 tablespoons mirin
1 teaspoon sugar
2 tablespoons cornflour
2 x 300 g (10 oz) blocks silken firm tofu, each block cut into 4 slices
250 g (8 oz) bok choy, chopped
150 g (5 oz) choy sum, chopped
2 spring onions, cut on the diagonal
wasabi, to serve

1 Heat 1 tablespoon of the oil in a saucepan. Add the garlic, ginger and mushrooms and fry for 1–2 minutes, or until softened. Add the dashi powder and 2 cups (500 ml/16 fl oz) water and simmer for 5 minutes.
2 Add the mushroom soy sauce, mirin and sugar and stir until the sugar has dissolved. Mix the cornflour with a little water to make a smooth paste. Pour into the soy sauce mixture and stir until thickened.
3 Heat 2 tablespoons of the oil in a

frying pan. Add the tofu and brown in batches for 2–3 minutes. Set aside. Heat the remaining oil, then add the bok choy, choy sum and spring onion. Cook for 2 minutes, or until wilted.
4 Place the greens in a bowl, top with the tofu and pour on the dashi sauce. Serve a little wasabi on the side.

NUTRITION PER SERVE
Protein 17 g; Fat 25 g; Carbohydrate 6 g;
Dietary Fibre 5 g; Cholesterol 0 mg;
1368 kJ (327 cal)

Stir the cornflour paste into the soy sauce mixture until it thickens.

Fry the slices of tofu in batches in the hot oil until they are brown on both sides.

SWEET AND SOUR TOFU

Preparation time: 15 minutes
Total cooking time: 20 minutes
Serves 4

600 g (1¼ lb) firm tofu
3–4 tablespoons soy bean oil
1 large carrot, cut into matchsticks
2 cups (150 g/5 oz) trimmed bean
   sprouts or soy bean sprouts
1 cup (90 g/3 oz) sliced button
   mushrooms
6–8 spring onions, cut diagonally
100 g (3½ oz) snow peas, cut in half
   on the diagonal

⅓ cup (80 ml/2¾ fl oz) rice vinegar
2 tablespoons light soy sauce
1½ tablespoons caster sugar
2 tablespoons tomato sauce
1½ cups (375 ml/12 fl oz) chicken or
   vegetable stock
1 tablespoon cornflour

1 Cut the tofu in half horizontally, then cut into 16 triangles in total. Heat 2 tablespoons of the oil in a frying pan. Add the tofu in batches and cook over medium heat for 2 minutes on each side, or until crisp and golden. Drain on paper towels. Keep warm.
2 Wipe the pan clean and heat the remaining oil. Add the carrot, bean sprouts, mushrooms, spring onion and snow peas and stir-fry for 1 minute. Add the vinegar, soy sauce, sugar, tomato sauce and stock and cook for a further 1 minute.
3 Combine the cornflour with 2 tablespoons water. Add to the vegetable mixture and cook until the sauce thickens. Serve the tofu with the sauce poured over the top.

NUTRITION PER SERVE
Protein 15 g; Fat 16 g; Carbohydrate 17 g;
Dietary Fibre 4 g; Cholesterol 0 mg;
1178 kJ (280 cal)

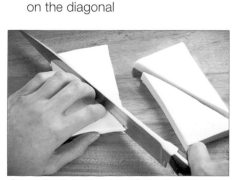

Cut the firm tofu slices into 16 triangles with a sharp knife.

Fry the tofu triangles on both sides until they are crisp and golden.

Stir the sauce and vegetables together until the sauce thickens.

TOFU IN BLACK BEAN SAUCE

Preparation time: 20 minutes
Total cooking time: 15 minutes
Serves 4

1/3 cup (80 ml/2³/4 fl oz) vegetable
 stock
2 teaspoons cornflour
2 teaspoons Chinese rice wine (see
 NOTE)
1 teaspoon sesame oil
1 tablespoon soy sauce
2 tablespoons peanut oil
450 g (14 oz) firm tofu, diced
2 cloves garlic, very finely chopped
2 teaspoons finely chopped fresh
 ginger
3 tablespoons fermented black beans,
 rinsed and very finely chopped
4 spring onions, cut on the diagonal
1 red capsicum, cut into cubes
300 g (10 oz) baby bok choy,
 chopped

1 Combine the vegetable stock, cornflour, rice wine, sesame oil, soy sauce, 1/2 teaspoon salt and freshly ground black pepper in a small bowl.
2 Heat a wok over medium heat, add the peanut oil and swirl to coat. Add the tofu and stir-fry in two batches for 3 minutes each batch, or until lightly browned. Remove with a slotted spoon and drain on paper towels. Discard any bits of tofu stuck to the wok or floating in the oil.
3 Add the garlic and ginger and stir-fry for 30 seconds. Toss in the black beans and spring onion and stir-fry for 30 seconds. Add the capsicum and stir-fry for 1 minute. Add the bok choy and stir-fry for a further 2 minutes. Return the tofu to the wok and stir gently.

Pour in the sauce and stir gently for 2–3 minutes, or until the sauce has thickened slightly. Serve immediately.

NUTRITION PER SERVE
Protein 13 g; Fat 14 g; Carbohydrate 4 g; Dietary Fibre 4 g; Cholesterol 0 mg; 850 kJ (205 cal)

NOTE: Chinese rice wine is an alcoholic liquid made from cooked glutinous rice and millet mash which has been fermented with yeast, then aged for a period of 10 to 100 years. With a sherry-like taste, it is used as both a drink and a cooking liquid.

Stir-fry the tofu cubes in batches until they are lightly browned.

Stir-fry the garlic, ginger, black beans and spring onion for 30 seconds.

Return the tofu to the wok and gently stir together with the vegetables.

HONEY AND BLACK PEPPER BEEF

Preparation time: 15 minutes
Total cooking time: 10 minutes
Serves 4

oil, for cooking
500 g (1 lb) round steak, cut into thin
    strips
2 cloves garlic, crushed
1 onion, sliced
300 g (10 oz) sugar snap peas

2 tablespoons honey
2 teaspoons soy sauce
2 tablespoons oyster sauce
3 teaspoons cracked black pepper

1 Heat the wok until very hot, add
1 tablespoon of the oil and swirl it
around to coat the side. Stir-fry the
beef in batches over high heat.
Remove and drain on paper towels.
2 Reheat the wok, add 1 tablespoon
of the oil and stir-fry the garlic, onion
and sugar snap peas until softened.
Remove from the wok and set aside.

3 Add the honey, soy sauce, oyster
sauce and cracked pepper to the wok.
Bring to the boil, then reduce the heat
and simmer for 3–4 minutes, or until
the sauce thickens slightly.
4 Increase the heat, return the meat
and vegetables to the wok, and toss
for 2–3 minutes, or until well
combined and heated through.

NUTRITION PER SERVE
Protein 30 g; Fat 15 g; Carbohydrate 20 g;
Dietary Fibre 4.5 g; Cholesterol 70 mg;
1400 kJ (335 cal)

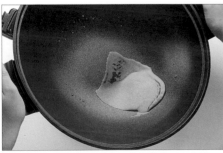

Heat the wok before adding the oil, then add the oil and swirl to coat the side.

Once the beef is cooked, remove it from the wok and drain on paper towels.

Add the honey, soy sauce, oyster sauce and cracked pepper and bring to the boil.

BARBECUED PORK AND BROCCOLI STIR-FRY

Preparation time: 25 minutes
Total cooking time: 10 minutes
Serves 4–6

1 tablespoon oil
1 large onion, thinly sliced
2 carrots, cut into matchsticks
200 g (6¹/₂ oz) broccoli, cut into bite-sized florets
6 spring onions, diagonally sliced
1 tablespoon finely chopped fresh ginger
3 cloves garlic, finely chopped

400 g (13 oz) Chinese barbecued pork, thinly sliced (see NOTE)
2 tablespoons soy sauce
2 tablespoons mirin
2 cups (180 g/6 oz) bean sprouts

1 Heat the wok until very hot, add the oil and swirl it around to coat the side. Stir-fry the onion over medium heat for 3–4 minutes, or until slightly softened. Add the carrot, broccoli, spring onion, ginger and garlic, and stir-fry for 4–5 minutes.
2 Increase the heat to high and add the barbecued pork. Toss constantly until the pork is well mixed with the vegetables and is heated through. Add the soy sauce and mirin, and toss until the ingredients are well coated. (The wok should be hot enough that the sauce reduces a little to form a glaze-like consistency.) Add the bean sprouts and season well with salt and pepper. Serve immediately.

NUTRITION PER SERVE (6)
Protein 20 g; Fat 15 g; Carbohydrate 6.5 g; Dietary Fibre 6 g; Cholesterol 40 mg; 920 kJ (220 cal)

NOTE: Chinese barbecued pork is available from Asian barbecue shops.

Peel the carrots, if necessary, and cut them into even-sized matchsticks.

Cut the pieces of Chinese barbecued pork into thin slices.

Add the pork to the wok and toss until it is well mixed with the vegetables.

BEEF WITH BLACK BEAN SAUCE

Preparation time: 20 minutes +
  30 minutes marinating
Total cooking time: 15 minutes
Serves 4

500 g (1 lb) rump steak, cut into thin
  strips
1 tablespoon cornflour
2 tablespoons sherry
2 tablespoons soy sauce
2 teaspoons sugar
oil, for cooking
1 onion, thinly sliced
2 cloves garlic, finely chopped
1 tablespoon finely chopped fresh
  ginger
1 red capsicum, thinly sliced
90 g (3 oz) drained bamboo shoots,
  sliced
6 spring onions, diagonally sliced
2 tablespoons salted black beans,
  rinsed and mashed

1 Put the beef in a non-metallic bowl. Combine the cornflour with the sherry, soy sauce and sugar, pour over the meat and mix well. Cover and refrigerate for 30 minutes.

2 Drain the meat, reserving the marinade. Heat the wok until very hot, add 2 teaspoons of the oil and swirl it around to coat the side. Stir-fry the meat in two batches for 2–3 minutes, or until browned and just cooked. Add more oil when necessary. Remove all the meat from the wok.

3 Reheat the wok, add 1 tablespoon of oil and stir-fry the onion over medium heat for 3–4 minutes, or until softened. Stir in the garlic, ginger and capsicum, then increase the heat to high and cook for 2–3 minutes, or until

the capsicum is just tender.

4 Add the reserved marinade, bamboo shoots, spring onion, black beans and 2–3 tablespoons water to the wok. Toss over high heat until the ingredients are well coated and the sauce is boiling. Return the beef to the wok and heat through. Season well.

NUTRITION PER SERVE
Protein 30 g; Fat 15 g; Carbohydrate 9 g;
Dietary Fibre 3 g; Cholesterol 85 mg;
1230 kJ (295 cal)

Drain the bamboo shoots and slice them with a sharp knife.

Thoroughly rinse the salted black beans under cold running water.

Add the garlic, ginger and capsicum to the softened onion.

173

TONKATSU

Preparation time: 35 minutes +
  2 hours refrigeration
Total cooking time: 12 minutes
Serves 4

500 g (1 lb) pork loin
1/2 cup (60 g/2 oz) plain flour
6 egg yolks, beaten with
  2 tablespoons water
2 cups (120 g/4 oz) Japanese dried
  breadcrumbs
2 spring onions
pickled ginger and pickled daikon
2 cups (90 g/3 oz) finely shredded
  Chinese or savoy cabbage
1 sheet nori
1 1/2 cups (375 ml/12 fl oz) oil
1 cup (250 ml/8 fl oz) Tonkatsu sauce

1 Cut the pork into 8 thin slices. Sprinkle with salt and pepper and lightly coat with flour.
2 Dip the pork in the egg and then the breadcrumbs, pressing the crumbs on with your fingertips for an even coating. Arrange in a single layer on a plate and refrigerate, uncovered, for at least 2 hours.
3 To prepare the garnishes, peel away the outside layers of the spring onions, then slice the stems very finely and place in a bowl of cold water until serving time. Slice the ginger and daikon and set aside with the shredded cabbage. Using a sharp knife, shred the nori very finely and then break into strips about 4 cm (1 1/2 inches) long.
4 Heat the oil in a heavy-based frying pan. Cook 2–3 pork steaks at a time until golden brown on both sides, then drain on kitchen towels. Slice the pork into strips and reassemble into the original steak shape. Top each one with a few nori strips. Serve with the Tonkatsu sauce, shredded cabbage, drained spring onions, pickled ginger, daikon and steamed rice.

NUTRITION PER SERVE
Protein 40 g; Fat 25 g; Carbohydrate 42 g;
Dietary Fibre 3 g; Cholesterol 325 mg;
2320 kJ (555 cal)

Use your fingertips to press the breadcrumbs onto the pork.

Slice the ginger and daikon finely and set aside with the shredded cabbage.

Shred the nori finely, and then break it into strips about 4 cm long.

Cook 2–3 steaks at a time until they are golden brown on both sides.

TEPPAN YAKI

Preparation time: 45 minutes
Total cooking time: 25 minutes
Serves 4

350 g (11 oz) scotch fillet, partially
    frozen
4 small ladyfinger eggplants
100 g (3¹/₂ oz) fresh shiitake
    mushrooms
100 g (3¹/₂ oz) baby green beans
6 baby yellow or green squash
1 red or green capsicum, seeded
6 spring onions
200 g (6¹/₂ oz) canned bamboo
    shoots, drained
3 tablespoons light vegetable oil
soy and ginger dipping sauce or
    sesame seed dipping sauce

1 Slice the steak very thinly. Mark a large cross on each slice of meat. Place the slices in a single layer on a large serving platter and season well.
2 Trim the ends from the eggplants and cut the flesh into long, very thin diagonal slices. Trim any tough stalks from the mushrooms and top and tail the beans. Quarter or halve the squash, depending on the size. Cut the capsicum into thin strips and slice the spring onions into long pieces. Trim the bamboo shoot slices to a similar size. Arrange the vegetables in separate bundles on a serving plate.
3 Heat an electric grill or electric frying pan until very hot and then lightly brush it with the oil. Quickly fry about a quarter of the meat, searing on both sides, and then push it over to the edge of the pan. Add about a quarter of the vegetables to the grill or pan and quickly stir-fry, adding a little more oil as needed. Serve a small portion of the meat and vegetables to each guest with sauces for dipping.

NUTRITION PER SERVE
Protein 25 g; Fat 20 g; Carbohydrate 8 g;
Dietary Fibre 6 g; Cholesterol 60 mg;
1220 kJ (290 cal)

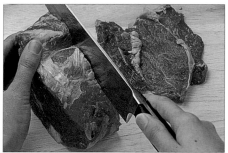
Partially freezing the steak will firm it up, making it easier to slice thinly.

Using the same knife, make a large cross on each slice of meat.

Carefully trim any hard stems from the fresh shiitake mushrooms.

Sear the meat quickly on each side, using tongs to turn it.

Stir-fry Sauces

The following sauces are suitable for many different meat and vegetable combinations. To make a stir-fry meal to feed four people, stir-fry roughly 500 g (1 lb) of meat and vegetables in a wok, add one of the following sauces and bring to the boil until thickened.

SAKE SAUCE

Soak 10 g (1/4 oz) sliced dried Chinese mushrooms in boiling water for 5 minutes. Drain and reserve 2 tablespoons of the liquid. Place 2 tablespoons sake, 2 tablespoons kecap manis, 1 tablespoon sweet chilli sauce, 1/2 teaspoon sesame oil, 1 small finely chopped red chilli, 2 teaspoons finely chopped lemon grass, 1 tablespoon lime juice, the mushrooms and the reserved liquid in a bowl and stir well.

CHILLI OYSTER SAUCE

Place 1 teaspoon sesame oil, 2 cloves crushed garlic, 1 tablespoon grated fresh ginger, 2 finely chopped small red chillies, 4 sliced spring onions, 2 tablespoons mirin and 1/2 cup (125 ml/4 fl oz) vegetable oyster sauce in a bowl and stir together well.

JAPANESE DRESSING

Place 10 dried shiitake mushrooms in a bowl and cover with 1 1/2 cups (375 ml/12 fl oz) boiling water. Soak for 10 minutes. Drain, reserving 1/4 cup (60 ml/2 fl oz) of the liquid and cut the mushrooms in quarters. Place 1/3 cup (80 ml/2 3/4 fl oz) Japanese soy sauce, 1 teaspoon grated fresh ginger, 1/3 cup (80 ml/2 3/4 fl oz) mirin, 2 tablespoons sugar and the reserved liquid in a bowl. Add the mushrooms and stir together well.

HOISIN SAUCE

Place 1/4 cup (60 ml/2 fl oz) hoisin sauce, 2 tablespoons vegetable stock, 1 tablespoon vegetable oyster sauce and 1 tablespoon sweet chilli sauce in a small bowl and stir together.

BLACK BEAN SAUCE

Place 2 teaspoons cornflour and 1/2 cup (125 ml/4 fl oz) vegetable stock in a small bowl and blend together. Drain and rinse a 170 g (5 1/2 oz) can of black beans, place in a bowl and lightly mash with a fork. Stir in the cornflour mixture, 1 tablespoon mushroom soy sauce, 2 teaspoons sugar and 2 crushed cloves of garlic.

GINGER OYSTER SAUCE

Combine 2 teaspoons cornflour and 2 teaspoons water. Add 1/2 cup (125 ml/4 fl oz) dry sherry, 1 chopped small red chilli, 1 tablespoon grated fresh ginger, 1/2 teaspoon sesame oil and 2 tablespoons vegetable oyster sauce and stir well.

Clockwise, from top left: Sake sauce; Chilli oyster sauce; Hoisin sauce; Ginger oyster sauce; Black bean sauce; Japanese dressing.

Grilled
& Steamed

PRAWNS STEAMED IN BANANA LEAVES

Preparation time: 30 minutes
  + 2 hours marinating
Total cooking time: 15 minutes
Serves 4

2.5 cm (1 inch) piece of fresh ginger,
  grated
2 small red chillies, finely chopped
4 spring onions, finely chopped
2 stalks lemon grass, white part only,
  finely chopped
2 teaspoons soft brown sugar
1 tablespoon fish sauce
2 tablespoons lime juice
1 tablespoon sesame seeds, toasted
2 tablespoons chopped fresh
  coriander
1 kg (2 lb) raw prawns, peeled and
  deveined
8 small banana leaves (see NOTES)

1 Process the ginger, chillies, spring onion and lemon grass in a food processor, in short bursts, until the mixture forms a paste. Transfer the paste to a bowl, stir in the sugar, fish sauce, lime juice, sesame seeds and coriander and mix well. Add the prawns and toss to coat. Cover, refrigerate and marinate for 2 hours.

2 Soak the banana leaves in boiling water for 3 minutes to soften. Drain, pat dry and use scissors to cut them into squares of about 18 cm (7 inches).
3 Divide the prawn mixture into eight, place a portion onto each banana leaf, fold the leaf up to enclose the mixture and then secure the parcels, using a bamboo skewer.
4 Cook the parcels in a bamboo steamer over simmering water for 8–10 minutes, or until the prawn filling is cooked.

NUTRITION PER SERVE
Protein 60 g; Fat 8 g; Carbohydrate 8 g;
Dietary Fibre 1 g; Cholesterol 355 mg;
1430 kJ (340 cal)

NOTES: Banana leaves are available from Asian food stores and speciality fruit and vegetable shops.
  If banana leaves are not available, the prawn mixture can be wrapped in aluminium foil or baking paper and steamed. If you are cooking them on a barbecue, use foil.
  The parcels can also be cooked on the barbecue.

STORAGE: The filled parcels can be made up a day in advance and stored, covered, in the refrigerator.

Use scissors to cut the banana leaves into squares, approximately 18 cm (7 inches).

Enclose the filling and secure the parcel with a bamboo skewer.

STEAMED LEMON GRASS AND GINGER CHICKEN WITH ASIAN GREENS

Preparation time: 25 minutes
Total cooking time: 40 minutes
Serves 4

200 g (6¹/₂ oz) fresh egg noodles
4 chicken breast fillets
2 stalks lemon grass, white part only
5 cm (2 inch) piece of fresh ginger, cut into matchsticks
1 lime, thinly sliced
2 cups (500 ml/16 fl oz) chicken stock
1 bunch (350 g/11 oz) choy sum, cut into 10 cm (4 inch) lengths
800 g (1 lb 10 oz) Chinese broccoli, cut into 10 cm (4 inch) lengths
¹/₄ cup (60 ml/2 fl oz) kecap manis
¹/₄ cup (60 ml/2 fl oz) soy sauce
1 teaspoon sesame oil
toasted sesame seeds, to garnish

1 Cook the egg noodles in a saucepan of boiling water for 5 minutes, then drain and keep warm.
2 Slice each chicken breast fillet horizontally to give 8 thin flat fillets.
3 Cut the lemon grass into lengths that are about 5 cm (2 inches) longer than the chicken fillets, then cut in half lengthways. Place one piece of lemon grass onto one half of each chicken breast fillet, top with some ginger and lime slices, then top with the other half of the fillet.
4 Pour the stock into a wok and bring to a simmer. Place two of the chicken fillets in a paper-lined bamboo steamer. Place the steamer over the wok and steam over the simmering stock for 12–15 minutes, or until the chicken is tender. Remove the chicken from the steamer, cover and keep

warm. Repeat with the other fillets.
5 Steam the greens in the same way for 3 minutes, or until tender. Bring the stock in the wok to the boil.
6 Whisk together the kecap manis, soy sauce and sesame oil.
7 Divide the noodles among four serving plates and ladle the boiling stock over them. Top with Asian greens and chicken and drizzle with the sauce. Sprinkle with toasted sesame seeds.

NUTRITION PER SERVE
Protein 65 g; Fat 7.5 g; Carbohydrate 37 g;
Dietary Fibre 9 g; Cholesterol 119 mg;
2045 kJ (488 cal)

Cut each chicken breast in half horizontally through the middle.

Top the bottom half of each fillet with lemon grass, ginger and lime.

Steam the lemon grass chicken fillets until cooked and tender.

POACHED COCONUT CHICKEN

Preparation time: 5 minutes +
  10 minutes resting
Total cooking time: 20 minutes
Serves 4

400 ml (13 fl oz) coconut milk
2 tablespoons fish sauce
1¹/₂ tablespoons grated palm sugar
1 tablespoon green peppercorns,
  drained and gently crushed

1 stalk lemon grass, white part only,
  split lengthways and bruised
4 chicken breast fillets
lime wedges, to serve

1 Place the coconut milk, fish sauce, sugar, peppercorns and lemon grass in a large saucepan and cook, stirring, over medium heat for 2 minutes, or until the sugar dissolves. Reduce the heat and keep at a low simmer.
2 Add the chicken fillets and cook for 10–15 minutes, turning halfway. To check if the fillet is cooked, press the

thickest section with your fingertips. The flesh should be springy to touch— if not, cook for 2 minutes. Remove from the heat and rest for 10 minutes.
3 Cut the fillets into thick slices and divide among four plates. (You can remove the lemon grass, if you prefer.) Spoon the liquid over the chicken. Serve with lime wedges.

NUTRITION PER SERVE
Protein 52 g; Fat 25 g; Carbohydrate 11 g;
Dietary Fibre 2 g; Cholesterol 110 mg;
2005 kJ (480 cal)

Cook the poaching liquid until the sugar has dissolved and then keep at a simmer.

Press the thickest section of the chicken with your fingertips.

Cut the chicken into thick slices and serve with the sauce and lime wedges.

181

INDIAN SPICED LAMB

Preparation time: 15 minutes +
  30 minutes marinating
Total cooking time: 20 minutes
Serves 4–6

3 tablespoons oil
2 tablespoons Madras curry powder,
  or to taste
4 lamb backstraps
1 tablespoon brinjal pickle (see
  NOTES)
250 g (8 oz) Greek-style plain yoghurt
350 g (11 oz) couscous
1/2 red capsicum, diced
4 spring onions, sliced

1 Mix together 2 tablespoons oil and
the curry powder. Place the lamb in a
non-metallic dish and brush the curry
oil over it. Cover and marinate for
30 minutes. Preheat the oven to
moderate 180°C (350°F/Gas 4).
2 Place the brinjal pickle and yoghurt
in a bowl and mix together well. Add
2 tablespoons water and set aside.
Heat the remaining oil in a frying pan,
add the lamb and cook for
2–3 minutes on each side to seal.
Transfer to an ovenproof dish and
cook in the oven for 10–12 minutes.
Remove from the oven and rest,
covered, for 5 minutes, then carve
into slices.
3 Meanwhile, place the couscous in a
bowl. Season with salt and cover with
450 ml (14 fl oz) boiling water. Leave
for 5 minutes, or until all the liquid is
absorbed. Fluff the couscous with a
fork to separate the grains. Cool, then

add the capsicum, spring onion and
half the yoghurt mixture. Serve the
lamb slices on a bed of couscous.
Drizzle the remaining yoghurt mixture
over the top.

NUTRITION PER SERVE (6)
Protein 30 g; Fat 16 g; Carbohydrate 45 g;
Dietary Fibre 3.5 g; Cholesterol 73 mg;
1881 kJ (450 cal)

NOTES: Brinjal pickle is made from
eggplant and is widely available. If
you can't find it, try mango chutney.

  With the couscous you can use
orange juice instead of water, and nuts
and sultanas instead of capsicums and
onions. If you are using a non-stick
frying pan to cook the lamb, no
oil is required as there is oil in
the marinade.

Put the lamb in a non-metallic dish and brush
with the curry oil.

Mix together the brinjal pickle and yoghurt with a
little water.

Add the capsicum, spring onion and half the
yoghurt to the couscous.

HOISIN BARBECUED CHICKEN

Preparation time: 10 minutes +
  2 hours marinating
Total cooking time: 25 minutes
Serves 4–6

2 cloves garlic, finely chopped
1/4 cup (60 ml/2 fl oz) hoisin sauce
3 teaspoons light soy sauce
3 teaspoons honey
1 teaspoon sesame oil
2 tablespoons tomato sauce or sweet
  chilli sauce
2 spring onions, finely sliced
1.5 kg (3 lb) chicken wings

1 To make the marinade, mix together the garlic, hoisin sauce, soy, honey, sesame oil, tomato sauce and spring onion. Pour over the chicken wings, cover and marinate in the refrigerator for at least 2 hours.
2 Cook the chicken on a barbecue grill or chargrill pan, turning once, for 20–25 minutes, or until cooked and golden brown. Baste with the marinade during cooking. Heat any remaining marinade in a pan until boiling and serve as a sauce.

NUTRITION PER SERVE (6)
Protein 26 g; Fat 8.5 g; Carbohydrate 9 g;
Dietary Fibre 1.5 g; Cholesterol 111 mg;
916 kJ (219 cal)

NOTE: The chicken can also be baked in a moderate 180°C (350°F/Gas 4) oven for 30 minutes. Turn halfway through cooking.

Mix together the garlic, hoisin sauce, soy, honey, sesame oil, tomato sauce and spring onion.

Pour the marinade over the chicken wings and leave in the fridge for at least 2 hours.

Cook the chicken wings on a barbecue grill or on a chargrill plate.

THAI DRUMSTICKS

Preparation time: 10 minutes +
    2 hours marinating
Total cooking time: 1 hour
Serves 6

3 tablespoons red curry paste
1 cup (250 ml/8 fl oz) coconut milk
2 tablespoons lime juice
4 tablespoons finely chopped fresh
    coriander leaves
12 chicken drumsticks, scored
2 bunches (1 kg/2 lb) baby bok choy
2 tablespoons soy sauce
1 tablespoon oil

1 Mix together the curry paste, coconut milk, lime juice and coriander. Place the chicken in a non-metallic dish and pour on the marinade. Cover and leave in the fridge for at least 2 hours.

2 Cook the chicken on a barbecue or chargrill plate for 50–60 minutes, or until cooked through.

3 Trim the bok choy and combine with the soy sauce and oil, then cook on the barbecue or in a wok for 3–4 minutes, or until just wilted. Serve the chicken on a bed of bok choy.

NUTRITION PER SERVE
Protein 30 g; Fat 20 g; Carbohydrate 3 g; Dietary Fibre 5 g; Cholesterol 105 mg; 1250 kJ (300 cal)

Put the chicken in a non-metallic dish with the marinade and leave for 2 hours.

Cook the chicken on a barbecue grill or chargrill plate for an hour, or until cooked through.

Cook the bok choy, soy sauce and oil in a wok or on the barbecue until wilted.

CHINESE BRAISED CHICKEN

Preparation time: 10 minutes
Total cooking time: 1 hour
Serves 4–6

1 cup (250 ml/8 fl oz) soy sauce
1 cinnamon stick
1/3 cup (90 g/3 oz) sugar
1/3 cup (80 ml/2³/4 fl oz) balsamic
    vinegar
2.5 cm (1 inch) piece of fresh ginger,
    thinly sliced
4 garlic cloves
1/4 teaspoon chilli flakes

1.5 kg (3 lb) chicken pieces on the
    bone (skin removed)
mixed Asian greens, to serve
1 tablespoon toasted sesame seeds,
    to garnish

1 Combine 1 litre water with the soy sauce, cinnamon, sugar, vinegar, ginger, garlic and chilli flakes in a saucepan. Bring to the boil, then reduce the heat and simmer for 5 minutes. Add the chicken and simmer, covered, for 50 minutes, or until cooked through. Serve on a bed of steamed greens, drizzled with the poaching liquid and sprinkled with toasted sesame seeds.

NUTRITION PER SERVE (6)
Protein 45 g; Fat 10 g; Carbohydrate 16 g;
Dietary Fibre 0.5 g; Cholesterol 140 mg;
1420 kJ (339 cal)

Poach the chicken in the spiced liquid for 50 minutes or until it is cooked through.

185

LIME STEAMED CHICKEN

Preparation time: 15 minutes
Total cooking time: 15 minutes
Serves 4

2 limes, thinly sliced
4 chicken breast fillets
1 bunch (500 g/1 lb) bok choy
1 bunch (500 g/1 lb) choy sum
1 teaspoon sesame oil
1 tablespoon peanut oil
1/2 cup (125 ml/4 fl oz) oyster sauce
1/3 cup (80 ml/2 3/4 fl oz) lime juice

1 Line the base of a bamboo steamer with the lime and place the chicken on top. Season. Place over a wok with a little water in the base, cover and steam for 8–10 minutes, or until the chicken is cooked through. Cover the chicken and keep warm. Remove the water from the wok.
2 Wash and trim the greens. Heat the oils in the wok and cook the greens for 2–3 minutes, or until just wilted.
3 Mix together the oyster sauce and lime juice and pour over the greens. Serve the chicken on top of the greens with some extra lime slices.

NUTRITION PER SERVE
Protein 60 g; Fat 12 g; Carbohydrate 10 g; Dietary Fibre 4.5 g; Cholesterol 120 mg; 1665 kJ (398 cal)

NOTE: The Asian green vegetables used in this recipe, bok choy and choy sum, can be replaced by any green vegetables, such as broccoli, snow peas, or English spinach.

Line the base of the steamer with lime slices and then arrange the chicken on top.

Heat the oils in a wok and stir-fry the Asian greens until they are just wilted.

Mix together the oyster sauce and lime juice and pour over the greens.

BEEF TERIYAKI WITH CUCUMBER SALAD

Preparation time: 20 minutes +
   30 minutes refrigeration
Total cooking time: 20 minutes
Serves 4

4 scotch fillet steaks
1/3 cup (80 ml/2³/4 fl oz) soy sauce
2 tablespoons mirin
1 tablespoon sake (optional)
1 clove garlic, crushed
1 teaspoon grated fresh ginger
1 teaspoon sugar
1 teaspoon toasted sesame seeds

CUCUMBER SALAD
1 large Lebanese cucumber, peeled,
   seeded and diced
1/2 red capsicum, diced
2 spring onions, sliced thinly
2 teaspoons sugar
1 tablespoon rice wine vinegar

1 Put the steaks in a non-metallic dish. Combine the soy, mirin, sake, garlic and ginger and pour over the steaks. Cover with plastic wrap and refrigerate for at least 30 minutes.
2 Put the cucumber, capsicum and spring onion in a bowl. Put the sugar, rice wine vinegar and 1/4 cup (60 ml/ 2 fl oz) water in a pan and stir over heat until the sugar dissolves. Increase the heat and simmer rapidly for 3–4 minutes, or until thickened. Pour over the cucumber salad, stir well and leave to cool completely.
3 Brush a chargrill or barbecue grill plate with oil and heat until very hot. Drain the steaks and reserve the marinade. Cook for 3–4 minutes on each side or to your taste. Rest the meat for 5–10 minutes before slicing.
4 Put the sugar and reserved marinade in a pan and heat, stirring, until the sugar has dissolved. Bring to the boil, then simmer for 2–3 minutes.
5 Slice each steak into strips and serve with the marinade, cucumber salad and a sprinkling of sesame seeds.

NUTRITION PER SERVE
Protein 23 g; Fat 5 g; Carbohydrate 6 g;
Dietary Fibre 1 g; Cholesterol 67 mg;
720 kJ (170 cal)

Combine the cucumber, capsicum and spring onion with the dressing.

Cook the steaks for 3–4 minutes on each side or until they are cooked to your taste.

STEAMED CHICKEN WITH SOY MUSHROOM SAUCE

Preparation time: 10 minutes +
   20 minutes soaking +
   1 hour marinating
Total cooking time: 20 minutes
Serves 4

8–10 g (1/4–1/2 oz) dried Chinese
   mushrooms
2 tablespoons light soy sauce
2 tablespoons rice wine
1/2 teaspoon sesame oil
1 tablespoon finely sliced fresh ginger
4 chicken breast fillets
450 g (14 oz) bok choy, ends removed
   and cut lengthways into quarters
1/2 cup (125 ml/4 fl oz) chicken stock
1 tablespoon cornflour

1 Soak the dried mushrooms in
1/4 cup (60 ml/2 fl oz) boiling water for
20 minutes. Drain and reserve the
liquid. Discard the tough stalks and
slice the caps thinly.
2 Combine the soy sauce, rice wine,
sesame oil and ginger in a non-
metallic dish. Add the chicken and
turn to coat. Cover and marinate for at
least 1 hour.
3 Line a bamboo steamer with baking
paper. Place the chicken on top,
reserving the marinade. Bring water to
the boil in a wok, then place the
steamer over the wok. Cover and
steam the chicken for 6 minutes, then
turn over and steam for a further
6 minutes. Place the bok choy on top
of the chicken and steam for
2–3 minutes.
4 Meanwhile, place the reserved
marinade, mushrooms and their
soaking liquid in a small saucepan and
bring to the boil. Add enough stock to

the cornflour in a small bowl to make
a smooth paste. Add the cornflour
paste and remaining stock to the pan
and stir for 2 minutes over medium
heat, or until the sauce thickens.
5 Place some bok choy and a chicken
fillet on each plate, then pour on a
little sauce to serve.

NUTRITION PER SERVE
Protein 46 g; Fat 6 g; Carbohydrate 5 g;
Dietary Fibre 2 g; Cholesterol 95 mg;
1085 kJ (260 cal)

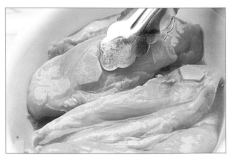

Turn the chicken fillets until they are well coated in
the marinade.

Place the lengths of bok choy in the bamboo
steamer on top of the chicken.

Stir the marinating liquid and chicken stock
mixture until the sauce thickens.

THAI-STYLE STEAMED FISH WITH SPICY TOMATO SAUCE

Preparation time: 25 minutes +
  30 minutes standing
Total cooking time: 40 minutes
Serves 4

6 cloves garlic
3 red Asian shallots
3 tomatoes
2 fresh long red chillies
1½ tablespoons lime juice
3½ tablespoons fish sauce
2 cloves garlic, extra
4 coriander roots
6 whole black peppercorns
4 snapper, fins trimmed, cleaned and
  gutted
1 cup (30 g/1 oz) fresh coriander
  leaves

1 Chargrill the skins of the garlic, shallots, tomatoes and chillies over an open gas flame, using a pair of metal tongs, or roast in a preheated very hot (230°C/450°F/Gas 8) oven for 15–20 minutes. When cool enough to handle, peel and discard the skins of all the vegetables. Roughly chop the vegetables and combine with the lime juice and 2 tablespoons of the fish sauce. Leave for 30 minutes.
2 Place the extra garlic, coriander roots and peppercorns in a mortar and pestle and grind to a smooth paste. Add the remaining fish sauce and stir to combine. Score each fish on both sides in a crisscross pattern. Rub the paste on both sides.
3 Line the bottom of a large bamboo steamer with baking paper. Place the fish on the paper and place the steamer over a wok of boiling water. Cover and steam for 15–20 minutes, or until the flesh flakes easily when tested with a fork. Remove the steamer from the wok and slide the fish onto a serving plate. Spoon the tomato sauce over the fish and sprinkle with fresh coriander leaves.

NUTRITION PER SERVE
Protein 34 g; Fat 3 g; Carbohydrate 4 g;
Dietary Fibre 3 g; Cholesterol 92 mg;
750 kJ (180 cal)

Once the vegetables have been chargrilled, peel off and discard the skins.

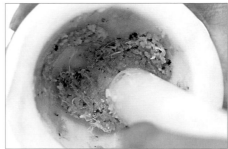

Grind the garlic, coriander roots and peppercorns until smooth.

CRUMBED FISH WITH WASABI CREAM

Preparation time: 25 minutes +
  15 minutes refrigeration
Total cooking time: 20 minutes
Serves 4

3/4 cup (60 g/2 oz) fresh breadcrumbs
3/4 cup (25 g/3/4 oz) cornflakes
1 sheet nori, roughly torn
1/4 teaspoon paprika
4 x 150 g (5 oz) pieces firm white fish
  fillets
plain flour, for dusting
1 egg white
1 tablespoon skim milk
1 spring onion, thinly sliced

WASABI CREAM
1/2 cup (125 g/4 oz) low-fat plain
  yoghurt
1 teaspoon wasabi (see NOTE)
1 tablespoon mayonnaise
1 teaspoon lime juice

1 Preheat the oven to moderate 180°C
(350°F/Gas 4). Combine the crumbs,
cornflakes, nori and paprika in a food
processor and mix until the nori is
finely chopped.
2 Dust the fish lightly with plain flour,
dip into the combined egg white and
milk, then into the breadcrumb
mixture. Press the crumb mixture on
firmly, then refrigerate for 15 minutes.
3 Line a baking tray with non-stick
baking paper and put the fish on the
paper. Bake for 15–20 minutes, or until

the fish flakes easily when tested.
4 To make the wasabi cream, mix
together all the ingredients. Serve a
spoonful on top of the fish and
sprinkle with spring onion.

NUTRITION PER SERVE
Protein 35 g; Fat 6 g; Carbohydrate 25 g;
Dietary Fibre 1 g; Cholesterol 105 mg;
1270 kJ (305 cal)

NOTE: Wasabi paste (a pungent paste,
also known as Japanese horseradish)
and nori (sheets of paper-thin dried
seaweed) are both available from
Japanese food stores.

Process the breadcrumbs, cornflakes, nori and
paprika together.

Dust the fish with flour, dip in the egg and milk,
then press in the breadcrumbs.

Thoroughly mix together all the ingredients for the
wasabi cream.

STEAMED TROUT WITH GINGER AND CORIANDER

Preparation time: 20 minutes
Total cooking time: 30 minutes
Serves 2

2 whole rainbow trout, cleaned and
    scaled
2 limes, thinly sliced
5 cm (2 inch) piece of fresh ginger, cut
    into matchsticks
1/4 cup (60 g/2 oz) caster sugar
1/4 cup (60 ml/2 fl oz) lime juice
rind of 1 lime, cut into thin strips
1/3 cup (10 g/1/4 oz) fresh coriander
    leaves

1 Preheat the oven to moderate 180°C
(350°F/Gas 4). Fill the fish cavities with
the lime slices and some of the ginger,
then place the fish on a large piece of
lightly greased foil. Wrap the fish
and bake on a baking tray for
20–30 minutes, or until the flesh flakes
easily when tested with a fork.
2 Combine the sugar and lime juice
with 1 cup (250 ml/8 fl oz) water in a
small pan and stir without boiling until
the sugar dissolves. Bring to the boil,
reduce the heat and simmer for
10 minutes, or until syrupy. Stir in the
remaining ginger and lime strips. Put
the fish on a plate. Top with coriander
leaves and pour the hot syrup over it.

NUTRITION PER SERVE
Protein 50 g; Fat 10 g; Carbohydrate 30 g;
Dietary Fibre 1 g; Cholesterol 120 mg;
1715 kJ (410 cal)

NOTE: You can ask the fishmonger to
remove the bones from the fish.

Peel the piece of fresh ginger and cut it into fine,
short matchsticks.

Fill the cavities of the trout with the lime slices and
some of the ginger.

Simmer the sugar in the lime juice and water to
make a hot syrup.

JAPANESE-STYLE SALMON PARCELS

Preparation time: 40 minutes
Total cooking time: 15 minutes
Serves 4

2 teaspoons sesame seeds
4 x 150 g (5 oz) salmon cutlets or
    steaks
2.5 cm (1 inch) piece of fresh ginger
2 celery sticks
4 spring onions
3 tablespoons mirin (see NOTE)
2 tablespoons tamari
1/4 teaspoon dashi granules

1 Cut baking paper into four squares large enough to wrap the salmon steaks. Preheat the oven to very hot 230°C (450°F/Gas 8). Lightly toast the sesame seeds under a grill or in the oven for a few minutes.
2 Wash the salmon and dry with paper towels. Place a salmon cutlet in the centre of each paper square.
3 Cut the ginger into paper-thin slices. Slice the celery and spring onions into short lengths, then lengthways into fine strips. Arrange a bundle of the prepared strips and several slices of ginger on each salmon steak.
4 Combine the mirin, tamari and dashi granules in a small saucepan. Heat gently until the granules dissolve.

Drizzle over each parcel, sprinkle with sesame seeds and carefully wrap the salmon, folding in the sides to seal in all the juices. Arrange the parcels on a baking tray and cook for about 12 minutes, or until tender. (The paper will puff up when the fish is cooked.) Do not overcook or the salmon will dry out. Serve immediately, as standing time can spoil the fish.

NUTRITION PER SERVE
Protein 20 g; Fat 14 g; Carbohydrate 0 g; Dietary Fibre 0.5 g; Cholesterol 85 mg; 935 kJ (225 cal)

NOTE: Mirin, tamari and dashi are all available from Japanese food stores.

Cut the celery sticks into short lengths, then lengthways into thin strips.

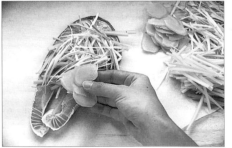

Arrange celery and spring onion strips on the fish and top with ginger slices.

Wrap the salmon in baking paper, folding the sides to seal in the juices.

LEMON GRASS AND CORIANDER FISH

Preparation time: 15 minutes
Total cooking time: 40 minutes
Serves 4

4 x 200 g (6¹/₂ oz) fish cutlets
plain flour, seasoned with salt and
    pepper
2–3 tablespoons peanut oil
2 onions, sliced
2 stalks lemon grass, white part only,
    finely chopped
4 kaffir lime leaves, finely shredded
1 teaspoon ground cumin
1 teaspoon ground coriander
1 teaspoon finely chopped red chilli
3/4 cup (180 ml/6 fl oz) chicken stock
1¹/₂ cups (375 ml/12 fl oz) coconut
    milk
¹/₄ cup (15 g/¹/₂ oz) chopped fresh
    coriander
2 teaspoons fish sauce

1 Preheat the oven to moderate 180°C (350°F/Gas 4). Toss the fish lightly in the flour. Heat half the oil in a large heavy-based frying pan and cook the fish over medium heat until lightly browned on both sides. Transfer to a shallow ovenproof dish.
2 Heat the remaining oil in the pan. Add the onion and lemon grass and cook, stirring, for 5 minutes, or until the onion softens. Add the lime leaves, ground spices and chilli and stir for about 2 minutes, or until fragrant.
3 Add the stock and coconut milk and bring to the boil. Pour over the fish, then cover and bake for 30 minutes, or until tender. Transfer to a plate.
4 Stir the coriander and fish sauce into the remaining sauce and season to taste. Pour over the fish to serve.

NUTRITION PER SERVE
Protein 35 g; Fat 40 g; Carbohydrate 6 g;
Dietary Fibre 1 g; Cholesterol 105 mg;
2040 kJ (490 cal)

NOTE: Kaffir lime leaves are glossy and dark green with double leaves and a floral citrus smell. They are tough and need to be very finely shredded before use. They can also be frozen.

Finely chop the white part of the lemon grass stems and shred the lime leaves.

Heat half the peanut oil and brown the lightly floured fish over medium heat.

Add the lime leaves, ground spices and chilli to the fried onions.

193

Curries

BUTTER CHICKEN

Preparation time: 10 minutes
Total cooking time: 35 minutes
Serves 4–6

2 tablespoons peanut oil
1 kg (2 lb) chicken thigh fillets,
    quartered
60 g (2 oz) butter or ghee
2 teaspoons garam masala
2 teaspoons sweet paprika
2 teaspoons ground coriander
1 tablespoon finely chopped fresh
    ginger
1/4 teaspoon chilli powder
1 cinnamon stick
6 cardamom pods, bruised
350 g (11 oz) puréed tomatoes
1 tablespoon sugar
1/4 cup (60 g/2 oz) plain yoghurt
1/2 cup (125 ml/4 fl oz) cream
1 tablespoon lemon juice

1 Heat a wok until very hot, add
1 tablespoon oil and swirl to coat. Add
half the chicken thigh fillets and stir-fry
for 4 minutes, or until browned.
Remove. Add extra oil, as needed, and
cook the remaining chicken. Remove.
2 Reduce the heat, add the butter to
the wok and melt. Add the garam
masala, sweet paprika, coriander,
ginger, chilli powder, cinnamon stick
and cardamom pods and stir-fry for
1 minute, or until fragrant. Return the
chicken to the wok and mix to coat in
the spices.
3 Add the tomato and sugar, and
simmer, stirring, for 15 minutes, or
until the chicken is tender and the
sauce has thickened.
4 Add the yoghurt, cream and juice
and simmer for 5 minutes, or until the
sauce has thickened slightly. Serve
with rice or poppadoms.

NUTRITION PER SERVE (6)
Protein 40 g; Fat 28 g; Carbohydrate 6 g;
Dietary Fibre 1 g; Cholesterol 140 mg;
1790 kJ (427 cal)

Stir-fry the chicken pieces in two batches until
they are browned.

Simmer until the chicken is tender and the sauce
has thickened.

THAI CHICKEN AND POTATO CURRY

Preparation time: 20 minutes
Total cooking time: 30 minutes
Serves 4–6

2 tablespoons oil
1 onion, chopped
1–2 tablespoons Thai yellow curry
    paste (see NOTES)
1/4 teaspoon ground turmeric
1²/₃ cups (410 ml/13 fl oz) coconut
    milk
300 g (10 oz) potatoes, peeled and
    cubed
250 g (8 oz) orange sweet potatoes,
    peeled and cubed
250 g (8 oz) chicken thigh fillets, diced
2 kaffir lime leaves (see NOTES)
2 teaspoons fish sauce
2 teaspoons soft brown sugar
1 tablespoon lime juice
1 teaspoon lime rind
1/3 cup (10 g/1/4 oz) fresh coriander
    leaves
1/3 cup (60 g/2 oz) roasted peanuts,
    roughly chopped

1 Heat the oil in a large heavy-based pan or wok and cook the onion until softened. Add the curry paste and turmeric and stir for 1 minute, or until aromatic.
2 Stir in the coconut milk and 1 cup (250 ml/8 fl oz) of water and bring to the boil. Reduce the heat and add the potato, sweet potato, chicken and kaffir lime leaves. Simmer for 15–20 minutes, or until the vegetables are tender and the chicken is cooked through.
3 Stir in the fish sauce, sugar, lime juice, rind and coriander leaves. Garnish with the peanuts to serve.

NUTRITION PER SERVE (6)
Protein 10 g; Fat 35 g; Carbohydrate 15 g;
Dietary Fibre 3 g; Cholesterol 40 mg;
1805 kJ (430 cal)

NOTES: Thai yellow curry paste is not as common as the red or green but is available from most Asian food stores.
    Kaffir lime leaves are now available in most supermarkets.

Peel the orange sweet potato and chop into bite-sized pieces.

When the onion has softened, stir in the curry paste and turmeric.

Reduce the heat and add the potato, sweet potato, chicken and lime leaves.

MADRAS BEEF CURRY

Preparation time: 20 minutes
Total cooking time: 1 hour 45 minutes
Serves 6

1 tablespoon vegetable oil
2 onions, finely chopped
3 cloves garlic, finely chopped
1 tablespoon grated fresh ginger
4 tablespoons madras curry paste
1 kg (2 lb) chuck steak, diced
1/4 cup (60 g/2 oz) tomato paste
1 cup (250 ml/8 fl oz) beef stock
6 new potatoes, halved
1 cup (150 g/5 oz) frozen peas

1 Preheat the oven to moderate 180°C (350°F/Gas 4). Heat the oil in a large heavy-based 3 litre flameproof casserole. Cook the onion over medium heat for 4–5 minutes. Add the garlic and ginger and cook, stirring, for 5 minutes, or until the onion is lightly golden, taking care not to burn it.
2 Add the curry paste and cook, stirring, for 2 minutes, or until fragrant. Increase the heat to high, add the meat and stir constantly for 2–3 minutes, or until the meat is well coated. Add the tomato paste and stock and stir well.
3 Bake, covered, for 50 minutes, stirring 2–3 times during cooking, and add a little water if necessary. Reduce the oven to warm 160°C (315°F/Gas 2–3). Add the potato and cook for 30 minutes, then add the peas and cook for another 10 minutes, or until the potato is tender.

NUTRITION PER SERVE
Protein 40 g; Fat 13 g; Carbohydrate 15 g;
Dietary Fibre 5.5 g; Cholesterol 112 mg;
1410 kJ (335 Cal)

Fry the onion, garlic and ginger until the onion is lightly golden.

Stir the cubes of steak into the curry paste until well coated.

Stir in the potato halves and cook for 30 minutes.

197

BOMBAY LAMB CURRY

Preparation time: 25 minutes
Total cooking time: 1 hour 25 minutes
Serves 4–6

1.5 kg (3 lb) leg lamb, boned (ask your
    butcher to do this)
2 tablespoons ghee or oil
2 onions, finely chopped
2 cloves garlic, crushed
2 small green chillies, finely chopped
5 cm (2 inch) piece of fresh ginger,
    grated
1½ teaspoons turmeric
2 teaspoons ground cumin
3 teaspoons ground coriander
½–1 teaspoon chilli powder
1–1½ teaspoons salt
425 g (14 oz) can crushed tomatoes
2 tablespoons coconut cream

1 Cut the meat into cubes, removing
any skin and fat. You will have about
1 kg (2 lb) meat remaining. Heat the
ghee or oil in a large heavy-based
frying pan. Add the onion and cook,
stirring frequently, over medium-high
heat for 10 minutes until golden
brown. Add the garlic, chillies and
ginger and stir for a further 2 minutes,
taking care not to burn them.
2 Mix together the turmeric, cumin,
coriander and chilli powder. Stir to a
smooth paste with 2 tablespoons water
and add to the frying pan. Stir for
2 minutes, taking care not to burn.
3 Add the meat a handful at a time,
stirring well to coat with spices. It is
important to make sure all the meat is
well-coated and browned.
4 Add the salt to taste and stir in the
tomatoes. Bring to the boil, cover and
reduce the heat to low. Simmer for
30 minutes and then stir in the coconut
cream. Simmer for another 30 minutes,
or until the lamb is tender.

NUTRITION PER SERVE (6)
Protein 58 g; Fat 13 g; Carbohydrate 5 g;
Dietary Fibre 1.5 g; Cholesterol 165 mg;
1565 kJ (375 cal)

STORAGE: Keep covered and
refrigerated for up to 3 days. The
flavour of curry improves if kept for at
least a day.

Cut the meat into bite-sized chunks, removing
any fat as you cut.

Once the onion is golden brown, stir in the garlic,
chilli and ginger.

Blend the ground spices to a smooth paste with
a little water.

Add the meat a handful at a time to make sure it
is thoroughly coated with the spices.

KASHMIR LAMB WITH SPINACH

Preparation time: 20 minutes
Total cooking time: 1 hour 30 minutes
Serves 4

2 tablespoons oil
750 g (1¹/₂ lb) diced leg of lamb
2 large onions, chopped
3 cloves garlic, crushed
5 cm (2 inch) piece of fresh ginger,
    grated
2 teaspoons ground cumin
2 teaspoons ground coriander
2 teaspoons turmeric
¹/₄ teaspoon ground cardamom

¹/₄ teaspoon ground cloves
3 bay leaves
1¹/₂ cups (375 ml/12 fl oz) chicken
    stock
¹/₂ cup (125 ml/4 fl oz) cream
2 bunches English spinach leaves,
    washed and chopped

1 Heat the oil in a heavy-based pan and brown the lamb in batches. Remove from the pan. Add the onions, garlic and ginger and cook for 3 minutes, stirring regularly. Add the cumin, coriander, turmeric, cardamom and cloves and cook, stirring, for 1–2 minutes or until fragrant. Return the lamb to the pan with any juices. Add the bay leaves and stock.

2 Bring to the boil and then reduce the heat, stir well, cover and simmer for 35 minutes. Add the cream and cook, covered, for a further 20 minutes or until the lamb is very tender.
3 Add the spinach and cook until the spinach has softened. Season to taste before serving.

NUTRITION PER SERVE
Protein 45 g; Fat 25 g; Carbohydrate 3 g;
Dietary Fibre 2 g; Cholesterol 165 mg;
1820 kJ (435 cal)

STORAGE: Curry is best cooked a day in advance and refrigerated. Do not add the spinach until reheating.

Return the browned lamb to the pan and add the bay leaves.

Stir in the cream and simmer, covered, until the lamb is very tender.

It will only take a few minutes for the spinach to soften and reduce.

199

THAI GREEN CHICKEN CURRY

Preparation time: 40 minutes
Total cooking time: 30 minutes
Serves 4–6

500 ml (16 fl oz) coconut cream, do not shake the can (see NOTE)
4 tablespoons Thai green curry paste
2 tablespoons grated palm sugar
2 tablespoons fish sauce
4 kaffir lime leaves, finely shredded
1 kg (2 lb) chicken thigh or breast fillets, cut into thick strips
200 g (6¹/₂ oz) bamboo shoots, cut into thick strips
100 g (3¹/₂ oz) snake beans, cut into short lengths
¹/₂ cup (15 g/¹/₂ oz) fresh Thai basil leaves

1 Open the can of coconut cream and lift off the thick cream from the top, you should have about ¹/₂ cup (125 ml/4 fl oz). Put in a wok or saucepan and bring to the boil. Add the curry paste, then reduce the heat and simmer for 15 minutes, or until fragrant and the oil starts to separate from the cream. Add the palm sugar, fish sauce and kaffir lime leaves.
2 Stir in the remaining coconut cream and the chicken, bamboo shoots and beans and simmer for 15 minutes, or until the chicken is tender. Stir in the Thai basil just before serving.

NUTRITION PER SERVE (6)
Protein 40 g; Fat 22 g; Carbohydrate 11 g;
Dietary Fibre 2 g; Cholesterol 85 mg;
1698 kJ (405 cal)

NOTE: Do not shake the can because good-quality coconut cream has a layer of very thick cream at the top. This has a higher fat content, which causes it to split or separate more readily than the rest of the coconut cream or milk.

Lift off the thick cream from the top of the can of coconut cream.

Simmer the coconut cream and curry paste until the oil separates.

THAI RED VEGETABLE CURRY

Preparation time: 10 minutes
Total cooking time: 25 minutes
Serves 4

1 tablespoon peanut oil
250 g (8 oz) broccoli florets, quartered
250 g (8 oz) cauliflower florets, quartered
500 g (1 lb) orange sweet potato, cut into even-size chunks
2 tablespoons red curry paste
500 ml (16 fl oz) coconut milk
1 tablespoon lime juice
1 tablespoon fish sauce, optional
3 tablespoons chopped fresh coriander

1 Heat a wok over high heat, add the oil and swirl to coat the sides. Add the broccoli, cauliflower and sweet potato in batches and stir-fry for 3 minutes. Add 1/4 cup (60 ml/2 fl oz) water and cover. Reduce the heat to low for 8–10 minutes to steam the vegetables.
2 Add the curry paste and cook over medium heat for 30 seconds or until fragrant. Stir in the coconut milk and simmer for 8 minutes or until slightly thickened. Add the lime juice, fish sauce and coriander.

NUTRITION PER SERVE
Protein 22 g; Fat 63 g; Carbohydrate 40 g; Dietary Fibre 18 g; Cholesterol 0.5 mg; 3434 kJ (820 cal)

Steam the vegetables in the wok until they are just cooked but still crunchy.

Add the coconut milk to the wok and simmer until slightly thickened.

LAMB KOFTA CURRY

Preparation time: 25 minutes
Total cooking time: 35 minutes
Serves 4

500 g (1 lb) minced lean lamb
1 onion, finely chopped
1 clove garlic, finely chopped
1 teaspoon grated fresh ginger
1 small fresh chilli, finely chopped
1 teaspoon garam masala
1 teaspoon ground coriander
1/4 cup (45 g/1 1/2 oz) ground almonds
2 tablespoons chopped fresh
   coriander leaves

SAUCE
2 teaspoons oil
1 onion, finely chopped
3 tablespoons Korma curry paste
400 g (13 oz) can chopped tomatoes
1/2 cup (125 g/4 oz) low-fat yoghurt
1 teaspoon lemon juice

1 Combine the lamb, onion, garlic, ginger, chilli, garam masala, ground coriander, ground almonds and 1 teaspoon salt in a bowl. Shape into walnut-sized balls with your hands.
2 Heat a large non-stick frying pan and cook the koftas in batches until brown on both sides—they don't have to be cooked all the way through.
3 To make the sauce, heat the oil in a saucepan over low heat. Add the onion and cook for 6–8 minutes, or until soft and golden. Add the curry paste and cook until fragrant. Add the tomatoes and simmer for 5 minutes. Stir in the yoghurt a tablespoon at a time and lemon juice.
4 Put the koftas in the tomato sauce. Cook, covered, over low heat for 20 minutes. Garnish with coriander.

NUTRITION PER SERVE
Protein 32 g; Fat 23 g; Carbohydrate 10 g;
Dietary Fibre 5 g; Cholesterol 88 mg;
1575 kJ (375 cal)

Roll the lamb mixture into walnut-sized balls with your hands.

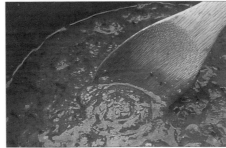

Add the chopped tomatoes and simmer for 5 minutes.

Add the koftas to the tomato sauce and cook over low heat for 20 minutes.

BEEF AND PINEAPPLE CURRY

Preparation time: 10 minutes
Total cooking time: 12 minutes
Serves 4

2 tablespoons peanut oil
500 g (1 lb) rump steak, thinly sliced
    across the grain
2 tablespoons Panang curry paste
2 onions, cut into thin wedges
2 cloves garlic, crushed
500 ml (16 fl oz) can coconut milk
8 kaffir lime leaves

2 cups (320 g/11 oz) chopped fresh
    pineapple
2 teaspoons soft brown sugar
2 tablespoons lime juice
1 tablespoon fish sauce
3 tablespoons chopped fresh
    coriander leaves

1 Heat a wok over high heat, add half
the oil and swirl to coat the sides. Add
the beef in batches and stir-fry for
2 minutes, or until browned. Remove.
2 Heat the remaining oil in the wok
over high heat, add the curry paste
and cook for 1 minute, or until
fragrant. Add the onion and garlic and

cook for 1–2 minutes, or until the
onion is soft.
3 Return the beef to the wok, add the
coconut milk, lime leaves and
pineapple and bring to the boil, then
reduce the heat and simmer for
5 minutes, or until the beef is just
cooked. Stir in the remaining
ingredients just before serving.

NUTRITION PER SERVE
Protein 47 g; Fat 53 g; Carbohydrate 23 g;
Dietary Fibre 7 g; Cholesterol 118 mg;
3137 kJ (749 cal)

Stir-fry the beef in batches over high heat until it is
all browned.

Add the onion and garlic to the wok and cook
until the onion is soft.

Stir in the coconut milk, lime leaves and
pineapple and simmer for 5 minutes.

PRAWN AND COCONUT CURRY

Preparation time: 30 minutes
Total cooking time: 20 minutes
Serves 4

1 onion, chopped
2 cloves garlic, crushed
1 stalk lemon grass, white part only,
    finely chopped
1/2 teaspoon sambal oelek
2 teaspoons garam masala
4 kaffir lime leaves, finely shredded
3 tablespoons chopped fresh
    coriander stems

1 tablespoon peanut oil
1 cup (250 ml/8 fl oz) chicken stock
400 ml (13 fl oz) coconut milk
1 kg (2 lb) raw prawns, peeled and
    deveined (see VARIATION)
1 tablespoon fish sauce
3 tablespoons fresh coriander leaves

1 For the curry paste, mix the onion, garlic, lemon grass, sambal oelek, garam masala, kaffir lime leaves, chopped coriander stems and 2 tablespoons water in a food processor until smooth.
2 Heat the oil in a saucepan, add the curry paste and cook for 2–3 minutes, or until fragrant. Stir in the stock and

coconut milk, bring to the boil, then reduce the heat and simmer for 10 minutes, or until slightly thickened.
3 Add the prawns and cook for 3–5 minutes, or until cooked through. Stir in the fish sauce. Sprinkle with fresh coriander leaves to serve.

NUTRITION PER SERVE
Protein 39 g; Fat 25.5 g; Carbohydrate 6 g;
Dietary Fibre 1.5 g; Cholesterol 261 mg;
1650 kJ (395 cal)

VARIATION: Instead of prawns, you can use bite-sized pieces of boneless ling or gemfish fillets. Cook for 3–5 minutes, or until cooked through.

Cut the kaffir lime leaves into fine shreds with a sharp knife.

Process the curry paste ingredients in a processor or blender until smooth.

Gently simmer the sauce over low heat until slightly thickened.

THAI GREEN FISH CURRY

Preparation time: 15 minutes
Total cooking time: 15 minutes
Serves 4

1 tablespoon peanut oil
1 onion, chopped
1¹/₂ tablespoons Thai green curry
  paste
1¹/₂ cups (375 ml/12 fl oz) coconut
  milk

750 g (1¹/₂ lb) boneless firm white fish
  fillets, cut into bite-sized pieces
3 kaffir lime leaves
1 tablespoon fish sauce
2 teaspoons grated palm sugar
2 tablespoons lime juice
1 long green chilli, finely sliced

1 Heat a wok until very hot, add the
oil and swirl to coat. Add the onion
and stir-fry for 2 minutes, or until soft.
Add the curry paste and stir-fry for
1–2 minutes, or until fragrant. Stir in
the coconut milk and bring to the boil.
2 Add the fish and lime leaves to the
wok, reduce the heat and simmer,
stirring occasionally, for 8–10 minutes,
or until the fish is cooked through.
3 Stir in the fish sauce, palm sugar
and lime juice. Scatter the chilli slices
over the curry before serving.

NUTRITION PER SERVE
Protein 39 g; Fat 29 g; Carbohydrate 4.5 g;
Dietary Fibre 1 g; Cholesterol 125 mg;
1820 kJ (435 cal)

To prevent skin irritation, wear rubber gloves
when slicing the chilli.

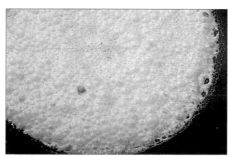

Heat the coconut milk to boiling point before
adding the fish.

Gently simmer the fish pieces, stirring
occasionally, until cooked through.

MALAYSIAN FISH CURRY

Preparation time: 25 minutes
Total cooking time: 25 minutes
Serves 4

5 cm (2 inch) piece of fresh ginger
3–6 medium red chillies
1 onion, chopped
4 cloves garlic, chopped
3 stalks lemon grass, white part only, sliced
2 teaspoons shrimp paste
1/4 cup (60 ml/2 fl oz) oil
1 tablespoon fish curry powder (see NOTE)
1 cup (250 ml/8 fl oz) coconut milk

1 tablespoon tamarind concentrate
1 tablespoon kecap manis
500 g (1 lb) firm white skinless fish fillets, cut into cubes
2 ripe tomatoes, chopped
1 tablespoon lemon juice

1 Slice the ginger and mix in a small food processor with the chillies, onion, garlic, lemon grass and shrimp paste until roughly chopped. Add 2 tablespoons of the oil and process until a paste forms, regularly scraping the side of the bowl with a spatula.
2 Heat the remaining oil in a wok or deep, heavy-based frying pan and add the paste. Cook for 3–4 minutes over low heat, stirring constantly, until

fragrant. Add the curry powder and stir for 2 minutes. Add the coconut milk, tamarind, kecap manis and 1 cup (250 ml/8 fl oz) water. Bring to the boil, stirring occasionally, then reduce the heat and simmer for 10 minutes.
3 Add the fish, tomato and lemon juice. Season, to taste, then simmer for 5 minutes, or until the fish is just cooked (it will flake easily).

NUTRITION PER SERVE
Protein 30 g; Fat 31 g; Carbohydrate 11 g;
Dietary Fibre 4 g; Cholesterol 89 mg;
1810 kJ (430 cal)

NOTE: Fish curry powder blend is available from speciality stores.

Add 2 tablespoons of oil to the chilli mixture and process to a paste.

Add the curry powder to the wok and stir for 2 minutes.

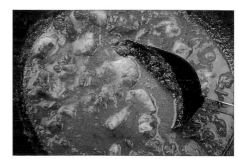
Add the fish, tomato and lemon juice to the wok and simmer until the fish is cooked.

THAI PRAWN CURRY

Preparation time: 30 minutes
Total cooking time: 10 minutes
Serves 4

5 cm (2 inch) piece of fresh galangal
1 small onion, roughly chopped
3 cloves garlic
4 dried long red chillies
4 whole black peppercorns
2 tablespoons chopped lemon grass, white part only
1 tablespoon chopped fresh coriander root
2 teaspoons grated lime rind

2 teaspoons cumin seeds
1 teaspoon sweet paprika
1 teaspoon ground coriander
3 tablespoons oil
1–2 tablespoons fish sauce
2 kaffir lime leaves
2 cups (500 ml/16 fl oz) coconut cream
1 kg (2 lb) raw prawns, peeled and deveined

1 Peel the galangal and thinly slice. Mix the onion, garlic, chillies, peppercorns, lemon grass, coriander root, lime rind, cumin seeds, paprika, coriander, 2 tablespoons oil and 1/2 teaspoon salt in a food processor

until a smooth paste forms.
2 Heat the remaining oil in a frying pan. Add half the curry paste and stir over medium heat for 2 minutes. (Leftover curry paste can be kept in the refrigerator for up to 2 weeks.) Stir in the fish sauce, galangal, kaffir lime leaves and coconut cream.
3 Add the prawns to the pan and simmer for 5 minutes, or until the prawns are cooked and the sauce has thickened slightly.

NUTRITION PER SERVE
Protein 42 g; Fat 40 g; Carbohydrate 9 g; Dietary Fibre 4 g; Cholesterol 280 mg; 2310 kJ (550 cal)

Add half the curry paste to the pan and stir over medium heat for 2 minutes.

Add the prawns to the pan and simmer until cooked through.

CHICKEN DUMPLINGS IN GREEN CURRY

Preparation time: 25 minutes +
  2–3 hours refrigeration
Total cooking time: 35 minutes
Serves 4

500 g (1 lb) chicken mince
3 spring onions, finely chopped
2 tablespoons small fresh coriander
  leaves
1 stalk lemon grass, white part only,
  finely sliced
3 tablespoons fish sauce
1 teaspoon chicken stock powder
1¹/2 cups (280 g/9 oz) cooked jasmine
  rice

1 egg plus 1 egg white
2 teaspoons oil
2 tablespoons Thai green curry paste
2 x 400 ml (13 fl oz) cans coconut milk
4 fresh kaffir lime leaves
¹/2 cup (30 g/1 oz) fresh basil leaves
1 tablespoon lemon juice

1 Mix together the chicken mince, spring onion, coriander leaves, lemon grass, 2 tablespoons of the fish sauce, stock powder and some pepper. Add the rice and mix well with your hands.
2 In a separate bowl, beat the egg and egg white with electric beaters until thick and creamy and then fold into the chicken mixture. With lightly floured hands, roll tablespoons of the mixture into balls. Place on a tray,

cover and refrigerate for 2–3 hours, or until firm.
3 Heat the oil in a large frying pan, add the green curry paste and stir over medium heat for 1 minute. Gradually stir in the coconut milk, then reduce the heat to simmer. Add the lime leaves and chicken dumplings to the sauce; cover and simmer for 25–30 minutes, stirring occasionally. Stir in the basil leaves, remaining fish sauce and lemon juice.

NUTRITION PER SERVE
Protein 40 g; Fat 50 g; Carbohydrate 65 g;
Dietary Fibre 6 g; Cholesterol 130 g;
3540 kJ (845 cal)

Beat the egg and egg white with electric beaters until thick and creamy.

Flour your hands and roll tablespoons of the mixture into balls.

When the sauce is simmering, add the lime leaves and chicken balls.

208

GINGERED DUCK CURRY

Preparation time: 30 minutes +
    30 minutes refrigeration + soaking
Total cooking time: 1 hour 30 minutes
Serves 4

1.8 kg (3 lb 10 oz) duck
1 clove garlic, crushed
1 teaspoon grated fresh ginger
1 tablespoon dark soy sauce
$1/2$ teaspoon sesame oil
8 dried Chinese mushrooms
5 cm (2 inch) piece of fresh ginger,
    thinly sliced
2 tablespoons Thai yellow curry paste
2 tablespoons chopped lemon grass,
    white part only
400 ml (13 fl oz) can coconut milk

4 kaffir lime leaves, shredded
100 g ($3^1/2$ oz) Thai pea eggplants
2 teaspoons soft brown sugar
2 teaspoons fish sauce
1 tablespoon lime juice

1 Cut the duck in half by cutting
down both sides of the backbone,
through the breastbone. Discard the
backbone. Cut each duck half into
four portions, removing any fat. Rub
the duck with the combined garlic,
ginger, soy sauce and oil. Refrigerate
for 30 minutes.
2 Soak the mushrooms in boiling
water for 20 minutes. Drain, remove
the stalks and cut the caps in half.
3 Heat a lightly oiled pan. Brown the
duck over medium heat. Leaving only
1 tablespoon of fat in the pan, stir-fry

the ginger, curry paste and lemon
grass for 3 minutes. Stir in the coconut
milk, lime leaves and $1/2$ cup (125 ml/
4 fl oz) water. Add the duck; cover and
simmer for 45 minutes. Skim well.
4 Remove the eggplant stems; add the
eggplants to the pan with the sugar,
fish sauce and mushrooms. Simmer,
partly covered, for 30 minutes, or until
tender. Stir in lime juice to taste.

NUTRITION PER SERVE (6)
Protein 50 g; Fat 40 g; Carbohydrate 6 g;
Dietary Fibre 1 g; Cholesterol 300 mg;
2330 kJ (560 cal)

NOTE: To reduce the fat in this dish,
use light coconut milk and skin the
duck before you start.

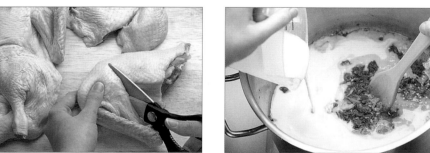

Cut the duck down the middle. Cut the legs and
breasts in half to give eight portions.

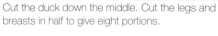

Stir the coconut milk, water and lime leaves into
the stir-fried spice mixture.

Remove the stems from the pea eggplants and
add the eggplants to the pan.

ROGAN JOSH

Preparation time: 25 minutes
Total cooking time: 1 hour 40 minutes
Serves 4–6

1 kg (2 lb) boned leg of lamb
1 tablespoon ghee or oil
2 onions, chopped
1/2 cup (125 g/4 oz) plain yoghurt
1 teaspoon chilli powder
1 tablespoon ground coriander
2 teaspoons ground cumin
1 teaspoon ground cardamom
1/2 teaspoon ground cloves
1 teaspoon ground turmeric
3 cloves garlic, crushed
1 tablespoon grated fresh ginger

400 g (13 oz) can chopped tomatoes
1/4 cup (30 g/1 oz) slivered almonds
1 teaspoon garam masala
chopped fresh coriander leaves, to
    garnish

1 Trim the lamb of any excess fat or
sinew and cut into small cubes.
2 Heat the ghee in a large saucepan,
add the onion and cook, stirring, for
5 minutes, or until soft. Stir in the
yoghurt, chilli powder, coriander,
cumin, cardamom, cloves, turmeric,
garlic and ginger. Add the tomato and
1 teaspoon salt and simmer for
5 minutes.
3 Add the lamb and stir until coated.
Cover and cook over low heat, stirring
occasionally, for 1–1 1/2 hours, or until

the lamb is tender. Uncover and
simmer until the liquid thickens.
4 Meanwhile, toast the almonds in a
dry frying pan over medium heat for
3–4 minutes, shaking the pan gently,
until the nuts are golden brown.
Remove from the pan at once to
prevent them burning.
5 Add the garam masala to the curry
and mix through well. Sprinkle the
slivered almonds and coriander leaves
over the top and serve.

NUTRITION PER SERVE (6)
Protein 40 g; Fat 13 g; Carbohydrate 5.5 g;
Dietary Fibre 2 g; Cholesterol 122 mg;
1236 kJ (295 cal)

Cook the onion in the ghee for 5 minutes, or until
it is soft.

Remove the lid from the pan and simmer until the
liquid thickens.

Toast the almonds in a dry frying pan, shaking
the pan gently until the nuts are golden brown.

MUSAMAN BEEF CURRY

Preparation time: 30 minutes
Total cooking time: 1 hour 45 minutes
Serves 4

1 tablespoon tamarind pulp
2 tablespoons oil
750 g (1½ lb) lean stewing beef,
    cubed
2 cups (500 ml/16 fl oz) coconut milk
4 cardamom pods, bruised
2 cups (500 ml/16 fl oz) coconut
    cream
2–3 tablespoons Musaman curry
    paste
8 pickling onions, peeled
8 baby potatoes, peeled
2 tablespoons fish sauce
2 tablespoons palm sugar
½ cup (90 g/3 oz) unsalted peanuts,
    roasted and ground
fresh coriander leaves, to garnish

1 Place the tamarind pulp and ½ cup
(125 ml/4 fl oz) boiling water in a
bowl and set aside to cool. When cool,
mash the pulp to dissolve in the water,
then strain and reserve the liquid.
Discard the pulp.
2 Heat the oil in a wok or a large
saucepan and cook the beef in batches
over high heat for 5 minutes, or until
browned. Reduce the heat and add the
coconut milk and cardamom, and
simmer for 1 hour, or until the beef is
tender. Remove the beef, strain and
reserve the beef and cooking liquid.
3 Heat the coconut cream in the wok
and stir in the curry paste. Cook for
5 minutes, or until the oil starts to
separate from the cream.
4 Add the pickling onions, potatoes,
fish sauce, palm sugar, peanuts, beef
mixture, reserved cooking liquid

and tamarind water, and simmer for
25–30 minutes. Garnish with fresh
coriander leaves to serve.

NUTRITION PER SERVE
Protein 52 g; Fat 77 g; Carbohydrate 35 g;
Dietary Fibre 7.5 g; Cholesterol 115 mg;
4324 kJ (1033 cal)

Mash the tamarind pulp with a fork, then strain
and reserve the liquid.

Cook the beef in batches over high heat until it is
all browned.

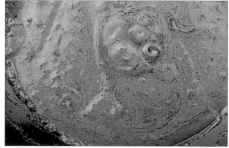

Cook the coconut cream and curry paste until the
oil starts to separate from the cream.

GREEN CURRY WITH SWEET POTATO AND EGGPLANT

Preparation time: 15 minutes
Total cooking time: 25 minutes
Serves 4–6

1 tablespoon oil
1 onion, chopped
1–2 tablespoons Thai green curry paste
1 eggplant, quartered and sliced
1½ cups (375 ml/12 fl oz) coconut milk

1 cup (250 ml/8 fl oz) vegetable stock
6 kaffir lime leaves
1 orange sweet potato, cut into cubes
2 teaspoons soft brown sugar
2 tablespoons lime juice
2 teaspoons lime rind

1 Heat the oil in a large wok or frying pan. Add the onion and green curry paste and cook, stirring, over medium heat for 3 minutes. Add the eggplant and cook for a further 4–5 minutes, or until softened. Pour in the coconut milk and vegetable stock, bring to the boil, then reduce the heat and simmer for 5 minutes. Add the kaffir lime leaves and sweet potato and cook, stirring occasionally, for 10 minutes, or until the eggplant and sweet potato are very tender.

2 Mix in the sugar, lime juice and lime rind until well combined with the vegetables. Season to taste with salt.

NUTRITION PER SERVE (6)
Protein 2.5 g; Fat 17 g; Carbohydrate 10 g;
Dietary Fibre 3 g; Cholesterol 0.5 mg;
835 kJ (200 cal)

Using a sharp knife, quarter and slice the eggplant before cooking until softened.

Stir-fry the onion and curry paste over medium heat for 3 minutes.

Cook, stirring occasionally, until the vegetables are tender.

BEEF AND SPINACH CURRY

Preparation time: 30 minutes
Total cooking time: 1 hour 15 minutes
Serves 4

2 tablespoons oil
1 onion, finely chopped
2 cloves garlic, finely chopped
2 teaspoons ground cumin
2 teaspoons ground coriander
2 teaspoons paprika
1 teaspoon garam masala
1 teaspoon turmeric
1/2 teaspoon finely chopped fresh red
    chilli
1 teaspoon finely chopped fresh green
    chilli

2 teaspoons grated fresh ginger
500 g (1 lb) lean beef or lamb mince
1 tomato, chopped
1 cup (250 ml/8 fl oz) beef stock or
    water
500 g (1 lb) English spinach, chopped
200 g (6½ oz) plain yoghurt

1 Heat 1 tablespoon of the oil in a large pan and cook the onion over medium heat until golden brown. Add the garlic, cumin, coriander, paprika, garam masala, turmeric, red and green chilli and the grated ginger and stir for 1 minute. Remove and set aside.
2 Heat the remaining oil in the pan and brown the meat in batches over high heat, breaking up any lumps with a fork or wooden spoon. Return the onion mixture to the pan and add the

tomato and stock or water.
3 Bring the mixture to the boil and then reduce the heat and simmer for about 1 hour. Season with salt, to taste. Meanwhile, cook the spinach. Just before serving, add the spinach to the mixture and stir in the yoghurt.

NUTRITION PER SERVE
Protein 35 g; Fat 15 g; Carbohydrate 5 g;
Dietary Fibre 5 g; Cholesterol 90 mg;
1270 kJ (300 cal)

NOTE: If possible, make the beef mixture in advance and refrigerate overnight for the flavours to develop.

Finely chop the chillies. Wear rubber gloves to prevent skin irritation.

Add the garlic, spices, red and green chilli and ginger to the pan and stir.

Add the tomato and stock or water to the pan and bring the mixture to the boil.

BEEF RENDANG

Preparation time: 20 minutes
Total cooking time: 2 hours 30 minutes
Serves 6

2 onions, roughly chopped
2 cloves garlic, crushed
400 ml (13 fl oz) coconut milk
2 teaspoons ground coriander seeds
1/2 teaspoon ground fennel seeds
2 teaspoons ground cumin seeds
1/4 teaspoon ground cloves
1.5 kg (3 lb) chuck steak, cubed
4–6 small red chillies, chopped
1 tablespoon lemon juice

1 stalk lemon grass, white part only,
  bruised, cut lengthways
2 teaspoons grated palm sugar or soft
  brown sugar

1 Mix the onion and garlic in a food
processor until smooth, adding water,
if necessary.
2 Put the coconut milk in a large
saucepan and bring to the boil.
Reduce the heat to medium and cook,
stirring occasionally, for 15 minutes, or
until reduced by half and the oil has
separated. Do not allow to brown.
3 Add the coriander, fennel, cumin
and cloves to the pan and stir for
1 minute. Add the meat and cook for

2 minutes, or until it changes colour.
Add the onion mixture, chilli, lemon
juice, lemon grass and sugar. Cook,
covered, over medium heat for
2 hours, or until the liquid has reduced
and the mixture has thickened. Stir
frequently to prevent sticking.
4 Uncover and cook until the oil from
the coconut milk begins to emerge
again, giving colour and flavour. Be
careful not to burn. The curry is
cooked when it is brown and dry.

NUTRITION PER SERVE
Protein 53 g; Fat 20 g; Carbohydrate 6 g;
Dietary Fibre 1.5 g; Cholesterol 168 mg;
1775 kJ (424 cal)

Mix the onion and garlic in a food processor until
smooth, adding water if necessary.

Cook the coconut milk over medium heat until
reduced and the oil has separated.

Continue to cook until the oil from the coconut
milk begins to emerge again.

PORK VINDALOO

Preparation time: 20 minutes
Total cooking time: 2 hours
Serves 4

1/4 cup (60 ml/2 fl oz) oil
1 kg (2 lb) pork fillets, cubed
2 onions, finely chopped
4 cloves garlic, finely chopped
1 tablespoon finely chopped fresh
   ginger

1 tablespoon garam masala
2 teaspoons brown mustard seeds
4 tablespoons vindaloo paste

1 Heat the oil in a pan, add the meat in small batches and brown over medium heat for 5–7 minutes. Remove all the meat from the pan.
2 Add the onion, garlic, ginger, garam masala and mustard seeds to the pan and cook, stirring, for 5 minutes, or until the onion is soft.
3 Return all the meat to the pan, add

the vindaloo paste and cook, stirring, for 2 minutes. Add 2¹/₂ cups (625 ml/ 21 fl oz) water and bring to the boil. Reduce the heat and simmer, covered, for 1¹/₂ hours until the meat is tender.

NUTRITION PER SERVE
Protein 58 g; Fat 20 g; Carbohydrate 4 g;
Dietary Fibre 2 g; Cholesterol 125 mg;
1806 kJ (430 cal)

Trim the pork of any excess fat or sinew and cut into cubes.

Cook the pork in small batches over medium heat until browned.

Add the vindaloo paste and cook the curry until the meat is tender.

JAPANESE PORK SCHNITZEL CURRY

Preparation time: 25 minutes
Total cooking time: 30 minutes
Serves 4

1 tablespoon oil
1 onion, cut into thin wedges
2 large carrots, diced
1 large potato, diced
60 g (2 oz) Japanese curry paste
    block, broken into small pieces
    (see NOTE)
plain flour, for coating
4 x 120 g (4 oz) pork schnitzels,
    pounded until thin
2 eggs, lightly beaten
150 g (5 oz) Japanese breadcrumbs
    (panko)
oil, for deep-frying
pickled ginger, pickled daikon,
    umeboshi (baby pickled plums),
    crisp-fried onion (see page 6),
    to garnish

1 Heat the oil in a saucepan, add the onion, carrot and potato and cook over medium heat for 10 minutes, or until starting to brown. Add 2 cups (500 ml/16 fl oz) water and the curry paste and stir until the curry paste dissolves and the sauce has a smooth consistency. Reduce the heat and simmer for 10 minutes, or until the vegetables are cooked through.
2 Season the flour well with salt and pepper. Dip each schnitzel into the flour, shake off any excess and dip into the beaten egg, allowing any excess to drip off. Coat with the Japanese breadcrumbs by pressing each side of the schnitzel firmly into the crumbs on a plate.
3 Fill a deep heavy-based saucepan one-third full of oil and heat to 180°C (350°F), or until a cube of bread browns in 15 seconds. Cook the schnitzels, one at a time, turning once or twice, for 5 minutes, or until golden brown all over and cooked through. Drain on crumpled paper towels.
4 Slice each schnitzel and then arrange in the original shape over rice. Ladle the curry sauce over the schnitzels. Garnish with fried onions and serve with the pickles on the side.

NUTRITION PER SERVE
Protein 38 g; Fat 22 g; Carbohydrate 40 g;
Dietary Fibre 5 g; Cholesterol 150 mg;
2145 kJ (513 cal)

NOTE: Japanese curry comes in a solid block or in powder form and is available in Asian supermarkets. It varies from mild to very hot.

Cook the onion, carrot and potato until they are starting to brown.

Coat the schnitzels in flour, egg and then Japanese breadcrumbs.

BALTI CHICKEN

Preparation time: 25 minutes
Total cooking time: 1 hour
Serves 6

1 kg (2 lb) chicken thigh fillets
1/3 cup (80 ml/2³/4 fl oz) oil
1 large red onion, finely chopped
4–5 cloves garlic, finely chopped
1 tablespoon grated fresh ginger
2 teaspoons ground cumin
2 teaspoons ground coriander
1 teaspoon ground turmeric
1/2 teaspoon chilli powder
425 g (14 oz) can chopped tomatoes
1 green capsicum, seeded and diced
1–2 small green chillies, seeded and
　　finely chopped
4 tablespoons chopped fresh
　　coriander
2 chopped spring onions, to garnish

1 Remove any excess fat or sinew from the chicken thigh fillets and cut into four or five even-sized pieces.
2 Heat a large wok over high heat, add the oil and swirl to coat the side. Add the onion and stir-fry over medium heat for 5 minutes, or until softened but not browned. Add the garlic and ginger and stir-fry for 3 more minutes.
3 Add the spices, 1 teaspoon salt and 1/4 cup (60 ml/2 fl oz) water. Increase the heat to high and stir-fry for 2 minutes, or until the mixture has thickened. Take care not to burn.
4 Add the tomato and 1 cup (250 ml/ 8 fl oz) water and cook, stirring often, for a further 10 minutes, or until the mixture is thick and pulpy and the oil comes to the surface.
5 Add the chicken to the pan, reduce the heat and simmer, stirring often, for

15 minutes. Add the capsicum and chilli and simmer for 25 minutes, or until the chicken is tender. Add a little water if the mixture is too thick. Stir in the coriander and garnish with the spring onion.

NUTRITION PER SERVE
Protein 40 g; Fat 17 g; Carbohydrate 5 g; Dietary Fibre 2 g; Cholesterol 83 mg; 1370 kJ (327 cal)

NOTE: This curry is traditionally cooked in a Karahi or Balti pan— a wok is a good substitute.

Remove any excess fat or sinew from the chicken, then cut into even-size pieces.

Add the spices, salt and water to the wok and cook until thickened.

Cook, stirring, until the curry thickens and the oil comes to the surface.

MALAYSIAN NONYA CHICKEN CURRY

Preparation time: 20 minutes
Total cooking time: 35 minutes
Serves 4

CURRY PASTE
2 red onions, chopped
4 small red chillies, seeded and sliced
4 cloves garlic, sliced
2 stalks lemon grass, white part only, sliced
5 cm (2 inch) piece galangal, sliced
8 kaffir lime leaves, roughly chopped

1 teaspoon ground turmeric
1/2 teaspoon shrimp paste, dry-roasted

2 tablespoons oil
750 g (1 1/2 lb) chicken thigh fillets, cut into bite-size pieces
400 ml (13 fl oz) coconut milk
3 tablespoons tamarind purée
1 tablespoon fish sauce
3 kaffir lime leaves, shredded

1 To make the curry paste, place all the ingredients in a food processor or blender and mix to a thick paste.
2 Heat a wok or large saucepan over high heat, add the oil and swirl to coat the side. Add the curry paste and cook, stirring occasionally, over low heat for 8–10 minutes, or until fragrant. Add the chicken and stir-fry with the paste for 2–3 minutes.
3 Add the coconut milk, tamarind purée and fish sauce to the wok, and simmer, stirring occasionally, for 15–20 minutes, or until the chicken is tender. Garnish with the lime leaves.

NUTRITION PER SERVE
Protein 45 g; Fat 35 g; Carbohydrate 8 g; Dietary Fibre 4 g; Cholesterol 94 mg; 2175 kJ (520 cal)

Place the curry paste ingredients in a food processor and mix to a thick paste.

Trim the chicken of any excess fat or sinew and cut into bite-sized pieces.

Add the chicken to the wok and stir-fry with the curry paste.

MALAYSIAN CHICKEN KAPITAN

Preparation time: 35 minutes
Total cooking time: 1 hour 20 minutes
Serves 4–6

1 teaspoon small dried shrimp
1/3 cup (80 ml/2³/4 fl oz) oil
6–8 red chillies, seeded and finely
    chopped
4 cloves garlic, finely chopped
3 stalks lemon grass, white part only,
    finely chopped
2 teaspoons ground turmeric
10 candlenuts
2 large onions, chopped
1 cup (250 ml/8 fl oz) coconut milk
1.5 kg (3 lb) chicken, cut into 8 pieces
1/2 cup (125 ml/4 fl oz) coconut cream
2 tablespoons lime juice

1 Put the shrimp in a frying pan and dry-fry over low heat, shaking the pan regularly, for 3 minutes, or until the shrimp are dark orange and are giving off a strong aroma. Transfer to a mortar and pestle and pound until finely ground. Alternatively, process in a food processor.

2 Mix half the oil, the chilli, garlic, lemon grass, turmeric and candlenuts in a food processor until very finely chopped, regularly scraping down the bowl with a rubber spatula.

3 Heat the remaining oil in a wok or frying pan, add the onion and 1/4 teaspoon salt and cook, stirring regularly, over low heat for 8 minutes, or until golden. Add the spice mixture and ground shrimp and stir for 5 minutes. If the mixture begins to stick to the bottom of the pan, add 2 tablespoons coconut milk. It is important to cook the mixture

thoroughly to develop the flavours.
4 Add the chicken to the wok and cook, stirring, for 5 minutes, or until beginning to brown. Stir in the remaining coconut milk and 1 cup (250 ml/8 fl oz) water and bring to the boil. Reduce the heat and simmer for 50 minutes, or until the chicken is cooked and the sauce has thickened

slightly. Add the coconut cream and bring the mixture back to the boil, stirring constantly. Add the lime juice before serving.

NUTRITION PER SERVE (6)
Protein 58 g; Fat 30 g; Carbohydrate 4 g;
Dietary Fibre 2 g; Cholesterol 125 mg;
2211 kJ (528 cal)

Dry-fry the shrimp over low heat until they turn dark orange.

Place the shrimp in a mortar and pestle and pound until finely ground.

Simmer until the chicken is cooked and the sauce has thickened slightly.

219

CHICKPEA CURRY

Preparation time: 10 minutes +
   overnight soaking
Total cooking time: 1 hour 15 minutes
Serves 6

1 cup (220 g/7 oz) dried chickpeas
2 tablespoons oil
2 onions, finely chopped
2 large ripe tomatoes, chopped
1/2 teaspoon ground coriander
1 teaspoon ground cumin
1 teaspoon chilli powder
1/4 teaspoon ground turmeric
1 tablespoon channa (chole) masala
   (see NOTE)
1 tablespoon ghee or butter
1 small white onion, sliced
fresh mint and coriander leaves, to
   garnish

1 Place the chickpeas in a bowl, cover with water and leave to soak overnight. Drain, rinse and place in a large saucepan. Cover with plenty of water and bring to the boil, then reduce the heat and simmer for 40 minutes, or until soft. Drain.

2 Heat the oil in a large saucepan, add the onion and cook over medium heat for 15 minutes, or until golden brown. Add the tomato, ground coriander and cumin, chilli powder, turmeric and channa (chole) masala. Add 2 cups (500 ml/16 fl oz) water and cook for 10 minutes, or until the tomato is soft. Add the chickpeas, season well with salt and cook for 7–10 minutes, or until the sauce thickens. Transfer to a serving dish. Place the ghee or butter on top and allow to melt before serving. Garnish with sliced onion and fresh mint and coriander leaves.

NUTRITION PER SERVE
Protein 8 g; Fat 11 g; Carbohydrate 17 g;
Dietary Fibre 6 g; Cholesterol 8.5 mg;
835 kJ (200 cal)

NOTE: Channa (chole) masala is a spice blend specifically used in this dish. It is available at Indian grocery stores. Garam masala can be used as a substitute if unavailable, but this will alter the final flavour.

Cook the onion in a large saucepan over medium heat until golden brown.

Add the chickpeas to the curry and cook until the sauce thickens.

CAULIFLOWER CURRY

Preparation time: 20 minutes +
  30 minutes marinating
Total cooking time: 20 minutes
Serves 6

MARINADE
1 large onion, roughly chopped
1 teaspoon grated fresh ginger
2 cloves garlic, crushed
3 green chillies, chopped
1/4 cup (60 g/2 oz) plain yoghurt

1 cauliflower, divided into florets
oil, for deep-frying

CURRY SAUCE
2 tablespoons ghee
1 onion, finely chopped
2 tablespoons tomato paste
2 tablespoons cream
1 teaspoon chilli powder
1 1/2 tablespoons garam masala

1 To make the marinade, place all the ingredients in a food processor and mix until smooth. Place the marinade in a bowl, add the cauliflower, toss to coat and leave for 30 minutes.

2 Fill a deep heavy-based saucepan one-third full of oil and heat to 160°C (315°F), or until a cube of bread dropped into the oil browns in 30–35 seconds. Cook the cauliflower in batches for 30 seconds until golden brown all over. Drain on paper towels.

3 Heat the ghee in a frying pan, add the onion and cook for 4–5 minutes, or until soft. Add the tomato paste, cream, chilli powder, garam masala, 1 1/2 cups (375 ml/12 fl oz) water and salt to taste. Cook, stirring constantly, over medium heat for 3 minutes.

4 Add the cauliflower and cook for 7 minutes, adding a little water if the sauce becomes dry.

NUTRITION PER SERVE
Protein 2.5 g; Fat 9 g; Carbohydrate 4.5 g; Dietary Fibre 2 g; Cholesterol 27 mg; 458 kJ (110 cal)

Mix all the marinade ingredients in a food processor until smooth.

Heat the oil until a cube of bread dropped into the pan browns in 30–35 seconds.

Cook the cauliflower in batches until golden brown all over.

Curry Pastes & Spices

MADRAS CURRY PASTE

Preparation time: 5 minutes
Total cooking time: Nil
Makes 1/2 cup

2 1/2 tablespoons coriander seeds,
   dry-roasted and ground
1 tablespoon cumin seeds,
   dry-roasted and ground
1 teaspoon brown mustard seeds
1/2 teaspoon cracked black
   peppercorns
1 teaspoon chilli powder
1 teaspoon ground turmeric
2 cloves garlic, crushed
2 teaspoons grated fresh ginger
3–4 tablespoons white vinegar

1 Place the ground coriander, ground
cumin, mustard seeds, cracked black
peppercorns, chilli powder, ground
turmeric, garlic, ginger and 1 teaspoon
salt in a small bowl and mix together
well. Add the vinegar and mix to a
smooth paste. Will keep in a clean
airtight container in the refrigerator
for up to a month.

GENERAL-PURPOSE INDIAN CURRY POWDER

Preparation time: 5 minutes
Total cooking time: 20 minutes
Makes 1/3 cup

2 teaspoons cumin seeds
2 teaspoons coriander seeds
2 teaspoons fenugreek seeds
1 teaspoon yellow mustard seeds
1 teaspoon black peppercorns
1 teaspoon cloves
1 teaspoon chilli powder
2 teaspoons ground turmeric
1/2 teaspoon ground cinnamon
1/2 teaspoon ground cardamom

1 Dry-fry the whole spices separately
in a small frying pan over medium
heat for 2–3 minutes, or until fragrant.
Place in a spice grinder, mortar and
pestle or small food processor with a
fine blade and grind to a fine powder.
2 Place in a small bowl with the pre-
ground spices and mix together well.
Store in an airtight container in a cool,
dark place.

SRI LANKAN CURRY POWDER

Preparation time: 5 minutes
Total cooking time: 20 minutes
Makes 1/3 cup

3 tablespoons coriander seeds
1 1/2 tablespoons cumin seeds
1 teaspoon fennel seeds
1/4 teaspoon fenugreek seeds
2.5 cm (1 inch) cinnamon stick
6 cloves
1/4 teaspoon cardamom seeds
2 teaspoons dried curry leaves
2 small dried red chillies

1 Dry-fry the coriander, cumin, fennel
and fenugreek seeds separately over
low heat until fragrant. It is important to
do this separately as all spices brown at
different rates. Make sure the spices are
well browned, not burnt.
2 Place the browned seeds in a food
processor, blender or mortar and pestle,
add the remaining ingredients and
process or grind to a powder. Store in
an airtight container in a cool, dry place.

VINDALOO PASTE

Preparation time: 10 minutes
Total cooking time: Nil
Makes 1/2 cup

2 tablespoons grated fresh ginger
4 cloves garlic, chopped
4 red chillies, chopped
2 teaspoons ground turmeric
2 teaspoons ground cardamom
4 cloves
6 peppercorns
1 teaspoon ground cinnamon
1 tablespoon ground coriander
1 tablespoon cumin seeds
1/2 cup (125 ml/4 fl oz) cider vinegar

1 Place all the ingredients in a food processor and mix for 20 seconds, or until well combined and smooth. Refrigerate for up to a month.

BALTI MASALA PASTE

Preparation time: 5 minutes
Total cooking time: 8 minutes
Makes 1 cup

4 tablespoons coriander seeds
2 tablespoons cumin seeds
2 cinnamon sticks, crumbled
2 teaspoons fennel seeds

2 teaspoons black mustard seeds
2 teaspoons cardamom seeds
1 teaspoon fenugreek seeds
6 cloves
4 fresh bay leaves
20 fresh curry leaves
1 tablespoon ground turmeric
2 cloves garlic, crushed
1 tablespoon grated fresh ginger
1 1/2 teaspoons chilli powder
1 cup (250 ml/8 fl oz) malt vinegar
1/2 cup (125 ml/4 fl oz) oil

1 Separately dry-fry the coriander seeds, cumin seeds, cinnamon sticks, fennel seeds, black mustard seeds, cardamom seeds, fenugreek seeds and cloves in a small frying pan over medium heat for 2–3 minutes, or until just starting to become fragrant.
2 Transfer all the spices to a food processor or mortar and pestle and mix or grind to a powder. Add the bay leaves, curry leaves, ground turmeric, garlic, ginger, chilli powder and 3/4 cup (185 ml/6 fl oz) vinegar and mix well.
3 Heat the oil in the pan, add the paste and cook, stirring, for 5 minutes. Stir in the remaining vinegar. Pour into clean, warm jars and seal. Will keep in the fridge for a month.

GARAM MASALA

Preparation time: 7 minutes
Total cooking time: 20 minutes
Makes 1/2 cup

2 tablespoons coriander seeds
1 1/2 tablespoons cardamom pods
1 tablespoon cumin seeds
2 teaspoons whole black peppercorns
1 teaspoon whole cloves
3 cinnamon sticks
1 nutmeg, grated

1 Dry-fry all the ingredients, except the nutmeg, separately in a frying pan over medium heat for 2–3 minutes, or until just becoming fragrant.
2 Remove the cardamom pods, crush with the handle of a heavy knife and remove the seeds. Discard the pods.
3 Place the fried spices, cardamom seeds and nutmeg in a food processor, blender or mortar and pestle, and process or grind to a powder. Store in an airtight container in a cool, dark place.

Left to right: Madras curry paste; General-purpose Indian curry powder; Sri Lankan curry powder; Vindaloo paste; Balti masala paste; Garam masala.

THAI YELLOW CURRY PASTE

Preparation time: 20 minutes
Total cooking time: Nil
Makes 1/2 cup

8 small green chillies
5 red Asian shallots, roughly chopped
2 cloves garlic, chopped
1 tablespoon finely chopped coriander stem and root
1 stalk lemon grass, white part only, chopped
2 tablespoons finely chopped fresh galangal
1 teaspoon ground coriander
1 teaspoon ground cumin
1/2 teaspoon ground turmeric
1/2 teaspoon black peppercorns
1 tablespoon lime juice

1 Mix all the ingredients to a paste in a food processor, blender or mortar and pestle. Will keep in an airtight container in the fridge for a month.

THAI GREEN CURRY PASTE

Preparation time: 30 minutes
Total cooking time: 10 minutes
Makes 1 cup

1 teaspoon white peppercorns
1 teaspoon cumin seeds
2 tablespoons coriander seeds
2 teaspoons shrimp paste, wrapped in foil
1 teaspoon sea salt
4 stalks lemon grass, white part only, finely chopped
2 teaspoons chopped fresh galangal
2 teaspoons finely shredded kaffir lime leaves
1 tablespoon chopped fresh coriander root
5 red Asian shallots, chopped
10 cloves garlic, chopped
16 large green chillies, chopped

1 Preheat the oven to 180°C (350°F/ Gas 4). Put the peppercorns, cumin, coriander seeds and shrimp paste in a dish and bake for 5–10 minutes until fragrant. Unwrap the shrimp paste.
2 Mix all the ingredients to a smooth paste in a food processor or mortar and pestle. Keep in an airtight container in the fridge for up to a month.

THAI RED CURRY PASTE

Preparation time: 20 minutes + soaking
Total cooking time: 10 minutes
Makes 1 cup

15 dried large red chillies
1 teaspoon white peppercorns
2 teaspoons coriander seeds
1 teaspoon cumin seeds
2 teaspoons shrimp paste, wrapped in foil
5 red Asian shallots, chopped
10 cloves garlic
2 stalks lemon grass, white part only, finely sliced
1 tablespoon chopped fresh galangal
2 tablespoons chopped fresh coriander root
1 teaspoon finely grated kaffir lime rind

1 Preheat the oven to 180°C (350°F/ Gas 4). Soak the chillies in boiling water for 10 minutes. Remove the seeds and roughly chop the flesh.
2 Put the spices and shrimp paste in a dish and bake for 5–10 minutes until fragrant. Unwrap the shrimp paste.
3 Mix all the ingredients to a smooth paste in a food processor or mortar and pestle. Will keep in an airtight container in the fridge for a month.

MUSAMAN CURRY PASTE

Preparation time: 20 minutes + soaking
Total cooking time: 5 minutes
Makes 1/2 cup

10 dried large red chillies
3 cardamom pods
1 teaspoon cumin seeds
1 tablespoon coriander seeds
1/4 teaspoon black peppercorns
1 teaspoon shrimp paste, wrapped
   in foil
5 red Asian shallots, chopped
1 stalk lemon grass, white part only,
   finely chopped
1 tablespoon chopped fresh galangal
10 cloves garlic, chopped
1/4 teaspoon ground cinnamon
1/2 teaspoon ground nutmeg
1/4 teaspoon ground cloves

1 Preheat the oven to 180°C (350°F/
Gas 4). Soak the chillies in boiling
water for 10 minutes, drain, remove
the seeds and roughly chop.
2 Put the spices, shrimp paste,
shallots, lemon grass, galangal and
garlic in a dish and bake for 5 minutes
until fragrant. Unwrap the paste.

3 Mix the chilli, roasted ingredients
and ground spices to a smooth paste
in a food processor, mortar and pestle
or spice grinder. If the mixture is too
dry add a little vinegar to moisten it.
Will keep in an airtight container in the
fridge for up to a month.

CHU CHEE CURRY PASTE

Preparation time: 20 minutes +
  soaking
Total cooking time: 5 minutes
Makes 1/2 cup

10 large dried red chillies
1 teaspoon coriander seeds
1 tablespoon shrimp paste, wrapped
   in foil
1 tablespoon white peppercorns
10 kaffir lime leaves, finely shredded
10 red Asian shallots, chopped
2 teaspoons finely grated kaffir lime
   rind
1 tablespoon chopped fresh coriander
   stem and root
1 stalk lemon grass, white part only,
   finely chopped
3 tablespoons chopped fresh
   galangal

1 tablespoon chopped Krachai (see
   NOTE), optional
6 cloves garlic, chopped

1 Preheat the oven to 180°C (350°F/
Gas 4). Soak the chillies in boiling
water for 10 minutes. Drain, remove
the seeds and roughly chop.
2 Place the coriander seeds, shrimp
paste and peppercorns on a foil-lined
baking tray and bake for 5 minutes
until fragrant. Unwrap the paste.
3 Mix all the ingredients to a smooth
paste in a food processor or mortar
and pestle. You may need to use a
little lemon juice if the paste is too
thick. Will keep in an airtight container
in the fridge for up to a month.

NOTE: Krachai (bottled lesser
galangal) is available from Asian
grocery stores. It can be omitted if
it is unavailable.

Left to right: Yellow curry paste; Green curry paste; Red curry paste; Musaman curry paste; Chu chee curry paste.

Side Dishes

MANGO CHUTNEY

Preparation time: 20 minutes
Total cooking time: 1 hour
Makes 3 cups (serves 36)

3 large green mangoes
1/2 teaspoon garam masala
1 1/2 cups (375 g/12 oz) sugar
1 cup (250 ml/8 fl oz) white vinegar
2 small red chillies, seeded and finely
    chopped
1 tablespoon finely grated fresh ginger
1/2 cup (90 g/3 oz) finely chopped
    dates

1 Cut the cheeks from the rounded side of each mango and use a large spoon to scoop out the flesh. Cut the remaining flesh from around the sides of the seed and chop all the flesh into large slices. Sprinkle with salt.
2 Mix together the garam masala and sugar. Place in a large saucepan with the vinegar. Bring to the boil, then reduce the heat and simmer for 5 minutes.
3 Add the mango slices, chilli, ginger and dates and simmer for 1 hour, or until the mango is tender. Stir often during cooking to prevent the chutney from sticking and burning on the bottom, especially towards the end of the cooking time.
4 Spoon immediately into sterilised jars (see NOTE) and seal. Turn the jars upside down for 2 minutes, then invert and leave to cool. Label and date. Will keep for up to six months.

NUTRITION PER SERVE
Protein 0.2 g; Fat 0 g; Carbohydrate 13 g;
Dietary Fibre 0.5 g; Cholesterol mg;
212 kJ (50 cal)

NOTE: To sterilise jars, preheat the oven to very slow 120°C (250°F/ Gas 1/2). Thoroughly wash the jars and lids in hot soapy water (or preferably in a dishwasher) and rinse well with hot water. Put the jars on baking trays and place them in the oven for 20 minutes, or until they are fully dried and you are ready to use them. Do not dry the jars, or the lids, with a tea towel.

HINT: Mango chutney is great with almost any Indian curry, especially the hotter ones. It also tastes delicious on sandwiches with roast lamb or beef.

Use a large metal spoon to scoop out the mango flesh from the cheeks.

Simmer the mixture for 1 hour, or until the mango is tender.

CUCUMBER RAITA

Preparation time: 5 minutes
Total cooking time: 1 minute
Makes 1¹/₃ cups (serves 10)

2 Lebanese cucumbers, peeled,
    seeded, finely chopped (see NOTE)
1 cup (250 g/8 oz) plain yoghurt
1 teaspoon ground cumin
1 teaspoon mustard seeds
¹/₂ teaspoon grated fresh ginger
paprika, to garnish

1 Mix together the cucumber and
yoghurt in a large bowl.
2 Dry-fry the ground cumin and
mustard seeds in a small frying pan
over medium heat for 1 minute, or
until fragrant and lightly browned,
then add to the yoghurt mixture. Stir in
the ginger, season to taste with salt
and pepper and mix together well.
Garnish with the paprika. Serve
chilled. Will keep in an airtight
container in the refrigerator for up to
three days.

NUTRITION PER SERVE
Protein 1 g; Fat 0.5 g; Carbohydrate 1 g;
Dietary Fibre 0 g; Cholesterol 4.5 mg;
54 kJ (13 cal)

NOTE: Raitas are deliciously soothing
and cooling Indian yoghurt-based side
dishes which cool the palate when
eating hot curries.

VARIATIONS: Add 2 tablespoons
chopped fresh coriander or mint
leaves to the cucumber raita.

Or, replace the cucumber with
1 bunch (500 g) English spinach. Bring
a large saucepan of water to the boil,
add the spinach and cook for
1–2 minutes. Drain the spinach,
squeezing out any excess water. Chop
finely and combine with the yoghurt.

To make a tomato raita, replace the
cucumber with 2 medium, seeded;
diced tomatoes. Add 1 tablespoon
very finely chopped onion as well.

Place the cucumber and yoghurt in a bowl and
mix together.

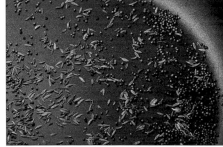

Dry-fry the ground cumin and mustard seeds
until fragrant and lightly browned.

CORIANDER CHUTNEY

Preparation time: 10 minutes
Total cooking time: Nil
Makes 1¹/₄ cups (serves 9)

90 g (3 oz) fresh coriander, including
    the roots, roughly chopped
3 tablespoons desiccated coconut
1 tablespoon soft brown sugar
1 tablespoon grated fresh ginger
1 small onion, chopped
2 tablespoons lemon juice
1–2 small green chillies, seeded

1 Place all the ingredients and
1 teaspoon salt in a food processor
and process for 1 minute, or until
finely chopped. Refrigerate until ready
to serve. Serve chilled.

NUTRITION PER SERVE
Protein 0.2 g; Fat 1 g; Carbohydrate 2 g;
Dietary Fibre 0.5 g; Cholesterol 0.5 mg;
75 kJ (18 cal)

NOTE: Chutneys are spicy, vegetarian
Indian relishes eaten as side dishes.
They are often used to perk up plain
dishes such as dhal or rice and are
traditionally made fresh for each meal.

VARIATIONS: There are numerous
variations, depending on region and
tastes. Try substituting 1 bunch of
roughly chopped fresh mint leaves for
the coriander in this recipe, or add
5 roughly chopped spring onions
(including the green part) instead of
the onion.

If you prefer more fire in your
chutney, do not remove the seeds
from the chillies. It is the seeds and
white fibrous tissue inside the chillies
that contain most of the heat.

Roughly chop the fresh coriander leaves, stems
and roots.

Place all the ingredients in a food processor and
mix until finely chopped.

229

DHAL

Preparation time: 15 minutes
Total cooking time: 35 minutes
Serves 4–6

200 g (6¹/₂ oz) red lentils
5 cm (2 inch) piece fresh ginger, cut
    into 3 slices
¹/₂ teaspoon ground turmeric
1 tablespoon ghee or oil
2 cloves garlic, crushed
1 onion, finely chopped
¹/₂ teaspoon yellow mustard seeds
pinch of asafoetida, optional
1 teaspoon cumin seeds
1 teaspoon ground coriander
2 green chillies, halved lengthways
2 tablespoons lemon juice
1 tablespoon chopped fresh coriander
    leaves

1 Put the lentils and 3 cups (750 ml/
24 fl oz) water in a pan and bring to
the boil. Reduce the heat, add the
ginger and turmeric and simmer,
covered, for 20 minutes or until tender.
Stir occasionally to prevent sticking.
Remove the ginger and stir in
¹/₂ teaspoon salt.

2 Heat the ghee in a frying pan, add
the garlic, onion and mustard seeds,
and cook over medium heat for
5 minutes, or until the onion is golden.
Add the asafoetida, cumin seeds,
ground coriander and chilli and cook
for 2 minutes.

3 Add the onion mixture to the lentils
and stir gently. Add ¹/₂ cup (125 ml/
4 fl oz) water, reduce the heat to low
and cook for 5 minutes. Stir in the
lemon juice and season. Sprinkle with
the coriander. Serve as a side dish with
Indian curries.

NUTRITION PER SERVE (6)
Protein 9 g; Fat 4 g; Carbohydrate 13 g;
Dietary Fibre 5 g; Cholesterol 8 mg;
505 kJ (120 cal)

Add the ginger and turmeric to the lentils and
cook until the lentils are tender.

Cook the garlic, onion and mustard seeds until
the onion is golden.

NAAN

Preparation time: 15 minutes +
  2 hours resting
Total cooking time: 10 minutes
Makes 8

4 cups (500 g/1 lb) plain flour
1 teaspoon baking powder
1/2 teaspoon bicarbonate of soda
1 egg, beaten
1/2 cup (125 g/4 oz) plain yoghurt
4 tablespoons ghee or butter,
  melted
1 cup (250 ml/8 fl oz) milk

1 Preheat the oven to moderately hot 200°C (400°F/Gas 6). Lightly grease two 28 x 32 cm (11 x 13 inch) baking trays. Sift together the flour, baking powder, bicarbonate of soda and 1 teaspoon salt. Mix in the egg, yoghurt and 1 tablespoon of the ghee and gradually add enough of the milk to form a soft dough. Cover with a damp cloth and leave in a warm place for 2 hours.

2 Knead the dough on a well-floured surface for 2–3 minutes until smooth. Divide into eight portions and roll each one into an oval 15 cm (6 inches) long. Brush with water and place, wet-side-down, on the baking trays. Brush with the rest of the melted ghee and bake for 8–10 minutes, or until golden brown. Serve with Indian curries.

NUTRITION PER NAAN
Protein 10 g; Fat 12 g; Carbohydrate 48 g;
Dietary Fibre 2.5 g; Cholesterol 55 mg;
1418 kJ (340 cal)

VARIATION: To make garlic naan, crush 6 garlic cloves and sprinkle evenly over the dough prior to baking.

Mix all the ingredients together with enough milk to form a soft dough.

Knead the dough on a well-floured surface until it is smooth.

Roll each of the eight portions into an oval about 15 cm long.

231

ROTIS

Preparation time: 45 minutes +
　2 hours resting
Total cooking time: 25 minutes
Makes 12

3 cups (375 g/12 oz) roti flour or plain
　flour (see NOTES)
2 tablespoons softened ghee or oil
1 egg, lightly beaten
oil, to brush
1 egg, extra, beaten
extra ghee or oil, for frying

1 Sift the flour into a large mixing bowl and stir in 1 teaspoon salt. Rub in the ghee with your fingertips or, alternatively, stir in the oil. Add the lightly beaten egg and 1 cup (250 ml/ 8 fl oz) warm water and mix together with a flat-bladed knife to form a moist dough. Turn the dough out on to a well-floured surface and knead for 10 minutes, or until you have a soft dough. Sprinkle the dough with more flour as necessary. Gently form the dough into a ball and brush lightly with oil. Place in an oiled bowl, cover with plastic wrap and leave to rest for 2 hours.

2 Remove the dough from the bowl. Working on a lightly floured work surface (use a clean bench top), divide the dough into 12 pieces and roll it into even-size balls. Take one ball and, working with a little oil on your fingertips, hold the ball in the air and work around the edge, pulling out the dough to form a 2 mm x 15 cm (1/8 inch x 6 inch) round. Lay the roti on a lightly floured surface and cover with plastic wrap so that it doesn't dry out while you are working with the rest of the dough. Repeat the process

with the remaining balls.

3 Heat a large frying pan over high heat and brush it with ghee or oil. Drape one of the rotis over a rolling pin and carefully place in the frying pan. Quickly brush the roti with some of the extra beaten egg. Cook for 1 minute, or until the underside is golden—this won't take long. Using an egg slice, slide the roti onto a plate and brush the pan with some more ghee or oil. Return the roti to the frying pan to cook the other side. Cook the roti for 50–60 seconds, or until that side is golden. Remove from the pan and cover to keep warm while cooking the rest.

NUTRITION PER ROTI
Protein 4 g; Fat 7 g; Carbohydrate 23 g; Dietary Fibre 1 g; Cholesterol 23 mg; 705 kJ (168 cal)

NOTES: Roti flour is a cream-coloured flour available from Indian food shops. It is used in Indian unleavened breads. Plain flour can be used as a substitute if roti flour is unavailable, but it will not have the same texture.

　Rotis are served as accompaniments to Indian curries and are great for mopping up wet sauces.

VARIATIONS: This recipe for plain roti can be flavoured by adding additional ingredients to the roti flour once it has been sifted and before you rub in the ghee with your fingertips. For coconut rotis (a popular Sri Lankan breakfast dish), add 1/2 cup (45 g/11/2 oz) desiccated coconut. For delicious spicy rotis, add 1 teaspoon finely chopped red chilli, 2 tablespoons finely chopped onion, 1/2 teaspoon ground turmeric and 1 teaspoon ground cumin.

Rub the softened ghee into the flour mixture with your fingertips.

Mix together with a flat-bladed knife to form a moist dough.

Knead the mixture on a well-floured surface until you have a soft dough.

Pull out the dough around the edges to form a 15 cm round.

Drape a roti over a rolling pin and carefully place in the frying pan.

Return to the heat and cook the roti on the other side until it is golden.

PURIS

Preparation time: 50 minutes +
   50 minutes standing
Total cooking time: 20 minutes
Makes 18

1½ cups (225 g/7 oz) wholemeal flour
1 cup (125 g/4 oz) plain flour
1 tablespoon ghee or oil
oil, for deep-frying

1 Sift the flours together with a pinch of salt. Discard the husks. Rub in the ghee with your fingertips, or stir in the oil. Gradually add ²/₃ cup (170 ml/ 5½ fl oz) water to form a firm dough. Knead on a lightly floured surface until smooth. Cover with plastic wrap and leave for 50 minutes.

2 Divide into 18 portions and roll into circles 2 mm (¹/₈ inch) thick and 14 cm (5½ inches) wide.

3 Fill a deep heavy-based saucepan one-third full of oil and heat to 180°C

(350°F) or until a cube of bread dropped into the oil browns in 15 seconds. Add the puris one at a time and cook, spooning oil over the top, for 30–60 seconds, or until puffed. Turn and cook until golden brown. Drain on paper towels. Serve immediately with Indian curries.

NUTRITION PER PURI
Protein 2 g; Fat 4 g; Carbohydrate 12 g;
Dietary Fibre 1.5 g; Cholesterol 3 mg;
360 kJ (85 cal)

Gradually add water to the sifted flours to form a firm dough.

Divide the dough into 18 portions and roll each into a 14 cm circle.

Cook the puris, spooning oil over them, until they puff up and swell.

CHAPATIS

Preparation time: 40 minutes +
50 minutes standing
Total cooking time: 1 hour 10 minutes
Makes 14

2^1/$_4$ cups (280 g/9 oz) atta flour (see NOTE)
melted ghee or oil, for brushing

1 Place the flour in a large bowl with a pinch of salt. Slowly add 1 cup (250 ml/8 fl oz) water, or enough to form a firm dough. Place on a lightly floured surface and knead until smooth. Cover with plastic wrap and leave for 50 minutes.
2 Divide into 14 portions and roll into 14 cm (5^1/$_2$ inch) circles. Heat a frying pan over medium heat and brush with the ghee or oil. Cook the chapatis one at a time over medium heat, flattening the surface, for 2–3 minutes on each side or until golden brown and bubbles appear. Serve with curries.

NUTRITION PER CHAPATI
Protein 2.5 g; Fat 3 g; Carbohydrate 10 g;
Dietary Fibre 2 g; Cholesterol 0 mg;
335 kJ (80 cal)

NOTE: Atta flour is also known as chapati flour and is a finely milled, low-gluten, soft-textured, wholemeal wheat flour used to make Indian flatbreads. If unavailable, use plain wholemeal flour—sift it first and discard the husks. This may result in heavier, coarser bread.

Add enough water to the flour mixture to form a firm dough.

Knead the dough on a lightly floured surface until it is smooth.

Flatten the surface of the chapati with a spatula while cooking.

Cook the chapati until it is golden brown and bubbles appear.

SAMBAL OELEK (HOT CHILLI PASTE)

Preparation time: 10 minutes
Total cooking time: 15 minutes
Makes 1 cup (serves 48)

200 g (6¹/₂ oz) small fresh red chillies
1 teaspoon sugar
1 tablespoon vinegar
1 tablespoon oil

1 Roughly chop the chillies, wearing gloves to protect your hands, then place in a saucepan with ¹/₂ cup (125 ml/4 fl oz) water and bring to the boil. Reduce the heat and simmer, covered, for 15 minutes.
2 Pour the chilli and the soaking liquid into a food processor or blender and add the sugar, vinegar, oil and 1 teaspoon salt. Finely chop. Pour immediately into a sterilised jar and carefully seal. Leave to cool. Will keep in the fridge for a month.

NUTRITION PER SERVE
Protein 0 g; Fat 0 g; Carbohydrate 0 g; Dietary Fibre 0 g; Cholesterol 0 mg; 23 kJ (5.5 cal)

NOTE: Sambal oelek is a very hot paste, so use it sparingly. It is used as a relish in Indonesian and Malaysian cooking and can also be used as a substitute for fresh chillies in most recipes. Each serve is only 1 teaspoon.

Wear gloves while chopping the chillies to protect your hands.

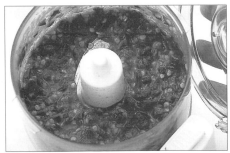

Process all the ingredients in a food processor until finely chopped.

Pour the mixture immediately into a sterilised jar. It can then be kept for up to a month.

CRISP-FRIED ONIONS

Preparation time: 15 minutes +
  10 minutes standing
Total cooking time: 10 minutes
Makes 1 cup (serves 12)

1 onion, sliced paper-thin
oil, for deep-frying

1 Drain the onion on paper towels for 10 minutes. Fill a deep, heavy-based saucepan one-third full of oil and heat to 160°C (315°F), or until a cube of bread dropped into the oil browns in 30–35 seconds. Cook the onion in batches for up to 1 minute or until brown and crispy. Drain on paper towels. Cool and store in an airtight container for up to two weeks.

NUTRITION PER SERVE
Protein 0.2 g; Fat 3 g; Carbohydrate 0.5 g; Dietary Fibre 0 g; Cholesterol 0 mg; 128 kJ (30 cal)

NOTE: Use as a garnish and flavour enhancer in Indonesian rice and noodle dishes.

Slice the onion into paper-thin slices so that it will fry to a crisp finish.

Heat the oil until a cube of bread dropped in it browns in 30–35 seconds.

Cook the onions until brown and crispy and drain on crumpled paper towels.

Desserts

CARAMEL STICKY RICE

Preparation time: 40 minutes +
  overnight soaking
Total cooking time: 1 hour 15 minutes
Serves 4

2 cups (400 g/13 oz) glutinous white
  rice
250 ml (8 fl oz) coconut milk
90 g (3 oz) palm sugar, grated
1/4 teaspoon salt
starfruit, finely sliced
3 tablespoons coconut cream
1 tablespoon sesame seeds, toasted

1 Rinse the rice until the water runs
clear. Put into a glass bowl, cover with
water and soak overnight, then drain.
2 Line a bamboo steamer with baking
paper or a damp tea towel and place it
over a water-filled wok. Spread the
rice over the base of the steamer, fold
the sides of the paper over the rice and
cover with another sheet of paper.
Tuck it in so the rice is completely
encased and cover with the bamboo
lid. Steam over medium heat for
50 minutes until just cooked, refilling
the water whenever necessary.
3 Stir the coconut milk, palm sugar
and salt in a small pan until boiling.
Reduce the heat and simmer for
15 minutes or until a thick caramel.
4 Pour one-quarter of the caramel
over the rice, fork it through, cover
again with the paper and lid and steam
for 5 minutes. Repeat with the
remaining caramel, cooking the rice
until plump and sticky. Press into a
square dish, leave to stand and then
cut into diamonds, or form into balls
and serve warm with starfruit, coconut
cream and sesame seeds.

NUTRITION PER SERVE
Protein 10 g; Fat 20 g; Carbohydrate 100 g;
Dietary Fibre 4 g; Cholesterol 0 mg;
2555 kJ (610 cal)

Wash the glutinous rice under running water until
the water runs clear.

Grate the palm sugar on the large holes of a
metal grater.

Cover the rice with baking paper, tucking in the
sides to encase the rice.

Pour about one-quarter of the caramel over the
steamed rice.

COCONUT ICE CREAM

Preparation time: 10 minutes +
  freezing
Total cooking time: 15 minutes
Serves 4

425 g (14 oz) can coconut cream
1¹/₂ cups (375 ml/12 fl oz) cream
2 eggs
2 egg yolks
¹/₂ cup (125 g/4 oz) caster sugar
¹/₄ teaspoon salt
1 teaspoon vanilla essence
fresh mint leaves and toasted,
    shredded coconut, to garnish

1 Put the coconut cream and cream in a pan. Stir over medium heat, without boiling, for 2–3 minutes. Set aside; cover and keep warm. Place the eggs, egg yolks, sugar, salt and vanilla in a large heatproof bowl. Beat with electric beaters for 2–3 minutes until frothy and thickened. Place the bowl over a pan of simmering water.
2 Continue to beat the egg mixture while gradually adding the warm coconut mixture, a little at a time, until all the coconut mixture is added. This will take about 10 minutes—continue until the custard thickens. The mixture will be the consistency of thin cream and should easily coat the back of a spoon. Do not boil or it will curdle.
3 Cover and set aside to cool. Stir the mixture occasionally while it is cooling. When cool, pour into a shallow tray, cover and freeze for about 1¹/₂ hours or until half-frozen.
4 Quickly spoon the mixture into a food processor and process for 30 seconds, or until smooth. Return to the tray or place in plastic containers; cover and freeze completely. Serve garnished with mint and coconut.

NUTRITION PER SERVE
Protein 5 g; Fat 60 g; Carbohydrate 40 g;
Dietary Fibre 2 g; Cholesterol 140 mg;
3000 kJ (900 cal)

STORAGE: Will keep for up to three weeks in the freezer. Allow to stand at room temperature for 10–15 minutes before serving.

Beat the mixture until it is thick and frothy, using electric beaters.

Cook the coconut mixture until it easily coats the back of a spoon.

Pour the cooled mixture into a shallow tray; cover and freeze until half-frozen.

Transfer the half-frozen mixture to a food processor and mix until smooth.

SPICY COCONUT CUSTARD

Preparation time: 20 minutes
Total cooking time: 1 hour
Serves 8

2 cinnamon sticks
1 teaspoon ground nutmeg
2 teaspoons whole cloves
300 ml (10 fl oz) cream
1/2 cup (125 g/4 oz) palm sugar,
    chopped
280 g (9 oz) can coconut milk
3 eggs, lightly beaten
2 egg yolks, lightly beaten

1 Preheat the oven to warm 160°C (315°F/Gas 2–3). Put the spices, cream and 1 cup (250 ml/8 fl oz) water in a pan. Bring to simmering point, then reduce the heat to very low and leave for 5 minutes to allow the spices to flavour the liquid.
2 Add the sugar and coconut milk to the pan, return to low heat and stir until the sugar has dissolved.
3 Whisk the eggs and egg yolks together. Pour the spiced mixture over the eggs and stir well. Strain, discarding the whole spices. Pour the custard mixture into eight 1/2-cup (125 ml/4 fl oz) dishes. Put the dishes in a roasting tin and pour enough boiling water into the tin to come halfway up the sides of the dishes. Bake for 40–45 minutes.
4 Poke a knife in the centre of one of the custards to check if they are set— the mixture should be only slightly wobbly. Remove the custards from the roasting tin and serve hot or chilled.

NUTRITION PER SERVE
Protein 5 g; Fat 26 g; Carbohydrate 3 g;
Dietary Fibre 0 g; Cholesterol 166 mg;
1080 kJ (260 cal)

STORAGE: The custards will keep, covered and refrigerated, for up to three days.

Place the cinnamon sticks, nutmeg, cloves, cream and water in a pan.

Stir in the sugar and coconut milk and return the pan to the heat.

Strain the custard into a jug and discard the whole spices.

Insert a knife in the centre of one of the custards to check if they are set.

BANANA TEMPURA WITH GREEN TEA ICE CREAM

Preparation time: 30 minutes + freezing
Total cooking time: 25 minutes
Serves 4

ICE CREAM
1/3 cup (10 g/1/4 oz) Japanese green
    tea leaves
2 cups (500 ml/16 fl oz) milk
6 egg yolks
1/2 cup (125 g/4 oz) caster sugar
2 cups (500 ml/16 fl oz) cream

BANANA TEMPURA
oil, for deep-frying
1 egg
3/4 cup (185 ml/6 fl oz) iced water
2/3 cup (90 g/3 oz) tempura flour
4 small bananas
caster sugar and honey, to serve

1 Combine the tea leaves and milk in a saucepan and bring to simmering point very slowly over low heat. Set aside for 5 minutes before straining.
2 Whisk the egg yolks and sugar in a heatproof bowl until thick and pale, then add the infused milk. Place the bowl over a saucepan of simmering water, making sure that the base of the bowl is not touching the water. Stir the custard until thick enough to coat the back of a spoon, then remove from the heat and cool slightly. Add the cream.
3 Pour the mixture into a metal tray and freeze for 1 1/2–2 hours, or until just frozen around the edges. Transfer to a chilled bowl, beat with electric beaters until thick and creamy, then return to the metal tray. Repeat the freezing and beating twice more. Transfer to a storage container, cover the surface with baking paper and freeze overnight. Alternatively, churn

in an ice-cream maker according to the manufacturer's instructions.
4 Heat the oil in a deep-fryer or heavy-based saucepan until a cube of bread browns in 20 seconds. Mix together the egg and water in a bowl, then stir in the tempura flour. Do not whisk the batter—it must be lumpy.
5 Split the bananas lengthways, then crossways. Dip the banana quarters into the batter and deep-fry a few at a time for about 2 minutes, or until crisp and golden. Drain on paper towels and sprinkle with caster sugar. Serve with a scoop of ice cream and drizzle with warmed honey.

NUTRITION PER SERVE
Protein 16 g; Fat 77 g; Carbohydrate 80 g; Dietary Fibre 3.5 g; Cholesterol 494 mg; 4413 kJ (1054 cal)

Whisk the egg yolks and sugar in a heatproof bowl until thick and pale.

Stir the custard until it is thick enough to coat the back of a spoon.

Deep-fry the bananas until crisp and golden, then drain on paper towels.

GINGER AND LYCHEE JELLY

Preparation time: 10 minutes +
    4 hours setting
Total cooking time: 5 minutes
Serves 6

500 g (1 lb) can lychees
2 cups (500 ml/16 fl oz) clear apple
    juice (no added sugar)
1/3 cup (80 ml/2 3/4 fl oz) strained lime
    juice
2 tablespoons caster sugar
5 cm (2 inch) piece of fresh ginger,
    thinly sliced
4 sheets gelatine
fresh mint, to garnish

1 Drain the syrup from the lychees and put 1 cup (250 ml/8 fl oz) of the syrup in a saucepan. Discard the remaining syrup. Add the apple juice, lime juice, sugar and ginger to the pan. Bring to the boil, then reduce the heat and simmer for 5 minutes. Strain into a heatproof bowl.

2 Place the gelatine sheets in a large bowl of cold water and soak for 2 minutes, or until they soften. Squeeze out the excess water, then add to the syrup. Stir until completely dissolved. Leave to cool.

3 Pour 2 tablespoons of the jelly into each of six 150 ml (5 fl oz) wine glasses and divide the lychees among the glasses. Refrigerate until set. Spoon the remaining jelly over the fruit and refrigerate until set. Before serving, garnish with mint leaves.

NUTRITION PER SERVE
Protein 1 g; Fat 0 g; Carbohydrate 31 g;
Dietary Fibre 0.5 g; Cholesterol 0 mg;
530 kJ (125 cal)

After soaking, squeeze the sheets of gelatine to remove any excess water.

Stir the gelatine sheets into the hot liquid until they have dissolved.

Divide the lychees among the wine glasses, gently dropping them into the jelly mixture.

SANSRIVAL (PHILIPPINE CASHEW MERINGUE CAKE)

Preparation time: 40 minutes + cooling
Total cooking time: 45 minutes
Serves 8–10

CASHEW MERINGUE
300 g (10 oz) cashews
8 egg whites
1¹/₂ cups (375 g/12 oz) caster sugar
2 teaspoons vanilla essence
2 teaspoons white vinegar

FILLING
250 g (8 oz) unsalted butter, softened
1 cup (125 g/4 oz) icing sugar
4 tablespoons Crème de Cacao
2 cups (500 ml/16 fl oz) cream
1 tablespoon orange liqueur
2 teaspoons vanilla essence
chocolate or cocoa, for decoration, optional

1 To make the meringue, preheat the oven to moderate 180°C (350°F/Gas 4). Spread the cashews on a baking tray and toast them in the oven for 5 minutes or until golden, stirring occasionally to turn them over. Check frequently to make sure they don't burn. Remove from the oven, allow to cool and then process in short bursts in a food processor, until finely ground. Reduce the oven temperature to slow 150°C (300°F/Gas 2). Line four oven trays with non-stick baking paper and draw a 21 cm (8¹/₂ inch) diameter circle onto each piece.

2 Beat the egg whites in a large clean dry bowl until soft peaks form. Gradually add the caster sugar, beating well after each addition, until the whites are thick and glossy. Using a metal spoon, fold in the vanilla, vinegar and ground cashews.

3 Divide the mixture evenly among the circles and carefully spread it to the edge of each circle. Bake the meringues for 45 minutes or until they are crisp. Turn the oven off and allow the meringues to cool in the oven, leaving the oven door ajar.

4 To make the filling, beat the butter, icing sugar and Crème de Cacao until light and creamy. In a separate bowl, beat the cream, orange liqueur and vanilla essence until soft peaks form.

5 Place a meringue circle on a serving plate and carefully spread with half of the Crème de Cacao mixture. Top with another meringue circle and spread with half of the orange cream mixture. Repeat with the remaining meringue circles and mixtures.

6 The top of the meringue cake can be decorated with chocolate curls and dusted lightly with cocoa.

NUTRITION PER SERVE (10)
Protein 8 g; Fat 57 g; Carbohydrate 60 g;
Dietary Fibre 2 g; Cholesterol 130 mg;
3160 kJ (760 cal)

VARIATION: The cashew nuts can be replaced with almonds, pecans or hazelnuts.

HINT: If your oven doesn't have four racks, cook two meringue circles at a time.

NOTE: Sansrival is a celebration cake always served at fiestas and special occasions in the Philippines. The cream filling may vary in each village.

Process the roasted cashews, after they have cooled, until finely ground.

Using a plate as a guide, draw a circle onto each piece of paper.

Fold the vanilla essence, vinegar and ground cashews into the egg whites.

Use a spatula to spread the meringue mixture to the edge of each circle.

Beat the butter, icing sugar and Crème de Cacao until light and creamy.

Spread the second layer of meringue with half the orange cream.

MANGO ICE CREAM

Preparation time: 20 minutes +
  freezing
Total cooking time: Nil
Serves 4

3 fresh mangoes
1/2 cup (125 g/4 oz) caster sugar
3 tablespoons mango nectar
300 ml (10 fl oz) cream

1 Peel the mangoes, cut into pieces
and purée in a food processor until
smooth. Transfer to a bowl and add
the sugar and nectar. Stir until the
sugar has dissolved.

2 Beat the cream until stiff peaks form
and then gently fold into the mango.

3 Spoon the mixture into a shallow
tray, cover and freeze for 1¹/₂ hours or
until half-frozen. Spoon into a food
processor and mix for 30 seconds, or
until smooth. Return to the tray or a
plastic container, cover and freeze
completely. Remove the ice cream
from the freezer 15 minutes before
serving, to allow it to soften a little.
Serve with fresh mango.

NUTRITION PER SERVE
Protein 2 g; Fat 35 g; Carbohydrate 80 g;
Dietary Fibre 5 g; Cholesterol 100 mg;
2150 kJ (640 cal)

STORAGE: Freeze the ice cream for at
least eight hours—it can be kept in the
freezer for up to three weeks.

VARIATION: Stir in some toasted,
desiccated coconut before freezing the
ice cream completely.

Put the mangoes in a food processor and mix
until smooth.

Fold the whipped cream through the mango with
a metal spoon to keep the volume.

Pour the processed ice cream back into the tray
and freeze completely.

STICKY BLACK RICE

Preparation time: 20 minutes
  + overnight soaking
Total cooking time: 40 minutes
Serves 8

2 cups (400 g/13 oz) black rice
2 cups (500 ml/16 fl oz) coconut
  milk
80 g (2³/₄ oz) palm sugar, grated
3 tablespoons caster sugar
3 fresh pandan leaves, shredded and
  knotted
3 tablespoons coconut cream
3 tablespoons creamed corn

1 Place the rice in a large glass or
ceramic bowl and cover with water.
Soak for at least 8 hours or overnight.
Drain and transfer to a medium pan
with 1 litre of water. Bring slowly to
the boil, stirring frequently, and
simmer for 20 minutes, or until
tender. Drain.

2 In a large heavy-based pan, heat the
coconut milk until almost boiling. Add
the palm sugar, caster sugar and
pandan leaves and stir until dissolved.
Add the rice and stir for 3–4 minutes
without boiling.

3 Turn off the heat, cover the pan and
allow to stand for 15 minutes to allow
the flavours to be absorbed. Remove
the pandan leaves. Serve warm with
coconut cream and creamed corn.

NUTRITION PER SERVE
Protein 5 g; Fat 14 g; Carbohydrate 50 g;
Dietary Fibre 3 g; Cholesterol 0 mg;
1445 kJ (345 cal)

NOTES: Black rice, palm sugar and
pandan leaves are all available from
Asian food speciality stores.

Creamed corn is traditionally served
with coconut cream and sticky rice.

One teaspoon of pandan essence or
vanilla essence can be used if fresh
pandan leaves are not available.

Soak the black rice in water for at least
8 hours, or overnight.

Add the palm sugar, caster sugar and pandan
leaves to the coconut milk.

Use tongs to remove the pandan leaves from
the mixture.

BANANA AND COCONUT PANCAKES

Preparation time: 20 minutes
Total cooking time: 30 minutes
Serves 6

1/3 cup (40 g/1 1/4 oz) plain flour
2 tablespoons rice flour
1/4 cup (60 g/2 oz) caster sugar
1/4 cup (25 g/3/4 oz) desiccated
   coconut
1 cup (250 ml/8 fl oz) coconut milk
1 egg, lightly beaten
4 large bananas
60 g (2 oz) butter
1/3 cup (60 g/2 oz) soft brown sugar
1/3 cup (80 ml/2 3/4 fl oz) lime juice
1 tablespoon shredded, toasted
   coconut, for serving
strips of lime rind, for serving

1 Sift the flours into a bowl. Add the sugar and coconut and mix through with a spoon. Make a well in the centre, pour in the combined coconut milk and egg and beat until smooth.
2 Heat a non-stick frying pan and melt a little butter in it. Pour 3 tablespoons of the pancake mixture into the pan and cook over medium heat until the underside is golden.
3 Turn the pancake over and cook the other side. Transfer to a plate and cover with a tea towel to keep warm while cooking the rest, buttering the pan when necessary. Keep warm while preparing the bananas.
4 Cut the bananas diagonally into thick slices. Heat the butter in the pan; add the bananas and toss until coated. Cook over medium heat until the bananas start to soften and brown. Sprinkle with the brown sugar and shake the pan gently until the sugar has melted. Stir in the lime juice. Divide the bananas among the pancakes and fold over to enclose. Sprinkle with toasted coconut and strips of lime rind.

NUTRITION PER SERVE
Protein 4 g; Fat 14 g; Carbohydrate 30 g;
Dietary Fibre 3 g; Cholesterol 30 mg;
1083 kJ (260 cal)

Beat the pancake mixture thoroughly, until it is completely smooth.

When the pancakes are cooked, transfer them to a plate and keep them warm.

Toss the bananas gently until they are well coated with the butter.

Sprinkle brown sugar over the bananas and shake the pan until the sugar dissolves.

FRUIT PLATTER

Preparation time: 25 minutes + chilling
Total cooking time: 20 minutes
Serves 6

1 small pineapple, peeled and
    chopped
1 pawpaw, peeled and chopped
3 starfruit, sliced
8 rambutans, peeled and seeded
2 cups (500 g/1 lb) caster sugar
2 tablespoons lemon or lime juice
5 cm (2 inch) strip lemon or lime rind
fresh mint leaves, to garnish

1 Place the prepared fruit in a large bowl, cover and chill for at least 30 minutes.
2 Place the caster sugar and 2 cups (500 ml/16 fl oz) water in a pan. Stir over low heat, without boiling, for 5 minutes or until the sugar has dissolved. Add the juice and rind to the pan and bring the mixture to the boil. Boil without stirring for 10 minutes or until the syrup has thickened slightly. Remove the rind from the pan and set the mixture aside to cool.
3 Just prior to serving, pour over enough cooled syrup to coat the fruit

and carefully fold it through. Arrange the fruit in a bowl or hollowed out melon. Garnish with mint leaves.

NUTRITION PER SERVE
Protein 1 g; Fat 0 g; Carbohydrate 96 g;
Dietary Fibre 4 g; Cholesterol 0 mg;
1575 kJ (375 cal)

STORAGE: The syrup can be prepared a day ahead, covered and refrigerated. However, the fruit is best prepared on the day of serving.

Peel the rambutans and use your fingers to remove the seeds.

Add the juice and rind and boil the syrup for 10 minutes, or until it thickens slightly.

Just before serving, pour over enough of the cooled syrup to coat the fruit.

CARROT MILK PUDDING

Preparation time: 5 minutes
Total cooking time: 1 hour
Serves 6

1 litre milk
1½ cups (225 g/7 oz) grated carrot
⅓ cup (60 g/2 oz) sultanas
½ cup (125 g/4 oz) caster sugar
¼ teaspoon ground cinnamon
¼ teaspoon ground cardamom
⅓ cup (80 ml/2¾ fl oz) cream
2 tablespoons shelled, chopped
    pistachios

1 Pour the milk into a large, heavy-based pan. Place over medium heat and stir as it comes to the boil. Reduce the heat to low and leave until the milk reduces to about half its original volume. Stir occasionally to prevent it catching on the pan bottom.
2 Add the carrot and sultanas and cook a further 15 minutes.
3 Add the sugar, cinnamon, cardamom and cream and cook, stirring, until the sugar dissolves. Serve warm, sprinkled with pistachios. This pudding doesn't keep well and should be served immediately.

NUTRITION PER SERVE
Protein 8 g; Fat 15 g; Carbohydrate 18 g;
Dietary Fibre 2 g; Cholesterol 40 mg;
980 kJ (235 cal)

HINT: Indian sweets are often made from reduced milk. A heavy pan and an even distribution of heat for boiling down the milk are important. A heavy, non-stick pan would be ideal.

Stir the milk as it comes to the boil and then leave over low heat until reduced.

Add the carrot and sultanas to the milk and cook for a further 15 minutes.

Add the sugar, cinnamon, cardamom and cream and cook until the sugar dissolves.

SAGO PUDDING

Preparation time: 20 minutes + 1 hour
  soaking + 2 hours refrigeration
Total cooking time: 20 minutes
Serves 6

1 cup (200 g/6¹/₂ oz) sago
1 cup (185 g/6 oz) soft brown sugar
1 cup (250 ml/8 fl oz) coconut cream,
  well chilled

1 Soak the sago in 3 cups (750 ml/
24 fl oz) of water for 1 hour. Pour into
a pan, add 2 tablespoons of the brown
sugar and bring to the boil over low
heat, stirring constantly. Reduce the
heat and simmer, stirring occasionally,
for 10 minutes. Cover and cook over
low heat, stirring occasionally, for
2–3 minutes, until the mixture is thick
and the sago grains are translucent.
2 Half-fill six rinsed (still wet) ¹/₂-cup
(125 ml/4 fl oz) moulds with the sago
mixture and refrigerate for 2 hours, or
until set.
3 Combine the remaining brown
sugar with 1 cup (250 ml/8 fl oz) water
in a small pan and cook over low heat,
stirring constantly, until the sugar
dissolves. Simmer for 5–7 minutes,
until the syrup thickens. Remove from
the heat and cool. To serve, unmould
and top with a little of the sugar syrup
and coconut cream.

NUTRITION PER SERVE
Protein 3 g; Fat 9 g; Carbohydrate 60 g;
Dietary Fibre 2 g; Cholesterol 0 mg;
1340 kJ (320 cal)

NOTE: Palm sugar can be used instead
of brown sugar—grate it on a cheese
grater, or shred with a sharp knife,
before using.

STORAGE: The syrup can be made
up to a day in advance, covered
and refrigerated.

Stir the sago constantly, over low heat, until it has
come to the boil.

Cook until the mixture thickens and the sago
grains are translucent.

Simmer the syrup for 5–7 minutes, until it has
thickened, then remove from the heat.

Index

USEFUL INFORMATION

The recipes in this book were developed using a tablespoon measure of 20 ml. In some other countries the tablespoon is 15 ml. For most recipes this difference will not be noticeable but, for recipes using baking powder, gelatine, bicarbonate of soda, small amounts of flour and cornflour, we suggest that, if you are using the smaller tablespoon, you add an extra teaspoon for each tablespoon.

The recipes in this book are written using convenient cup measurements. You can buy special measuring cups in the supermarket or use an ordinary household cup: first you need to check it holds 250 ml (8 fl oz) by filling it with water and measuring the water (pour it into a measuring jug or a carton that you know holds 250 ml). This cup can then be used for both liquid and dry cup measurements.

Liquid cup measures

1/4 cup	60 ml	2 fluid oz
1/3 cup	80 ml	2 3/4 fluid oz
1/2 cup	125 ml	4 fluid oz
3/4 cup	180 ml	6 fluid oz
1 cup	250 ml	8 fluid oz

Spoon measures

1/4 teaspoon	1.25 ml
1/2 teaspoon	2.5 ml
1 teaspoon	5 ml
1 tablespoon	20 ml

Nutritional Information

The nutritional information given for each recipe does not include any garnishes or accompaniments, such as rice or pasta, unless they are included in specific quantities in the ingredients list. The nutritional values are approximations and can be affected by biological and seasonal variations in foods, the unknown composition of some manufactured foods and uncertainty in the dietary database. Nutrient data given are derived primarily from the NUTTAB95 database produced by the Australian and New Zealand Food Authority.

Oven Temperatures

You may find cooking times vary depending on the oven you are using. For fan-forced ovens, as a general rule, set oven temperature to 20°C lower than indicated in the recipe.

Note: Those who might be at risk from the effects of salmonella food poisoning (the elderly, pregnant women, young children and those suffering from immune deficiency diseases) should consult their GP with any concerns about eating raw eggs.

Weight

10 g	1/4 oz	220 g	7 oz	425 g	14 oz
30 g	1 oz	250 g	8 oz	475 g	15 oz
60 g	2 oz	275 g	9 oz	500 g	1 lb
90 g	3 oz	300 g	10 oz	600 g	1 1/4 lb
125 g	4 oz	330 g	11 oz	650 g	1 lb 5 oz
150 g	5 oz	375 g	12 oz	750 g	1 1/2 lb
185 g	6 oz	400 g	13 oz	1 kg	2 lb

Alternative names (UK/US)

bicarbonate of soda	—	baking soda
besan flour	—	chickpea flour
capsicum	—	red or green bell pepper
chickpeas	—	garbanzo beans
cornflour	—	cornstarch
fresh coriander	—	cilantro
single cream	—	cream
aubergine	—	eggplant
flat-leaf parsley	—	Italian parsley
hazelnut	—	filbert
minced beef	—	ground beef
plain flour	—	all-purpose flour
polenta	—	cornmeal
prawn	—	shrimp
Roma tomato	—	plum or egg tomato
sambal oelek	—	chilli paste
mangetout	—	snow pea
spring onion	—	scallion
thick cream	—	heavy cream
tomato purée	—	tomato paste
courgette	—	zucchini

Published by Murdoch Books® , GPO BOX 1203, Sydney, NSW 1045, AUSTRALIA
Ferry House, 51–57 Lacy Road, London SW15 1PR, UK

Editor: Jane Price **Designer:** Annette Fitzgerald **Publisher:** Kay Scarlett **Chief Executive:** Juliet Rogers
National Library of Australia Cataloguing-in-Publication Data. The complete Asian cookbook. Includes index. ISBN 1 74045 156 2 and 1 74045 155 4 (pbk) 1 Cookery. Asian. 641.595 Printed by Toppan Printing Hong Kong Co. Ltd. PRINTED IN CHINA.